KW-621-706

# The Philosophical Treatise of William H. Ferris

## Selected Readings from *The African Abroad or, His Evolution in Western Civilization*

Tommy J. Curry

ROWMAN &
LITTLEFIELD
INTERNATIONAL
*London • New York*

BIRMINGHAM CITY UNIVERSITY LIBRARY

Published by Rowman & Littlefield International Ltd
Unit A, Whitacre Mews, 26-34 Stannary Street, London SE11 4AB
www.rowmaninternational.com

Rowman & Littlefield International Ltd. is an affiliate of Rowman & Littlefield
4501 Forbes Boulevard, Suite 200, Lanham, Maryland 20706, USA
With additional offices in Boulder, New York, Toronto (Canada), and Plymouth (UK)
www.rowman.com

Selection and editorial matter © 2016 by Tommy J. Curry

*All rights reserved.* No part of this book may be reproduced in any form or by any electronic or mechanical means, including information storage and retrieval systems, without written permission from the publisher, except by a reviewer who may quote passages in a review.

**British Library Cataloguing in Publication Data**

A catalogue record for this book is available from the British Library

ISBN: HB 978-1-78660-032-5
PB 978-1-78660-033-2

**Library of Congress Cataloging-in-Publication Data**

Names: Ferris, William Henry, 1873–1941, author. | Curry, Tommy J., 1979– author.
Title: The philosophical treatise of William H. Ferris : selected readings from The African abroad or, his evolution in western civilization / Tommy J. Curry.
Other titles: African abroad. Selections.
Description: Lanham, Md : Rowman & Littlefield International, [2016] | Series: Creolizing the canon | Includes index.
Identifiers: LCCN 2016014001 (print) | LCCN 2016017623 (ebook) | ISBN 9781786600325 (cloth : alk. paper) | ISBN 9781786600332 (pbk. : alk. paper) | ISBN 9781786600349 (electronic)
Subjects: LCSH: African Americans—History. | Ferris, William Henry, 1873–1941. African abroad—History and criticism. | Blacks—History. | Black race.
Classification: LCC E185 .F392 2016 (print) | LCC E185 (ebook) | DDC 973/.0496073—dc23
LC record available at https://lccn.loc.gov/2016014001

∞ ™ The paper used in this publication meets the minimum requirements of American National Standard for Information Sciences—Permanence of Paper for Printed Library Materials, ANSI/NISO Z39.48-1992.

Printed in the United States of America

# Contents

# Acknowledgments

As with any text, the content and motivations far exceed those of merely one author. William H. Ferris's work has been a passion of mine since graduate school. I found his work fascinating and in stark contrast to that of Josiah Royce in the mid-2000s. I initially stumbled upon Ferris's *The African Abroad* by accident, as I walked the stacks of Southern Illinois University's library. Southern Illinois University, Carbondale, actually had signed copies of both volumes 1 and 2. After reading Ferris, I thought, "My God! Here is an adamant Black idealist nationalist—a Hegelian, no less." This book is the product of my decade-long reading and digging into the ideas and thought of William H. Ferris and the evolutionary science of ethnology.

I have to thank my then classmate and now colleague Dwayne Tunstall for his patience and attention to my rants over the willful ignorance of American philosophy toward the work of William H. Ferris. Bill Lawson spoke to me with great interest and support about the insights of William H. Ferris year after year. I have to thank my wife, Gwenetta Curry, for her support while I worked to find and document Ferris's missing citations. My first graduate student, Ms. Judith Bohr, was an indispensable resource and supporter of this project. Her endless work in formatting and correcting the editorial mistakes of Ferris's text drove the project forward. I would be remiss if I also did not thank Ken Stikkers for his conversations and Randy Auxier for his challenges concerning Royce, which drove me to dig deeper into Ferris. The late Helen Tartar and Doug Anderson deserve much credit for the publication of this work. Their support and belief in the need to republish the primary texts of turn-of-the-century Black philosophers remain motivational. Lastly, I would like to thank Jane Gordon and Neil Roberts, the reviewers, and Rowman & Littlefield for their belief in this project.

I wish to acknowledge my indebtedness to the Melbern G. Glasscock Center for Humanities Research at Texas A&M University for awarding the primary works of William H. Ferris publication support and recognition.

This is book represents my republication of a text, but it has been driven by a community of thinkers who have supported the findings and discussions that have emerged beyond the pages.

*Author's Preface*

# Deliberate Misreadings

## Derelictical Avoidance, William H. Ferris, and the Need to Expand the Geography of Black Nationalism to Comprehend *The African Abroad*

*Tommy J. Curry*

> When the American comes to the Negro problem, he settles that offhand, without any thorough investigation. He merely passes it by, with a contemptuous wave of the hand, or toss of the head. Why, any petty clerk, or office boy or newsboy or bootblack, knows what ought to be done with the Negro, knows what kind of education the Negro needs! The prevailing sentiments seems to be that anyone, no matter how ignorant, is fitted to grapple with the various Negro problems.
>
> —William H. Ferris, *The African Abroad*

As with the introduction of any historic Black thinker into the fray of philosophical recognition, there is hesitancy. This hesitancy is the consequence of knowing that what will make a Black thinker a philosopher is not what he or she teaches the world about the history or reality of Black people or American racism, but rather their closeness to canonical white figures. In the case of William H. Ferris, how he thought about the world will be irrelevant. He will be accepted by the extent to which he is able to be revised and imagined as the pupil of already admired white thinkers and their ideals. In short, Ferris will be recognized as a philosopher only insofar as he can be made into the racial daemon of already established philosophical thought. While it is undeniable that William H. Ferris read the works of the white thinkers of his day, some of whom have also come to form the canon of American philosophy, an interpretive problem arises when an intellectual giant like Ferris is determined to be a philosopher by the extent to which his thought is understood as being derived from the white thinkers he has read. This tendency is not as abstract as one might think. In a white supremacist discipline like philosophy, the introduction of Black philosophers' text and the situating of their place within already established canons are fraught with difficulty. Rather than being a particular example of the richness of the Black philosophical tradition, or how Black thought and Black thinkers have evolved with the changing times and new problems of Black existence in America, the value of new Black philosophers remains a redemptive exercise that seeks to prove that Black thinkers were in fact inspired by ideals offered by white philosophers—a new opportunity to guard their cherished white figures from charges of racism and a means to prove the exceptionalism of their heroes and heroines and to extricate them from the racial milieu of their times through their white figures' association (friendship) with said Black thinkers—this is the disciplinary problem of dereliction.[1] For a long time, these apologetics had to be accepted by Black philosophers as the only means possible for introducing historic Black philosophers into the field of "American philosophy." Today, however, such practices only continue to erase Black theorists, devalue the intellectual history of African-descended people throughout the centuries, and concede the power of interpretation to white disciplines that define the reality of Black thought not only in our present but also, I fear, well into the future.[2]

## THE EFFECT OF UNDERSPECIALIZATION ON THE GENEALOGICAL ACCOUNTS OF BLACK PHILOSOPHY

Given the aforementioned tendency of "American philosophy," the recovery of William H. Ferris's *The African Abroad* presents an opportunity in that it

1. Tommy J. Curry, "On Derelict and Method: The Methodological Crisis of Africana Philosophy's Study of African Descended People under an Integrationist Milieu," *Radical Philosophy Review* 14, no. 2 (2011): 139–64; Tommy J. Curry, "The Derelictical Crisis of African American Philosophy: How African American Philosophy Fails to Contribute to the Study of African Descended People," *Journal of Black Studies* 42, no. 3 (2011): 314–33.

2. Tommy J. Curry, "Concerning the Under-specialization of Race Theory in American Philosophy: An Essay Outlining Ignored Bibliographic Sources Addressing the Aforementioned Problem," *Pluralist* 5, no. 1 (2010): 44–64.

contributes to the growth of the archival materials available for study, just as readily as it poses a risk of tragedy, since gauging Ferris's usefulness as a philosopher remains dependent on his closeness to the perspectives of the canonical figures who make his unique perspective on Black Nationalism and his independence of thought an inconvenience in the efforts to make his thinking mirror the views of his white contemporaries. Most of the supposedly new contributions to Black philosophy simply restate old declarations using current jargon and the sexy theoretical apparatuses of the day. There are relatively few new materials introduced into contemporary debates—just the rewriting, reorganizing, and revamping of key texts to fit the decided political moralism of the day.

For decades, Black philosophers have suffered under this academic practice. Their ancestors, who fought for political and cultural freedom, have been turned into caricatures, their great contributions to American society reduced to the maxim "Love your oppressors." W. E. B. Du Bois becomes a Hegelian multiculturalist, an interpretation that ignores his work on the Atlanta Sociological Laboratory and his later rejection of integration and whites' power to educate Black children. Martin R. Delany, long considered the father of Black Nationalism, becomes a Rawlsian integrationist,[3] and Martin Luther King Jr. is sanitized into a colorblind seeker of love rather than the adamant anti-imperialist thinker he was. Such practices and the literature that evidences this dominant mode of thinking about Black thinkers know no boundaries. Philosophy, as a discipline, does not require Black thinkers to be situated entities within the thoughts and problems of their lifetimes. Their projects are irrelevant to their disciplinary end, which is to place them in close proximity and participation with white traditions (e.g., existentialism, pragmatism). As I have argued previously, "Black philosophers should require and maintain standards of interpretive rigor that demand the philosophical approaches toward our thinkers to be understood in totality and within the cultural genealogy of their own thought."[4] It is my hope that by announcing it, assaulting it, and urging the Black philosophers of today and the Black thinkers of tomorrow to reject it, we can develop, write, and articulate the thinking of our intellectual ancestors with historical integrity and intellectual fortitude.

For decades, American and Continental philosophical traditions have invented connections between Du Bois and G. W. F. Hegel, Du Bois and Josiah Royce, and Du Bois and pragmatism through his study with William

3. See Tommie Shelby, *We Who Are Dark: The Philosophical Foundations of Racial Solidarity* (Cambridge, MA: Belknap Press, 2005).

4. Curry, "Concerning the Under-specialization of Race Theory in American Philosophy," 58.

James. Whereas Du Bois specifically rejects these connections, Ferris acknowledges his fascination with the Western canon explicitly, while simultaneously announcing to the reader the ineffectiveness of looking to the theories of the Western canon to explain the history and philosophical anthropology of African-descended peoples. The account of the historical presence and civilization of African-descended people must be left to African-descended people. Years before Du Bois made similar arguments in *The Negro* and "The Propaganda of History," in his magnum opus *Black Reconstruction*, Ferris announced that the white account of history, because of its need to reify the myth of white superiority, could not be trusted. This insight by Ferris is a radical break from any attempts to read his works as derivative of his training at Harvard and Yale. Ferris, like Alexander Crummell, like Du Bois, like Booker T. Washington, took the race problem to have both historical and sociological explanations. Insofar as whites were committed to the propagation of the myth of their racial superiority and their need to culturally impose their history on the darker races, their philosophy, being a reflection of their racial character, could not be used to explain the existence of and dictate the future for African-descended people.

William H. Ferris offers the reader an interesting and nuanced account of Black Nationalist thought. His militancy and resistance to the theories of white supremacy, segregation, and the social repression that resulted from this regime came in the form of cultural criticism. For Ferris, intelligently written criticism against racism and the differing modes of Black leadership were just as important as organization for racial uplift. There is no ambiguity in his words; he adamantly insisted upon the brilliance of the men and women of his time, but he did not censor his intent or measure his penning of criticism against these same thinkers on various matters and philosophical differences in his day. Ferris wrote for the uplift of Black people even when doing so meant confronting in no small measure the scholarship produced by giants like Booker T. Washington, Alexander Crummell, Kelly Miller, Reverdy Ransom, and W. E. B. Du Bois. In sharp contrast to the ideological charges usually waged against Black political theory as being synonymous with essentialist calls for racial solidarity (preference), Ferris shows how his Black Nationalism, or his support and criticism of his peers, resists this quotidian simplification. Confronted with seemingly endless barriers to academic training and education and racial violence against the attempts of Blacks to politically organize, Ferris presents an idealist account of racial improvement and uplift that differs significantly from the idealism of some of his contemporaries, like Anna Julia Cooper, while mirroring that of others, like Alexander Crummell.

Idealism has long been connected to the theological pull the individual has to his or her communion with God. The philosophy of Hegel and the Hegelianism of Josiah Royce have both been noted traditions that have defined American idealism. Ferris, while sharing the Hegelian orientation of many American idealists around the turn of the twentieth century, interestingly resists the redemptive theology of suffering and deliverance embraced by many Black theologians and taken to be the consequence of the master-slave dialectic by many white philosophers. God was of no small consequence for Ferris, but he did not see the salvation of Black folks to be a matter of unwarranted hope and idle faith. Rather, God was a catalyst, and their elevation was predicted by the laws of history. Ideas, or, more precisely, the move of the race toward understanding the role of ideas in history, provide the inspiration an individual has toward truth, and for Black individuals, toward their racial history and subsequent uplift. In other words, theology was useful, though not insofar as it produced moral advancement among Black people, but rather for how morality meant care for and attention to the foundations of civilization, the development of history as the account of Black genius, and racial uplift for Black people.

William H. Ferris was a complex thinker, a prolific cultural commentator, and a pivotal figure in Black political thought at the turn of the century. He was involved in every major Black school of thought (race organization) in the twentieth century. He was an editor for William Monroe Trotter's anti-accommodationist (anti-Washington) newspaper, the *Boston Guardian*. He was a member of the American Negro Academy and the Negro Society for Historical Research and an editor of *Negro World*, the newspaper of Marcus Garvey's Universal Negro Improvement Association (UNIA). While *The African Abroad* does not capture the totality of his thinking, as it was written in 1913 and Ferris remained an active scholar throughout the 1920s, it does give the reader a substantial sense of his temperament, his political philosophy, his nationalist theology, and his reflections about the types of leadership Black people needed in order to overcome racism and, of particular concern to Ferris, the racist accounts of history presented as fact at the turn of the century. Rather than attempt to frame Ferris for the reader, I have intended only to announce the figures and associations of his time that provide context for his thinking. In bringing *The African Abroad* to academic audiences, I hope to resist the suppressive traditions of interpreting Black thinkers like Ferris, not to replace this practice with a fixed Black perspective (be it nationalism, Afrocentrism, and so forth), but rather to free the reader to accurately and creatively think through Ferris without constraint.

## THE PROXEMICS OF RACIAL THOUGHT: WHAT ESTABLISHES THE DISTANCE BETWEEN WILLIAM H. FERRIS AND W. E. B. DU BOIS

What establishes the distance between two thinkers or their proximity to each other? What marks Ferris as standing apart and distinct from how contemporary scholars read the canon of Du Bois from the turn of the twentieth century forward? Ferris and Du Bois have a complicated personal relationship that stains, so to speak, their intellectual and political differences. For some scholars, it is easier to read W. E. B. Du Bois and William H. Ferris as kindred minds, for they were both original members of the American Negro Academy, were both admirers and followers of Reverend Alexander Crummell, and were both among the Ivy League–educated Black leadership class at the turn of the twentieth century. Among the list of notable influences on his thought, Ferris does name Du Bois. He writes, "Professor DuBois has had as much influence over my ideals as any other man. When I heard him read his paper upon 'The Conservatism of Race Traits, and Tendencies of the Negro,' at a meeting of the American Negro Academy in Washington, in March, 1897, I trained my guns upon DuBois and severely criticised him. But the more I reflected the more truth I saw in his views."[5] This is but a brief mention in *The African Abroad* and demonstrates that there was some degree of influence, alongside stark disagreements between the two thinkers. The extent of this influence can only be hypothesized. Because *The African Abroad* was written at various times as an accumulation of multiple essays, there is no reliable way to understand the text linearly or to know the thought shared with Du Bois.

Ferris admires Du Bois for emerging as a stern voice against Negro compromise in the late 1890s. "When the industrial surrender, civil and political rights wave swept over the country fifteen years ago, most of the educators, preachers, editors and politicians of the race lost their moorings and drifted with it. To DuBois belongs the honor of being the man who stayed the advancing tide of compromise that would have engulfed and submerged the entire Negro race,"[6] writes Ferris. But this honor was cause not for celebration but for caution. Throughout the various correspondence and writings between Ferris and Du Bois, which expressed division over the quality of

5. William H. Ferris, *The African Abroad; or His Evolution in Western Civilization: Tracing His Development under Caucasian Milieu* (New Haven, CT: Tuttle, Morehouse & Taylor Press, 1913), 1:340.

6. Ibid., 2:774.

mind necessary to lead the Black race forward and ensure its progression and survival in the coming century, there was a reoccurring concern raised by Ferris—namely, the position from which Du Bois observed and studied the Negro.

The most obvious explanation for this division between Ferris and Du Bois would simply be to suggest that Ferris changed politically, or as time passed Ferris gained some intellectual distance from the scholars of the American Negro Academy and Du Bois himself. One could go as far to posit this as the result of Ferris's shift to Garveyism and Du Bois's resistance to it in the 1920s. However, there is evidence as early as volume 2 of *The African Abroad*, in the chapter titled "Dr. W. E. B. Du Bois and the Other Colored Leaders: The Warring Gods on Mount Olympus—Dr. DuBois's Place in History," that Ferris believed the mantle of Black leadership offered to Du Bois after Frederick Douglass was misplaced. Ferris believed that Du Bois "lacked the magnetism to gather the many of the race around him, lacked the fire and force to electrify vast crowds, and lacked the generalship to bind the masses together."[7]

Despite this criticism, Ferris does not deny the talent and eloquence in Du Bois's *The Souls of Black Folk* and other turn-of-the-century works. In fact, Ferris expresses a remarkable earnestness when he writes, "I think that as a literary craftsman, a magician in words and a verbal prestidigitator, DuBois is the equal of the famous masters of English and American prose, and that his brilliant style has as its substratum solid learning. Indeed, his scholarship is equal to that of the average Yale or Harvard professor."[8] Ferris believes Du Bois to be stunning as an intellectual and race man. In this regard, remarks Ferris, "No man in the race can show up better on social, semi-social and semi-literary occasions as an example of a cultured and refined colored gentleman."[9] While Ferris paid Du Bois handsome comments, he nonetheless remained suspicious of his ability to lead the Black race and fill the void he created by his condemnation of Booker T. Washington. "Will Dr. DuBois, the Mars who was so conspicuous in the struggle that resulted in the downfall of Jupiter Tonans, [rise] to fill the vacant throne,"[10] asks Ferris. Despite the proclamations and writings by Du Bois, specifically *The Souls of Black Folk*, Ferris was simply not convinced that Du Bois's intellectual attributes made him a race leader or voice for the Black race—politically or intellectually. Ferris writes,

7. Ibid., 2:910–23, 911.
8. Ibid., 2:913.
9. Ibid.
10. Ibid.

> But I am not quite sure whether this polished and refined scholar is endowed with the combination of qualities which make one a leader of men. He has the keen intellectual perceptions, the sensitive aesthetic perceptions, which cause one to be a superb literary, musical and art critic and social arbiter. But that very intellectual and aesthetic sensitiveness causes him to be hypersensitive of a jar or discord, and hypercritical. And the leader of men, while conscious of the defects and limitations of a man, sees in him material at his disposal to be utilized as means to realize an end.[11]

Du Bois was not the intellectual and prophetic leader of the Black race that many scholars of today suggest. Regarding Du Bois's place in history, Ferris remarks, "DuBois is the Ernest Renan of the Negro race. But the Mirabeaus have been the makers of history."[12] Such remarks are not unduly caustic in Ferris's writings. As a student of psychology, Ferris regarded Du Bois as "an intellectual giant, with the aesthetic sensibility of an artist or poet";[13] however, as a pupil of human history, Ferris was doubtful—unable to predict—that Du Bois was in fact "a leader who will fill individuals in his race with the thought that they, too, can climb the mount of human achievement."[14] This was more than a disagreement of political vision. For Ferris, this was a failure of the kind of mind Du Bois possessed and called into question the effect his scholarly proclamations held for the race. While Ferris held Du Bois to be "the most gifted writer our race in America has yet produced, [and] one of the greatest living American Negroes,"[15] Ferris was not willing to place his perspectives on racial progress in line with those of Du Bois.

Following the publication of Du Bois's *Darkwater*, Ferris penned a lengthy response to this work in the *Africa and Orient Review*. In this review, Ferris argues, "*Darkwater* is neither a philosophical, psychological, scientific, historical, or sociological masterpiece, for philosophical analysis is not Du Bois' forte."[16] Ferris claims that his review is only of Du Bois's *Darkwater*; it will not consider "whether Oswald Garrison Villard was spiritually blind when he regarded Du Bois as the only intellectual luminary in the African plane . . . whether Du Bois is too aristocratic and hypercritical, too touchy and sensitive, too dainty and fastidious, too high and holy to lead the masses of his race . . . [or] whether Du Bois did or did not make fatal blunders when

11. Ibid., 2:917.
12. Ibid., 2:918.
13. Ibid.
14. Ibid.
15. Ibid., 2:910.
16. William H. Ferris, "Dr. DuBois's *Darkwater*," *Africa and Orient Review* (June 1920): 20–24, 21.

he attempted to referee the work and worth of other coloured men and to determine 'who was who' in the Negro race."[17] Ferris does, however, insist in his review that "if our Anglo-Saxon friends and well-wishers will cease trying to select leaders for the Negro race, thereby putting men in positions which their natural tastes and aptitudes and inclinations and previous training and preparation unfit them for, there would be more peace and harmony within the black ranks."[18]

Ferris is now more explicit about his concern over Du Bois's leadership and the white philanthropists supporting him. Du Bois's work, while captivating, lacks intimate connection with the Negro and instead represents only his own personal strivings between whiteness and his Blackness. What then does Ferris think of the book? He believes it to be an extravagant work, "an amazing revelation of the soul of a cultured, refined Negro of mixed blood."[19] In his words, "We see in [*Darkwater*] the agony of soul of a Negro of mixed blood, writhing and twisting and turning in the cage in which the Anglo-Saxon has confined it. It is the white blood of Du Bois crying for its own. It is the disinherited coloured offspring and offshoot of the Caucasian, weeping and wailing and cursing and damning because he has been disinherited by his Caucasian brother."[20] This intimate need for the recognition of whites is what weakens Du Bois's conviction for the Negro in Ferris's view. Black and brown races the world over resent economic exploitation, lynching, jim crowism, and segregation, but "they are not as sensitive about social ostracism as Du Bois and the mulattoes, quadroons, and octoroons are."[21] *Darkwater* illustrates to Ferris that Du Bois has failed as a leader of the Negro because he desires a proximity to whites more than closeness to Blacks.

The book also suffers from the poetic style of Du Bois as a "captious critic." Drawing on Du Bois's autobiographical chapter in *Darkwater*, titled "The Shadow of Years," Ferris argues that the "captious critic explains Du Bois' attitude towards the members of his own race. He was interested in them, but seemingly felt himself immeasurably superior to them, and looked down upon them from the august heights of his superiority in a patronizing manner."[22] Describing Du Bois's prose as witchery that lures the reader into an idealistic critique that lacks practical force, Ferris notes that Du Bois is

17. Ibid., 21.
18. Ibid.
19. Ibid., 22.
20. Ibid.
21. Ibid.
22. Ibid., 24.

very good at describing the ills and problems that haunt the Negro in America but lacks any plan or program to get them out of this racial condition.[23] Ferris believes that "men who are in trouble, whether that trouble is moral, religious, social, physical, financial, or political, desire a way of escape or a plan of salvation. They want, whether they know it or not, some Messianic hope,"[24] and this remains lacking in Du Bois's *Darkwater*. Ferris then says, "I intimated in the *African Abroad* that Dr. Du Bois lacked a philosophy of history, lacked what theologians call the vision of God. No oppressed or suppressed or ostracised race or nation can rise in a day or generation. The Negro race must progress and struggle upwards through a long, slow, and painful progress. It must cry out for justice and acquire what the races on top have in their possession—the weapons of destiny."[25] Ferris concludes that Du Bois's sentiments are far reaching but directed toward establishing himself within the purview of the white race, a position that does not necessarily serve to remedy the conditions that Black Americans find themselves in. Ferris ends this review by stating, "Not a great sociologist or philosopher, Dr. Du Bois is a remarkably well-read and widely informed man, and he possesses that magic of style and witchery of phrase which will not only give him a permanent place in Negro literature, but a high place in American literature."[26]

Du Bois's reaction to Garvey's Universal Negro Improvement Association was another instance when Ferris argues that Du Bois's sentiment of superiority can be easily observed. In 1923, Ferris penned "Dr. DuBois's Ten Mistakes." In this editorial for the *Negro World*, Ferris writes that Du Bois's attacks on the UNIA are "written from the standpoint of a disinterested white man who studied the UNIA from long range and not from the standpoint of a race leader who has kept his finger on the pulsebeat of the race that it is supposed to represent."[27] Again emphasizing the distance Du Bois has from the condition of everyday rank-and-file Negroes, Ferris suggests that Du Bois is more interested in organizations and endeavors that involve recognition by and support from whites. This criticism of Du Bois by Ferris was well known to their contemporaries. In 1921, J. Osman Oriyo wrote a letter to Ferris in which he criticized Du Bois's Pan-African meetings as a "false congress." Oriyo told Ferris to tell Du Bois that West Africans "care not to know what

23. Ibid., 23.

24. Ibid.

25. Ibid.

26. Ibid., 24.

27. William H. Ferris, "Dr. DuBois's Ten Mistakes," in *African Fundamentalism: A Literary and Cultural Anthology of Garvey's Harlem Renaissance* (Dover: Majority Press, 1983), 73–78, 77.

is Dr. DuBois' attainment in scholarship. Tell DuBois that the Negroes at home never recommend him, for even their messenger, to say nothing about leadership."[28] This letter offers some evidence that Ferris was a well-known detractor of Du Bois, as well as some indication that others felt confident in sharing correspondences critical of Du Bois with him.

This magnanimous slighting was not offered by Ferris alone, for Du Bois made equally harsh criticisms of Ferris. Du Bois was polite in his review of Ferris's book in *The Crisis* in 1913, but in his letter to Ferris on March 23, 1912, Du Bois was extremely harsh and discouraging. Du Bois's letter is a response to several previously unanswered letters sent by Ferris. The letters must have addressed some ongoing dispute between the two, because Du Bois begins by telling Ferris, "You must remember that I have in certain ways the utmost sympathy with you, but the real criticism that I have to make is not that you are 'peculiar' or dynamic or anything of that sort, but that you are lazy and will not keep clean."[29] "These are elementary things which simply shut you out of proper companionship with people of your intellectual level," writes Du Bois.[30] Concerning *The African Abroad*, Du Bois disagreed with Ferris's "begging" for the money for his book, suggesting that he "would have more respect for himself in the long run if he worked for it."[31]

These were not simply personal disagreements but also questions over the generative force directing Negro intellectuals—their spiritual strivings. Ferris argues throughout *The African Abroad* that the Black race is oppressed because Blacks lack a claim to civilization and history. Ferris is adamant that the Negro is "ostracised, despised, segregated and persecuted as a race in America, regarded as an inferior social unit and imprisoned within certain caste limitations because *we have no grand and glorious history behind us in this country, because we have produced few illustrious and distinguished men, because we have made few contributions to the world's civilization or stock of ideas, because we lack prestige and standing.*"[32] The Negro is unknown to the world, but this is a condition that can be remedied with representative and philosophically trained Black men and women. Ferris argues that the Negro must rise in order to command the respect of others. Ferris explains, "When he is obscure and unknown, he has to come to the world; when he acquires prestige and standing, the world will come to him;

28. J. Osman Oriyo, "J. Osman Oriyo to William H. Ferris," in *The Marcus Garvey and Universal Negro Improvement Association Papers*, ed. Robert A. Hill (Berkeley: University of California Press, 1995), 9:283–84, 283.

29. Letter from Du Bois to Ferris, March 23, 1912.

30. Ibid.

31. Ibid.

32. Ferris, *The African Abroad*, 2:921 (emphasis added).

when he is in humble circumstances, he seeks other men; when he becomes distinguished, other men seek him."[33] The cultivation of man through philosophy and history is the task of race work. It is necessary to raise up the race through talented race men and women. It is in this demonstration of racial advance that the Negro is made known to the world and noted by history. Ferris explains, "But when he becomes famous, the rich and haughty, the proud and the aristocratic will vie with each other in lionizing him and giving banquets and receptions in his honor. To secure recognition this poor unknown youth must secure prestige and standing. That is what the African abroad, evolving in western civilization, must do."[34]

It is in this sense, this difference between Ferris's racial vision and Du Bois's renderings of race, that readers finds themselves drawn toward one interpretive lens or the other. I have chosen to frame Ferris and Du Bois in opposition to each other because of the various differences I find philosophically, politically, and ethnologically between the two thinkers. The benefit of introducing Ferris as a critic of Du Bois is that there will be no end to the debate as to how far such divisions can go. If I am correct, Africana philosophy, Black history, and various historiographies have a new figure from which to originate various accounts of knowledge, God, and race leadership. If I am wrong, then the field now has a polemic that can be used to generate endless accounts of the shared ideas and values between Ferris and Du Bois. Either way, scholarship on Ferris should be stimulated. My intent is simply to motivate thought, and in so doing, it may be revealed that what was once maintained as true or most likely is no longer tenable, given the evidence presented by others. But it is this waiting, the anticipation of new work on Ferris, that is the most exciting, especially when it allows us to expand upon traditions like Black Nationalism or the Black radical tradition.

## WILLIAM H. FERRIS AND THE EXPANSION OF THE BLACK NATIONALIST TRADITION

William H. Ferris was a central intellectual figure in the evolution of Black Nationalism at the turn of the twentieth century. His participation in the founding of the American Negro Academy and his editing of *Negro World*, the chief publication of Marcus Garvey's UNIA in 1919, show an intellectual

33. Ibid.
34. Ibid.

and philosophical range of thought bridging two of the most notable organizational embodiments of Black Nationalist thought in America. As Kevin K. Gaines argues in *Uplifting the Race: Black Leadership, Politics, and Culture in the Twentieth Century*, "Ferris's writings and career illustrate the intersection of Black [N]ationalism and racial uplift ideology, particularly in the equation of race progress and respectability with patriarchal authority."[35] While it is nonetheless true that racial manhood, or the ability of the race (specifically its men) to demonstrate various European-derived characteristics of gender, was the aim of racial uplift politics and ethnology, Ferris's masculine ideas—his writings—cannot be reduced to this one construct. He, like all Black intellectuals of his time (both male and female), assumed that such divisions between the sexes were in fact the goal of race progress beyond slavery. What gender looked like among newly free Blacks was part of the emerging questions heading into the twentieth century. What we now term gender, more accurately described in Ferris's time as the role and duty of manhood and womanhood, was a new construct being debated among poor Blacks and aspiring middle-class Black people at the turn of the century. Just as Ferris called for "manhood" for the race, Anna Julia Cooper called for the rise of Black male "chivalry" to protect the purity of Black women in the South, while Edward Blyden championed African matriarchy over the Christian notions of Black Americans.[36] These were ideas debated between Black men and women and not expressed only by one sex. Some Black women supported strong manhood and imperialism, while some Black men did not, and vice versa.[37] As Michelle Mitchell notes in *Righteous Propagation*, "A range of African American discourse was therefore gendered and sexualized during the period of American expansionism. . . . [M]anliness and manhood were frequently used by [B]lack and white Americans as generic terms that could included women."[38] Such a view is evident when we read how even Black women of the time, like Anna Julia Cooper, used manhood to mean the level of civilization attained by the race. As she argues in her chapter on womanhood in *The Voice from the South*, "The race is just twenty-one years removed from the conception and experience of a chattel, just at the age of

35. K. Gaines, *Uplifting the Race: Black Leadership, Politics, and Culture in the Twentieth Century* (Chapel Hill: University of North Carolina Press, 1996), 101–2.

36. See Anna Julia Cooper, *The Voice of Anna Julia Cooper* (Lanham, MD: Rowman & Littlefield, 1998).

37. Michelle Mitchell, *Righteous Propagation: African Americans and the Politics of Racial Destiny after Reconstruction* (Chapel Hill: University of North Carolina Press, 2004).

38. Ibid., 58.

ruddy manhood."[39] William H. Ferris had many intellectual associations and overlaps with various Black men and women of his time, and he was influenced by (and sought to determine) many of these debates. As Kevin K. Gaines suggests, "This extensive diasporic network suggests that Black Nationalism was a fluid intellectual discourse that held appeal for many within the Talented Tenth. An appreciation of the diversity of Black Nationalism intellectuals renders pointless the attempts of some students to construct a Black Nationalist genealogy of singular messianic (and invariably male) leaders in the quasi-biblical, familial sense of who begat whom."[40]

The dominant view of Black Nationalism as solely a political movement is most likely the product of imagining the political activism of the 1960s and 1970s as the historiographic lens through which to view the nineteenth-century origins of such movements and revolts. However, this view is largely mythological, not only mistaking the self-determinacy asserted by Blacks from the civil rights era as political, rather than cultural and intellectual, but also elevating specific historiographic claims about gender and Black militancy above the historical record of the late nineteenth and early twentieth centuries, which demonstrates vastly different ideas, notions, and aims from those motivating the 1960s radicalism that end up framing the scholarship of our day. This imagining of Black radicalism found in the civil rights leaders of the 1960s and 1970s, like Malcolm X and Stokely Carmichael, concerning Black Power and self-determination, and the iconic Black Panther Party ideas symbolized by Huey P. Newton, Eldridge Cleaver, Bobby Seale, and the earlier work of Robert F. Williams, have an effect of excluding a figure like Ferris from being thought of as a Black Nationalist. "As a writer and consumer of racial uplift texts, Ferris preferred the heroic associations of historical romance. He longed for a disinterested Black leadership, philosopher-kings in ebony, unfettered by social constraints."[41] William H. Ferris was an idealist; he was moved by the tides and products of history—its triumphant civilizations, the individuals who became the heroes and heroines of their times, and the legacies of generations beyond time which we now know as legend.

If we look to the original thinkers of Black Nationalist thought, we find a striking similarity between William H. Ferris's philosophy and those of the earliest thinkers of Black Nationalism, like Reverend Lewis Woodson. For many scholars, Martin R. Delany serves as the beginning of the Black Nationalist intellectual tradition, largely due to his political analysis and emigrationist program, but others have argued quite convincingly that it was

39. Cooper, *The Voice of Anna Julia Cooper*, 61.
40. Gaines, *Uplifting the Race*, 103–4.
41. Ibid., 104.

Delany's teacher and mentor, Reverend Lewis Woodson, who deserves recognition as the father of Black Nationalist thought in America.[42] Since the late 1820s, Black thinkers have asserted the existence and capacity of the Black soul that was in need of both religious and intellectual cultivation through the removal of ignorance. David Walker, for instance, argued in his famous *Appeal* that "man, in all ages and all nations of the earth, is the same. Man is a peculiar creature—he is the image of his God, though he may be subjected to the most wretched condition upon earth, yet the spirit and feeling which constitute the creature, man, can never be entirely erased from his breast."[43] Hosea Easton agrees with Walker's argument but stresses the need for principles to cultivate the mind in *A Treatise on the Intellectual Character, Civil and Political Condition of Colored People of the United States* (1837). Easton holds that the mind of the African is doomed to inaction without cultivation through liberal principles; he says, "Nothing but liberal, generous principles, can call the energies of an African mind into action. And when these principles are overruled by a foreign cause, they are left without any thing to inspire them to action, other than the cravings of their animal wants."[44]

This idea of cultivation is shared by Reverend Lewis Woodson, who wrote at the same time as Hosea Easton. This view of cultivation insisted on moral work beyond the physical constraints of slavery and racism. It was a view that suggested that education and the principles of civilization must be assimilated within the soul and mind of the African far beyond criticisms of white religion or government. Woodson argues, "The mere circumstance of our not being slaves, and of other people's not being prejudiced against us, does not necessarily constitute us elevated and worth. All moral worth is inherent, and never entirely depends for its existence on external circumstances."[45] Woodson is insisting that elevation is about not just the removal of external obstacles to equality but also the cultivation of inherent qualities within the self, such that the self improves through its moral labors. It is important to understand that Woodson is arguing for the cultivation of Black moral character by

---

42. See Floyd J. Miller, "The Father of Black Nationalism: A New Contender," *Civil War History: A Journal of the Middle Period* 17, no. 4 (1971): 310–19.

43. David Walker, "Walker's Appeal," in *The Ideological Origins of Black Nationalism*, ed. Sterling Stuckey (Boston: Beacon Press, 1972), 38–117, 99.

44. Hosea Easton, *A Treatise on the Intellectual Character, and Civil and Political Condition of Colored People of the United States: and the Prejudice Exercised towards Them: With a Sermon on the Duty of the Church to Them* (Boston: Isaac Knapp, 1837), 20.

45. Rev. Lewis Woodson (Augustine), "Ten Letters by Augustine: Moral Work for Colored Men," in Stuckey, *The Ideological Origins of Black Nationalism*, 118–48, 118.

Black people; any attempt to allow white abolitionists to direct or any effort to imitate other racial characteristics dooms Black people to failure. Elevation is simultaneously the duty and the burden of races seeking to rise within civilization.

While Woodson does infamously share the basis of Delany's assertion that Blacks are a "nation within a nation" by accepting that "the relation in which we [Blacks] have for generations been held in this land constitutes us as a distinct class,"[46] he is nonetheless interested in the general or national character of Blacks in America. Woodson asserts, "The general character of any nation or class of men, is determined by the private character of a majority of the individuals who compose it,"[47] and to change the national character of a people, Blacks must lead and direct their own moral improvement and elevation. As shown by Woodson's thinking, the issue is not that Ferris's theories fail to align with Black Nationalism and the sentiments that arose during the nineteenth century. In the nineteenth century, Ferris would be easily recognizable as a nationalist. However, in our present orders of knowledge, or what we call disciplines, his position is unrecognizable, because the various visions of Black self-development that emerged in Ferris's day challenge our present viewing of Black Nationalism as a political outgrowth of the 1960s, and not the philosophical disposition of a nineteenth-century Black intellectual tradition. William H. Ferris has a multitude of sentiments and assumptions to explore within the confines of the Black intellectual tradition, which preceded him by almost a century. Just as there is a claim to read Ferris among the Black interlocutors and white influences of his day, there is a need to read him as part of the long tradition he draws from to substantiate his tone and style of thought. To reduce the investigations into Ferris's brilliance to only those figures disciplines have fashioned as appropriate for association would rob Ferris of the poetic eloquence springing forth from his Black soul. It would make platitudes of sonnets and render that which is empyreal simple and mundane.[48]

## CONCLUSION

How, then, does one free an author's work, or rather repel the compulsion to read (whiteness/disciplinarity/Europe/Reason/détente) into a Black text the

46. "Ten Letters by Augustine," 118.

47. Ibid., 121.

48. Dwayne Tunstall's recent research, tentatively titled "The Cosmically Significant Negro: William H. Ferris's Philosophy of History," posits William H. Ferris's racial ideal-

preexisting/determined/configured iterations of racial assuagement, thereby disarming the interpretation of the editor, the truth of the original author, and the milieu of their day? How does one prevent this compulsion, which arms itself against the text with the intention to subdue its words and calm its dissent so that it may be of some use to this day? Perhaps such a question is beyond the hermeneutic as an art of suspicion, as limitation to the reader's will to exercise power over the text—the very meaning it will come to have as a "philosophical work." Perhaps it is the optimism, the enlargement of the meanings of the text, presumed to be democratic in nature, explored by one's foundationless participation in the understanding of (Black) words, and the draw of *rhetorica*, the pull of the audience, the discipline, toward the assimilation of Black figures, that worry me. Or maybe Black texts, in their very existence, are liminal: both what they are and what they are not insofar as they are *made*—the sociogenic extensions of meanings tied to the melaninated flesh of their creators. The Black text, then, seems to comprise words that both speak to Blackness and resist being stained by its voice. The introductory essay and textual annotations made to this volume have been written with this problem in mind. I have attempted to write the annotations and footnotes as signposts to lead the reader toward the texts and issues Ferris himself relied upon to complete this work. My intent is not to persuade the reader of my interpretation but to articulate the conditions that surround the thinking and attempts to create a methodological study of Black people in the early twentieth century.

The disciplinary regimes of knowledge, be they internalized by scholars reading this text or externalized in the form of the peer-review community hearing it, urge assimilation and conformity. Even new works, never before seen or written about, are expected to converge with the already existing forms of knowledge we confidently know, or claim to know, as true and useful to our disciplinary arrangements and projects. Ferris's *The African Abroad* will certainly be claimed to be an extension of many of these preexisting configurations. He mentions the works of Hegel and Immanuel Kant, as well as of William James and Josiah Royce. He cites extensively from his mentor at Yale, George Trumball Ladd, and even considers himself to be an idealist. His text then, according to most standards of philosophy, is compatible with the overarching structure of what we desire to know as philosophical. Yet, Ferris attends solely to the problem of the Negro. He urges us to think of

---

ism as a corrective to the thinking of American philosophers like Royce and investigates the function of race in Ferris's philosophy of history. This research deserves some mention, since it will be among the first theoretical contributions to Ferris scholarship in philosophy over the next several years.

Black folk beyond the minds of his white interlocutors, specifically reaching beyond Kantian physiognomy toward the heavens. He is attendant to the Black soul and asks the reader to care for its spiritual strivings. Ferris demands that we move beyond the quotidian imploring by nonspecialists, the newsboy at the market, toward the social scientific study and philosophical explanations of the Black American.

## *Author's Introduction*

# The Racial Idealism of William H. Ferris

## An Idealist Philosophy of History Rooted in the Ethnological Era

*Tommy J. Curry*

> Plato wrote over the door of the entrance to his lectures upon philosophy: "Let no one enter here who has not studied Geometry," thinking that a man who has not studied geometry could not understand philosophy. And I would like to engrave this axiom over the door of every Negro school-house, college, church and newspaper office, "No one who is not a profound student of sociology and human history is fit to be a leader of the Negro race. The blind cannot lead the blind."
>
> —William H. Ferris

Since its inception, African American philosophy has been fixated on an almost singular Du Boisian axis, the consequence of which is an unabated and unchecked revisionism of W. E. B. Du Bois's lifework that creatively transforms any and all of his writings into the "stuff that philosophical dreams" are made of, so to speak. Because the institutional legitimacy of African American thought remains chained to the integration of primarily two of Du Bois's texts ("Conservation of Races" and *The Souls of Black Folk*) into the disciplinary themes of white academia, there have been few opportunities to seriously explore, contrast, and place in conflict the ideas and philosophical systems of other prominent Black thinkers at the dawn of the twentieth century. While some attention has, of course, been paid to Alain

Locke and Frederick Douglass, with brief commentaries on the work of Booker T. Washington, these writings together do not compare to the amount of literature on Du Bois placing him next to canonical white figures (e.g., John Dewey, G. W. F. Hegel, Jane Addams, Josiah Royce). This singular focus, however, is not without cost. In order to fit within the prescribed limitations of American philosophical interest, Du Bois has had to become a Hegelian, a pragmatist, and a liberal progressive on the race question. While many of the scholars and much of the scholarship on Du Bois make no apologies for the creative interpretations of Du Bois's works, despite textual evidence where he adamantly rejects the aforementioned labels, there is not only a danger of underspecializing the field of African American philosophy in creating erroneous labels of interpretation but also a greater risk of perpetuating ignorance of the complexities and diversity of ideas that comprise African American philosophical thought as the foundation of African American philosophy's disciplinary legitimacy.

African American/Africana philosophy is in need of a wider survey of the primary texts and conceptual delineations articulated by various Black thinkers at the turn of the century. As the small recovery of William H. Ferris's work demonstrates, the specific thoughts and methods of inquiry embraced by historical Black figures of study vary to quite a large extent. Currently, African American philosophy is burdened by the overwhelming weight of the white discipline to simply interpret Black historical figures as the melaninated incarnations of their white heroes. Because Du Bois took classes with Josiah Royce and William James, he is taken to be the Black James, the Black Royce. Just as Frederick Douglass, because he appeals to the natural rights of Black manhood, is linked to the Lockean and social contractarianism of the Enlightenment and deemed the Black Locke in most philosophical discussions. Currently, these views intentionally eviscerate the substance of the relationships and debates that Black philosophers had with one another.

As evidenced by his own writings and tributes, Du Bois was heavily influenced by Alexander Crummell, Henry McNeal Turner, Booker T. Washington, and his debates with Marcus Garvey. His close personal relationships with George Padmore and Paul Robeson were equally important but are never discussed as having philosophical relevance to his thought and his evolving theories of American racism. But Du Bois is not the only victim of this disciplinary tendency in American philosophy. Booker T. Washington is made into a pragmatist despite his relationship with the militant agitationist T. Thomas Fortune and his funding of the political activities of the Afro-American League. Frederick Douglass is lauded for his idealism and optimism about America's promises without any attention to his connection to James McCune Smith. The same lack of genealogical inquiry can be pointed to with any of the Black historical figures taken to be "worthy" of philosophical study—Ida B. Wells, Anna Julia Cooper—as well as those excluded, deemed unworthy of philosophical attention, like Kelly Miller, Hubert Harrison, Ellen Irene Diggs, Drucilla Dunjee Houston, Henry McNeal Turner, Charles Victor Roman, John Edward Bruce, and Arthuro Schomburg. Because of this tendency to "make Black historical thinkers, especially W. E. B. Du Bois, into whatever white thought they have associated with," there is a lack of rigorous research into the annals of Black history for Black philosophers who specifically articulated philosophical insights into America's race problem beyond the caricaturized position of Booker T. Washington.

This republication of William H. Ferris's *The African Abroad; or His Evolution in Western Civilization, Tracing His Development under Caucasian Milieu* aims to complicate the historical account and widen the conceptual geography surveyed by Black thinkers engaging America's race problem. Here enters the lifework of a premier Black philosopher at the dawn of the twentieth century, William H. Ferris, and his racial idealism.

## LIFE AND WORK

William H. Ferris was born in New Haven, Connecticut, on July 20, 1874. He graduated from Hillhouse High School in New Haven and immediately sought admission to Yale, where he earned an AB in 1895. Ferris did pursue a graduate school education. According to his obituary, published in the *Journal of Negro History* in 1941, Ferris attended the Harvard Divinity School from 1897 to 1899, but Harvard's graduate school of journalism, to which he transferred in 1899, would ultimately award him a master's of arts at the turn of the century.[1] Until now, Ferris has primarily garnered limited historical interest by scholars for his work as an editor of Marcus Garvey's *Negro World* magazine from 1919 to 1923, but the conceptual frameworks and ideas set forth in volumes 1 and 2 of *The African Abroad* provide the foundation

1. See "William H. Ferris," *Journal of Negro History* 26, no. 4 (1941): 549–50. There is some discrepancy as to which Harvard school (graduate or divinity) William H. Ferris received his master's degree from. In Randall K. Burkett's *Black Redemption: Churchmen Speak for the Garvey Movement* (Philadelphia: Temple University Press, 1978), Ferris's academic credentials follow those given in Carter G. Woodson's *Journal of Negro History*, but according to Kevin K. Gaines, in *Uplifting the Race: Black Leadership, Politics, and Culture in the Twentieth Century* (Chapel Hill: University of North Carolina Press, 1996), 101, "Ferris received his M.A. from Harvard's Divinity School in 1900."

for his cultural and literary criticisms, articulated years later under Garvey. This historical focus, pursued by scholars like Kevin K. Gaines and Wilson Moses, while giving philosophers substantial materials for study, did not note the influence of the American Negro Academy on his thinking or the consequences of his relationships with the great thinkers of his day for the philosophy set forth in *The African Abroad.* As Gaines notes, "Ferris was an active member of a nationalistic circle of intellectuals that included John E. Bruce, former slave, journalist, and a founder in 1913 of the Negro Society for Historical Research, Pauline Hopkins, Anna Julia Cooper, and American Negro Academy member John Wesley Cro[m]well, William S. Scarborough, Archibald Grimke, Alexander Crummell, Alain Locke, and W. E. B. DuBois . . . [and] Puerto Rican bibliophile Arthur A. Schomburg."[2] These associations not only reveal why *The African Abroad* reflects such intricate and elaborate intellectual heritage but also suggest that the current absence of William H. Ferris from philosophical conversations that seek to recover the intellectual heritage and political philosophy of African Americans at the turn of the century has produced inquiries that can only be found wanting.

William H. Ferris was a well-known Black intellectual of the early twentieth century. He was a founding member of the American Negro Academy and a noted commentator on the major scholarly works of his time. While he is and will remain a somewhat tragic figure, another great Black thinker who died penniless and alone, never receiving the critical acclaim of his contemporaries, his life's work, *The African Abroad*, did deserve and receive some attention and remark by the intellectual giants of his day. It was advertised in the *Crisis* magazine and touted as "Ferris's Vindication," likely by then editor W. E. B. Du Bois.[3] Given the life of Ferris, it comes as no surprise that his work is idiosyncratic, championing the thought of his teachers and colleagues, while suggesting their shortsightedness and urging even their contrasting thoughts toward his eccentric conceptualizations of a Black philosophy of history. It would be a mistake to understand *The African Abroad* as the product of an isolated mind. Ferris takes great care to remark upon and carefully categorize the thinkers of his time. In many ways, *The African Abroad* reads as a philosophically acute cultural criticism of Black literature

2. Gaines, *Uplifting the Race*, 103.

3. Ferris's *The African Abroad* was reviewed in *Crisis* 7, no. 3 (1914): 147. The advertisement for *The African Abroad* appears on p. 155 of the aforementioned volume. Other reviews of Ferris's work include F. H., "The African Abroad by William H. Ferris," *Journal of the Royal African Society* 13, no. 51 (1914): 343–45; Jerome Dowd, "The African Abroad by William H. Ferris," *American Journal of Sociology* 20, no. 2 (1914): 274.

and the role this literature plays in demonstrating and developing the racial personality of African-descended people throughout history.

The success of Ferris's work lies in its ability to provide a remarkable framing of Black thought at the turn of the century. Every major school of Black intellectual thought is remarked upon. Booker T. Washington, W. E. B. Du Bois, Kelly Miller, William Monroe Trotter, and Reverend Reverdy Ransom are all spoken of with high regard, but rather than idle adulation, Ferris offers readers a nuanced commentary on their thought, works, and activities. In the same vein, Ferris makes just as careful a reading and notation of his intellectual influences from Harvard and Yale under his white professors. His writings show great respect for his teachers. William Graham Sumner, William James, Josiah Royce, William Henry Harrison Hart, and George Trumball Ladd are all remarked upon with a noted indebtedness from Ferris. Far from simply imitating the works and ideas of these previous thinkers, Ferris's work shows a remarkable ability to synthesize. His thinking about race, his call for the scientific (sociological) study of the Negro problem, and his philosophy of history show a mastery of previous works by Black and white scholars alike. One of his earliest published pieces demonstrates his indebtedness to ethnology in his move toward idealism.

## FERRIS'S "TYPICAL NEGRO TRAITS" (1908) AS THE BASIS OF HIS PHILOSOPHICAL TREATISE, *THE AFRICAN ABROAD*

Contrary to the ethnological thinking of his times, which still debated the origins of race and the distance the individual's racial stock placed him from (white) humanity, Ferris begins "Typical Negro Traits" by noting, "The fact that strikes us as we study history is the solidarity of the human race. . . . All have an innate longing for life and liberty, all grope towards the Eternal and reach in their soaring aspirations the thought of some Great Mysterious Power, who is the creator of this universe, all strive to express and give utterance to what is deepest and most fundamental within them; all shudder at the mystery of death."[4] The fate of humanity resists simple ethnological accounts in Ferris's view. Race, rather than being one condemnation to the pigment of one's flesh, is drawn out from the body toward these higher ideals. Ferris is of the core belief that "the Negro shares these hopes, strivings, aspirations with other human beings."[5] Unlike such ethnological works as

4. William H. Ferris, "Typical Negro Traits," *American Missionary* 62, no. 4 (1908): 99–102.

5. Ibid.

Martin R. Delany's *Principia of Ethnology: The Origins of Races and Color* (1879) and Edward Blyden's *African Life and Customs* (1908), published in the same year as "Typical Negro Traits," which sought to respond to the alleged biological inferiority of the African through a reclamation of African culture and African civilization, and the sociological works of W. E. B. Du Bois, conducted from the mid-1890s forward at Atlanta University, Ferris suggests that Negroes' humanity can be determined not from their physiology but rather from their philosophical ontogeny—the conceptual development and growth of a young race toward maturity through an understanding and embracing of the ideal.[6] This is not to say that Ferris completely jettisoned the racial archetypes of ethnological psychology but to suggest that, rather than simply appealing to African civilizations for racial vindication or refuting the biologism still behind the assumption of sociological findings, Ferris aimed to demonstrate the conceptual evolution of the Negro beyond an assumed racial personality toward the universal ideals that linked and drove human civilization. The question of the time revolved around whether racial difference marked the Negro's inhumanity. As Ferris asserts, while "the Negro has race traits and tendencies peculiar to himself alone; I do not believe that he is outside of the pale of humanity."[7]

During the late nineteenth century, the study of human variation or races was confined to the field of ethnology.[8] According to A. H. Keane in *Ethnology: Fundamental Ethnical Problems; the Primary Ethnical Groups* (1896),

6. See Martin R. Delany, *Principia of Ethnology: The Origins of Races and Color* (Baltimore: Black Classics Press, 1991); Edward Blyden, *African Life and Customs* (Baltimore: Black Classics Press, 1994). For an account of the theories proposed and the work done by the Atlanta Sociological Laboratory, see Earl Wright Jr., "The Atlanta Sociological Laboratory, 1896–1924: A Historical Account of the First American School of Sociology," *Western Journal of Black Studies* 26, no. 3 (2002): 165–74; Earl Wright Jr., "Deferred Legacy! The Continued Marginalization of the Atlanta Sociological Laboratory," *Sociology Compass* 2, no. 1 (2008): 195–207; Earl Wright Jr., "W. E. B. Du Bois and the Atlanta University Studies on the Negro, Revisited," *Journal of African American Studies* 9, no. 4 (2006): 3–17; Earl Wright Jr. and Thomas Calhoun, "Jim Crow Sociology: Toward and Understanding of the Origin and Principles of Black Sociology via the Atlanta Sociological Laboratory," *Sociological Focus* 36, no. 1 (2006): 1–18.

7. Ferris, "Typical Negro Traits," 99.

8. In "Race and the Concept of Progress in Nineteenth Century American Ethnology," *American Anthropologist* 73 (1971): 710–24, 710, J. S. Haller explains, "Ethnology was the comparative and developmental study of social man and his culture. Concerning himself with the science of culture, the ethnologist enumerated the conditions and modes of existence of specific non-Western peoples, and only touched tangentially upon the contemporary problems of Western life."

ethnology is a specialized field of anthropology dedicated to understanding the "structural differences, which have to be gauged by comparative anatomical studies."[9] Rather than simply studying the physical manifestations of humankind, presupposing the wholeness of the species as differing from other animals, as anthropology does, ethnology is "that branch of general anthropology which deals with the relations of the different varieties of mankind to each other . . . from both the physical and psychological sides."[10] In the nineteenth century, ethnology dealt with a myriad of racial questions and "proceeds by the comparative method, coordinating its facts with a view to determining such general questions as the antiquity of man; monogenism or polygenism; the geographical centre or centres of evolution of dispersion; the number and essential characteristics of the fundamental human types; the absolute and relative value of racial criteria: miscegenation; the origin and evolution of articulate speech and its value as a test of race; the influence of the environment on the evolution of human varieties, on their pursuits, temperament, religious views, grades of culture; the evolution of the family, clan, tribe and nation."[11]

Rather than simply a decadent system used only to substantiate the social Darwinism of the day, ethnology was utilized by Black thinkers to scientifically challenge the scientific racism of the day. While W. E. B. Du Bois's "Conservation of Races" (1897) is routinely read as a revolutionary statement of race theory in line with twentieth-century understandings of race and racial identity, nothing could be farther from the truth. In fact, Alexander Crummell's Occasional Paper No. 3 published two talks together, titled "Civilization, the Primal Need of the Race" and "The Attitude of the American Mind toward the Negro Intellect," respectively. In his second address, "The Attitude of the American Mind toward the Negro Intellect," Crummell briefly thanks Kelly Miller for his research refuting Frederick Hoffman's "Race Traits and Tendencies," then dedicates two paragraphs to commenting on the brilliance of Du Bois's "Conservation of Races." According to Crummell, "The treatise of Prof. DuBois upon the 'Conservation of Race,' separated itself, in tone and coloring, from the ordinary effusions of literary work in this land. It rose to the dignity of philosophical insight and deep historical inference. He gave us, in a most lucid and original method, and in a condensed form, the long settled conclusion of Ethnologists and anthropologists

9. A. H. Keene, *Ethnology: Fundamental Ethnical Problems; the Primary Ethnical Groups* (Cambridge: Cambridge University Press, 1909), 2.

10. Ibid.

11. Ibid.

upon the question of Race."[12] Crummell's comments indicate that the American Negro Academy not only was well versed in the ethnological research of the day but also adapted it to members' own use. William H. Ferris's "Typical Negro Traits" resonates with this appropriation of ethnological sciences taking hold in the ANA from 1897 to 1908. This insight comes from Ferris's own mouth in 1926 in an essay titled "The Myth of the New Negro," which reacts to the recent ongoing popularity of Alain Locke's *The New Negro*. Ferris thinks, "If the papers read before the American Negro Academy in March, 1897, when Dr. Alexander Crummell spoke on 'Civilization, the Primal Need of the New Negro,' and 'The Attitude of the American Mind toward the Negro Intellect,' Dr. DuBois on 'The Conservation of Races,' and Prof. Kelly Miller on 'Hoffman's Race Traits and Tendencies of the American Negro' . . . could be published in a single volume, the scholarship, philosophical analysis, sociological insight displayed would have startled the world and made as strong an impression as the essays on the New Negro."[13] Ferris concludes his review of Alain Locke's *The New Negro* (1925) stating, "The Black Man has been revealing his mind for the past thirty years; but the country did not take the revelation seriously."[14]

Ferris's 1908 essay seeks to advance the mind and passions of the Negro beyond the racial personality traits that refuse to give way to civilization. So whereas the work of Du Bois emphasizes the duality of the Negro soul, this double-consciousness, a concept which continues to overdetermine Du Bois's *The Souls of Black Folk* (1903)—the Negro "feels his two-ness—an American, a Negro; two souls, two thoughts, two unreconciled strivings; two warring ideals in one dark body, whose dogged strength alone keeps it from being torn asunder"[15]—Ferris appeals to assimilationism as the means by which the Negro is civilized away from Africanity. For example, in "The Conservation of Races," Du Bois argues that while "race differences have followed mainly physical race lines . . . [t]he deeper differences are spiritual, psychical, differences—undoubtedly based on the physical, but infinitely transcending them. The forces that bind together the Teuton nations are, then,

12. Alexander Crummell, "The Attitude of the American Mind toward the Negro Intellect," *American Negro Academy Occasional Papers 1–22* (New York: Arno Press and New York Times, 1969), 1–19, 18.

13. William H. Ferris, "The Myth of the New Negro," in *Blacks at Harvard: A Documentary History of African-American Experience at Harvard and Radcliffe*, ed. Werner Sollors, Caldwell Titcomb, and Thomas A. Underwood (New York: New York University Press, 1993), 148–51, 149–50.

14. Ibid., 151.

15. W. E. B. Du Bois, *The Souls of Black Folk* (New York: Dover, 1994), 2.

first, their race identity and common blood; secondly, and more important, a common history, common laws and religion, similar habits of thought and a conscious striving together for certain ideals of life."[16] Du Bois sees the ethnological purview of races and racial personalities to be the effect of the historical growth and development of racial ideals. Racial ideals are formed through the historical differentiation of groups into cities, and cities into nations. In the development of a people into a nation, Du Bois contends, "the spiritual and physical differences of race groups which constituted the nations became deep and decisive."[17] Being true to the focus that ethnology places on the psychology and racial personalities of these various groups, Du Bois sees the ontogeny of races to be growth, where "the great characteristic of this growth has been the differentiation of spiritual and mental differences between great races of mankind and the integration of physical differences."[18] Ferris, on the other hand, saw the taking on of the civilization of the dominant race as the means by which the Negro race specifically could—or, more appropriately, would—develop.

Common to the dozens of essays and manuscripts dedicated to the meaning of the "Conservation of Races" is their failure to attend to the difference between ethnological theories of race and the liberal environmentalism gaining popularity in the mid-twentieth century. The cultural and intellectual contextualization of "race theory" is important so as not to overstate Ferris's project in *The African Abroad*. Ferris's own mind on the development and preservation of the Negro's temperament was in many ways characteristic of his times, with one exception. He saw a genuine need for Negroes to rise above their conditions and toward their genius through the practice of philosophy—the mastering of the techniques of civilization. He turns this lens specifically to understanding what truly makes up the genius, racial gifts, and temperament of the Negro. According to Ferris, "Nine special race traits are often attributed to the Negro. He is said to be immoral, to have a happy-go-lucky disposition, to be jealous of his fellows, to be deceitful, to be imaginative, oratorical, musical, emotionally religious and imitative."[19] Ferris, however, resists simply accepting these common notions attributed to Negroes as their racial personality. Pursuing more stringent evaluation, Ferris concludes, "The first four traits or qualities certainly are not peculiar to the Negro. We cannot call those traits or qualities typical which the colored man shares with

16. W. E. B. Du Bois, "The Conservation of Races," *American Negro Academy Occasional Papers 1–22* (New York: Arno Press and New York Times, 1969), 3–14, 8.

17. Ibid., 8.

18. Ibid., 7.

19. Ferris, "Typical Negro Traits," 99.

all undeveloped peoples that have not long been brought under the refining influence of civilization, but those race traits which are not destroyed by civilization, and which persist in a modified form, in a cultured individual, these only can be called race traits."[20] Ferris takes great care in this work in 1908, as in his magnum opus, to delineate that which is simply attributed to the Negro and that which is an attribute of the Negro. Civilization cannot destroy that which is innate to the racial character of the Negro. Just as the French have a love of art and literature, the Irishman the gift of wit and humor, so, too, thinks Ferris, is the Negro a contributor to the personalities of humanity and marked by his own racial sentiments. In ignorance, we mistake the ills of the Negro's condition for his personality; so it is in the midst of civilization, in the throes of Anglo-Saxon antagonism against the Negro soul, that his gifts emerge—clear and unmistakable as "those Black traits."

Following this line of reasoning, Ferris argues that the Negro is in fact in possession of five race traits. He is "imaginative, possesses the gift of gab, is musical, is religious, and imitative."[21] Ferris likens the imagination of the Negro to that of the ancient Greek. He admits that "the Negro race is not as practical and hard-headed as the Anglo-Saxon, that the black man has not the grim dogged determination and bull dog tenacity of purpose of the white man; but neither had the Greeks of long ago. . . . The Negro race is by nature as imaginative, versatile and imitative as the Greek was, although he has not, as yet, developed his constructive and creative genius."[22] The subtle construction of critique is masterful throughout Ferris's text. The gifts of the Negro are more so in line with that which creates and ushers in what we know as philosophy.

Laying the foundation of his forthcoming Egyptological interventions, Ferris posits the capacity of the Negro to innovate and create as lying at the base of his capabilities to be at the origin of thought. But the thought of the Negro, unlike that of his Anglo-Saxon antagonist, is convey not through the formal pronouncements of civilization and war but through words. The Negro has "a native poetic imagination."[23] The Negro has a voice illuminated by imagery, or, as Ferris more eloquently puts it, "his imagination is tropical in its fertility and luxuriant richness. He is gifted with graphic descriptive power. He is a vivid word painter."[24] There is a somewhat unexpected repetition of this language in W. E. B. Du Bois's book review, titled "The Souls of Black

20. Ibid., 99–100.
21. Ibid., 100.
22. Ibid., 100.
23. Ibid.
24. Ibid.

Folk," published one year after his manuscript by the same name. In that review, Du Bois describes the style he used in writing *The Souls of Black Folk*, saying, "In its larger aspects the style is tropical-African. This needs no apology. The blood of my fathers spoke through me and cast off the English restraint of my training and Surroundings."[25] Here again we see the ethnological parallels and utilizations of the Negro gifts, like prose and gospel, as proof of Du Bois's and ultimately Ferris's point. This gift of gab is as musical as it is poetic. It conveys the spiritual suffering of the Negro in sound, as would pen to pad, and it is this oration—the pull of the Negro voice—that makes its ministers and preachers grasp the ear of even the most indifferent listener. The celebrations of the Negro's gifts, however, are not without pause. Just as the Negro is an aesthetic creature, he is also imitative of the white race. Ferris worries the Negro is too complacent within the milieu of his oppression: "I have met few colored men who were original thinkers. They could sit in judgment upon the American civilization and critically dissect and analyze the ideas upon which it is based."[26]

In his philosophical sensibilities, his ability to critically assess, the Negro is found wanting. In order to uplift himself, the Negro must move beyond his imitativeness. According to Ferris, "In order for a man to pass from the imitative to the reflexive stage of self-consciousness, in order for him to set up a higher ideal than his own age and country affords, he must take a deep dive into history and philosophy. He must drink deeply of the Pierian springs. Then only can he compare and contrast the American civilization with the civilization of other times and other countries."[27] This is not to say imitation is in itself a negation of the spiritual life of the Negro—quite the contrary. Ferris warns, "The fact must not be overlooked that most of the ideas underlying the Anglo-Saxon civilization do not originate in Anglo-Saxon brains."[28] Imitation, however, is only the stepping-stone of the Negro toward his ascension past the Anglo-Saxon. Ferris's ultimate aim is for the Negro to cultivate himself beyond the civilization demonstrated by the Anglo-Saxon: "The Negro should continue to absorb, assimilate and appropriate the highest elements of Anglo-Saxon civilization as he has done for the past forty years. And he must retain his buoyant, hopeful, optimistic nature, his warm sympathy and rich emotional equipment and endowment. With education he must preserve the type. Then, indeed the prophecy of Mr. E. H. Clement may be realized when he declares that 'The Negroes surpass the Whites in artistic

25. W. E. B. Du Bois, "The Soul of Black Folk," *Independent* 57 (November 17, 1904): 1152

26. Ferris, "Typical Negro Traits," 102.

27. Ibid.

28. Ibid.

temperament, and with education and refining may become what the Greeks were to the Romans in their later centuries.' "[29]

Ferris thus sets in motion the intellectual motivation in his penning of *The African Abroad*, offering the reader not only the foundation from which he theorizes but also the ultimate aim of his text. It is this rich ethnological understanding that entails a use of the recently acknowledged capacity of a nonwhite race to assimilate and appropriate (white) civilization without being destroyed by it that stands out in Ferris's work. What is the American Negro but the Negro who controls the laws of civilization to climb above the levees of white civilization standing before him? Throughout the text this nationalistic tone, his insistence upon the conceptual foundations of the Black race, its manhood, its spiritual strivings, returns to this central motivation.

## *THE AFRICAN ABROAD*: THE JOURNEY UPWARD AND BEYOND

The first section of Ferris's *The African Abroad* is a rigorous attempt to construct a philosophy of history where the Negro does not exist at the periphery of modernity but constitutes its dynamic center. Civilization is a fickle caricature of its time, always in flux, remembered only through the pen and words of lifetimes, inevitably written, rewritten, and erased. The mythology of white supremacy, the cherished legend of the Anglo-Saxon, is no different in this regard. Ferris begins his text with precisely this understanding of the laws underlying the centuries, and this knowledge informs what is at stake in articulating race within the dynamism of history and the rise and fall of civilizations. As he says, "Perhaps in that distant time scholars may write books to prove that the world-renowned and world-conquering Anglo-Saxon race never really existed, except in the imagination of rapt poets, and was only a mythical, legendary race. Yes, in the course of time—in the course of five thousand centuries, the races and men now familiar to every schoolboy and girl will be swallowed up in oblivion."[30] What, then, drives a race, no less than an individual, to strive, to develop beyond its present state? "If the great races only dominate the world for a few centuries, and then give way to fresher, stronger races, if even after a few thousand years the great figures in history are forgotten, what is the use of the striving of man?"[31]

29. Ibid.

30. William H. Ferris, *The African Abroad; or His Evolution in Western Civilization: Tracing His Development under Caucasian Milieu* (New Haven, CT: Tuttle, Morehouse & Taylor Press, 1913), 10.

31. Ibid.

Ferris believes the answer to the inevitability of one's passing away, the condemnation of races to oblivion, is quite simple. Eternity of one's kind lives on through the *idea*. Ferris eloquently offers a steadiness in his idealism. He asks the reader to consider that "though nations rise and fall, though they pass off the stage of existence, they yet live in the ideas they have bequeathed to civilization. Though great individuals die and are forgotten, they yet live in the thoughts they have thrown out, which constitutes our intellectual inheritance. Though teachers and preachers are forgotten, they yet live in the lives they inspire, and they kindle a flame that burns in the breasts of countless generations. So our striving is not vain. It ultimately becomes a part of the structure of civilization."[32] The ideas, the concepts birthed in the striving of man and civilization, are the foundation of the architecture for that which we call history. Ideas are the material from which civilizations rise and the basis from which any civilization itself can be challenged and fall. Following Samuel E. Stevens's *The Philosophy of the Great Unconscious*, Ferris understands these laws of civilization as part of the divine substructure of reason and faith. Like Stevens, Ferris believes that the laws of the universe function independently of human understanding. As Stevens famously states, "Whether Man or Mind are evolved, being immaterial to the infinite processes of Nature—which pause not, cease not, rest not, regard not, respect not, care not."[33] One does not simply intuit the eternal mechanisms of civilization through an acceptance of a personal God; rather, such a realization comes as the individual, as a vestibule of the race, is developed and becomes conscious of these directives of God. Similarly, "we cannot believe that the stream can rise higher than its source. We must believe in the cause adequate to produce the effect."[34] God, then, sustains the infinite laws of nature and the universe from which civilization grows. The great unconscious, what Stevens has deemed a more fitting understanding of God, is the basis of the relation the physical world has to purpose—it is the inexplicable continuity of physical phenomena into the manifold of human consciousness, what holds reality together for our perceiving of it.

Spiritual striving, the developing of a race's manhood in history, reaches toward the divine—the Absolute—the eternal scope of the immaterial (God's) mind. In aiming for that beyond the self and the time of the flesh, Ferris conceptualizes the spirit-idea as that part of the divine captured by the conscious of man. Ferris argues, "In developing our manhood, we are not

---

32. Ibid., 10–11.

33. Samuel Eugene Stevens, *The Philosophy of the Great Unconscious* (Boston: Old Corner Bookstore, 1908), 41.

34. Ibid.

only realizing our latent potentialities and developing the germs of divinity that slumber in our natures, but we are developing a bit of the Absolute. If we share in the life of the Absolute, and are partakers of his divine nature, what is more natural than that we should share in and partake of his eternity and immortality?"[35] The spiritual strivings of the human then exhibit the purpose and "meant to be" will of the divine creator. Ferris's substantiation of "man" through God allows for a powerful appeal to the role uplift has in making the Negro fit—not only worthy of political or social equality but also cosmologically significant and necessary to the overall move of history.

> Every living thing fulfills the laws of its being and realizes the immanent idea that Nature implants in it. The grass grows; the seed buds and blossoms into fruit and leaf and flower; the acorn develops into the wide-spreading oak; the majestic lion stalks the forests, monarch of all he surveys; the eagle soars aloft on his powerful wings and sights his prey from afar, and man develops from a babbling babe into a Godlike being, in whom reason and conscience are inthroned. The plant and animal do this unconsciously, obeying their instincts. Man does this consciously, through the guidance of reason, and by the power of choice.
>
> The ideals which man consciously sets up before himself and endeavors to realize in his life and character spring from the abysmal depths of a superhuman source. Man wills whether or no to register, incarnate and embody these institutions and ideals in his life and character, but they come from the eternal God. We must remember that this earth is a stage on which a world drama is being enacted and that our little lives not only have significance for our poor finite selves but also for the universe which begat us.[36]

God then is revealed to us not simply by faith but in the inexplicable quality of the ideas which substantiate us—our striving toward that something—beyond but within our mortal lives upon Earth. It is the endurance of the idea, its transmission beyond the flesh and throughout minds of various times, that commits Ferris to connecting the importance of spiritual striving among the races with the intended, deliberate will of God to sustain history through the rise and fall of civilizations—the birth and demise of ideas and the races which carried them.

Much of Ferris's thinking about history, race, and the idea itself was generated by two central questions. The first two-part question—"What is the meaning of History; Is the hand of God revealed in the movement of history?"—seems to be a common philosophical query asked from the Enlightenment forward, specifically in Hegel. The second question, however, is a much more complicated inquiry that resonates throughout his corpus and

---

35. Ferris, *The African Abroad*, 17.
36. Ibid., 19.

his thinking about "the race"—namely, "Does the way in which man has moved along in his historical development, does the influence of great men upon history, does the moral order that is revealed in history, does the fact that history shows that religion is the deepest thing about man prove anything with regard to the nature of the world ground?"[37] Ferris's second question is a groundwork, so to speak, of the development of racial morals and ideas within the philosophy of history broadly understood. While such a view seems to commit him to the limitations of "choice" and "free will" within the movement of history, it sustains a novel view—namely, that the Negro's development, his gifts, are divinations meant to define a moral order for the world. These questions centralize the basis from which God and the striving of the Negro actively contour the civilizational dictum of the world. Ferris holds, "All human history is inexplicable and incapable of being explained if human history is not the manifestation of the self-revealing life of an Immanent God, who is the center and source of all human progress, because he is the Immanent Source and Ground of the ideals and instincts which have been the propelling cause of human progress."[38] He goes on to say, "If history is to be understood, if human history is to be interpreted, it can only be so as we recognize, in a dim way though it may be, the presence of God in human nature and history."[39]

Because of disciplinary tendencies, the dialectical tone of Ferris will inevitably be read as an example of his Hegelianism, but his thought must also be considered within the ethnological and religious teleological thinking of his day. While Ferris is clear that Hegel is one of his influences, this intellectual affinity must not overshadow the actual intellectual heritage and complexity involved in Ferris's thinking.[40] Ferris was also largely indebted to the work of George Trumball Ladd, who argued, "It is the soul of man which makes history what it is. History is a study of the development of the free spirit of man. It cannot be explained on biological, anthropological and statistical grounds alone. Some of the most important economical changes have been

37. Ibid., 24.

38. Ibid.

39. Ibid., 25.

40. This is, of course, not to dismiss Hegel's influence on Ferris's thinking. In a lesser-known article titled "The Influence of a Weltanschauung upon a Philosophy of Education and Its Bearing upon Negro Education," *School Journal* 81, no. 1 (1913/14): 87–88, Ferris argues, "As we survey the development of man in history we may say with Hegel that 'History is the development of human individuality'" (87). Again many would see a tension between the individual and the race, but under ethnological maxims what is true of the race, the family, is also true of the individual. It is through the race that the individual aspires toward ideas and finds his or her spiritual strivings.

due to the fact that man is a religious being. History is the resultant of the entire complex development of man considered as body and mind and determining his own development."[41] Ladd sees philosophy, the study of the spiritual ends or purposes of man, to be centrally related to the productive capacities of the soul. The human condition, its freedom to become, is the author of history. Ladd holds, "Man's philosophy, his science, his art, his ethics and religion are not caused by mechanical forces external to himself; but they arise out of the depth of the human soul. The intellectual, moral and spiritual characteristics of the human soul are what is of main account in history."[42] Ferris is heavily influenced by this aspect of Ladd's thinking. We can even see connections to his earlier 1908 piece, "Typical Negro Traits," since all the productions of races necessarily indicate the capacity and potentiality of the soul. From this aspect of Ladd's thinking, Ferris argues for a specific racial capacity, the specific gifts, from which the Negro(saxon) can contribute to humanity and literally make history.

It must be emphasized that Ferris is not a determinist in a strict sense of the word. While it is true that he believes that God is behind the move of civilization and the cosmic canvas that holds the reality of the world in relation, he is not arguing that God has already determined the ends of history or the Black race. He wants to believe in the potential and power of human freedom, a power that closely aligns his view of freedom and reason with that of Kant. In his *Anthropology from a Pragmatic Point of View*, Kant argues,

> Such an anthropology, considered as knowledge of the world, which must come after our schooling, is actually not yet called pragmatic when it contains an extensive knowledge of things in the world, for example, animals, plants, and minerals from, various lands and climates, but only when it contains knowledge of the human being as a citizen of the world.
>
> Therefore, even knowledge of the races of human beings as products belonging to the play of nature is not yet counted as pragmatic knowledge of the world, but only as theoretical knowledge of the world.[43]

Ferris parallels Kant's pragmatic anthropology more than a pure dialectical Hegelian mode of consciousness, which depends on a strong egoism and othering of subjects. Ferris embraces dialectic modes of thinking between the individual and the race, the race and civilization, and history and God, but

41. Ibid., 27.

42. Ibid.

43. Immanuel Kant, *Anthropology from a Pragmatic Point of View*, trans. Robert Louden (Cambridge: Cambridge University Press, 2006), 4.

this is due not to a strong objectification of the "other" category but rather to a dynamism that posits friction between the categories as necessary for development and *assimilation*, a blending together and unfolding, of the self *as* race, the race *as* humanity, history *as* civilization and God. Because Ferris recognizes the overdeterminism of race—the Negro, the African—to savagery, darkness, and barbarism, he aims to introduce the capacity of the American Negro, what he will develop later in this text as the "Negrosaxon," as beyond the theoretical taxonomies of the world, which place the Negro in state of inferiority by the hand of nature. It is precisely this *making* of the Negro, his ability to *be* a vessel of civilization and conduit of God through his spiritual strivings, that draws Ferris into this idealist tradition. Ferris takes the freedom that so occupied Kant's thought in his *Anthropology from a Pragmatic Point of View* and deploys it to escape the anthropological—or, more accurately, ethnological—hierarchy established between the races. It is in the spiritual development that the Negrosaxon aims for that he elevates and establishes the race beyond the racist taxonomy of *white* civilization and becomes a new being that contributes to *human* civilization.

This freedom that man enjoys finds in itself a tie to God. Ferris is set upon a teleological investigation into the movement of history through the strivings and development of one's kind, or race. As he says, "It is because God is operating in and through the laws of organic life that man comes into being. Man is finally produced on this earth because God had him in mind from the beginning."[44] The development of man follows the laws of the nature, just as God sustains or makes those laws possible. Ferris, like Ladd, believes that God uses the laws of nature, or evolution, to drive the perpetual unfolding of the world before us. Through these mechanisms of nature, man finds his place among the productions of God's will, not as its center.

> The question, is there a teleological movement in the world, admits of but one answer. That man is one of the final purposes that this universe was intended to realize, does not admit of a doubtful answer. But when we ask, is man the only final purpose that this universe was intended to serve, or is he the supreme final purpose that this universe was intended to serve, we are asking far different questions. The fact that Nature, in her obedience to inexorable laws, never swerves from her path to please man, that she frustrates his most cherished hopes and dearest wishes, ruthlessly and permanently destroys the fairest flowers of human blossom when her laws are disobeyed or man happens to stand athwart the path of her titanic forces, such as the cyclone, volcano, lightning or angry waves, forbids us believing that the only purpose this earth exists for is to produce man. Nor again can we ever know whether the creation and eternal preservation of finite moral personality was the supreme and

44. Ferris, *The African Abroad*, 58.

> most important final purpose God had in mind when he manifested himself through this universe.[45]

Nature is not married to the will of man. The political, the historical, the philosophical grasp of nature and ultimately God is frustrated and obscured within human experience, precisely because the mortality of the human species—its people, its races, its individuals—is incapable of truly understanding the ends God intends. This is not, however, a condemnation of mankind into ignorance. While Ferris believes, as Herbert Spencer indicates, that the human cannot know the absolute, he does not see knowledge or its pursuit throughout human life as meaningless, despite the limitation of the human to grasp Truth. Perhaps the greatest testament to Ferris's commitment to the study of man, what is best expressed as a philosophical anthropology comprised of a sociology and history of mankind, is his own query upon the matter: "How do we know man? We know him through the works that he does,—so we can know God."[46] The study of man is the beginning of the inquiry into God and the absolute.

## TOWARD THE RIGOROUS STUDY OF THE NEGRO: FERRIS'S HISTORICAL IDEALIST SOCIOLOGY

It would be a gross misrepresentation of Ferris's thinking to place his idealism against empirical fields of study like sociology. Throughout *The African Abroad*, Ferris references the importance of sociology to the study of the Black race but warns that in focusing on the conditions of man, or race, we must not believe that these entities are predetermined and fixed—incapable of change and development regardless of social condition and historical racial disposition. The study of the Negro must be based on the actual conditions of racism, segregation, and race hatred that were created in America, and his striving against these conditions, rather than on the intuitive responses that hold the Negro to be inferior, backward, and outside civilization. Ferris sees the problem as follows: "When the American comes to the Negro problem, he settles that offhand, without any thorough investigation. He merely passes it by, with a contemptuous wave of the hand, or toss of the head. Why, any petty clerk, or office boy or newsboy or bootblack, knows what ought to be done with the Negro, knows what kind of education the Negro needs! The

45. Ibid., 59.
46. Ibid., 60.

prevailing sentiment seems to be that anyone, no matter how ignorant, is fitted to grapple with the various Negro problems."[47] Ferris argues that specialists, people valued for their opinion on the Negro, need not actually know anything about the Negro or the race problem in America. Much in keeping with our contemporary disciplinary problems of underspecialization in race theory, where thinkers who lack a basic grasp of the historical problems and sociological scope of racism are regarded as specialists,[48] Ferris points out that any position regarding race becomes synonymous with an authoritative and valuable contribution to dealing with Black folk. His criticism is paradigmatic, pointing to the failure America has in understanding racism, an understanding that would require one to know about the history, sociology, and psychology of Black people to become an authority on Black people. In short, Ferris wages an epistemological assault on what we take to be knowledge of the Negro and the political problems that confront his rise within civilization.

Why does this problem of studying the Negro so occupy Ferris? Ferris understands the Negro to be a contributor to the overall knowledge of civilization and humanity, but the false notions of Negro uplift, based in tradition rather than sociology, history, theology, or philosophy, doom the Negro race to ignorance. While there is certainly an elitism in this view, Ferris states clearly, "If we seek to get the Irishman's opinion regarding Ireland, we don't go to the ignorant immigrant fresh from Ireland; but we generally go to the Irishmen of the finest minds, who have had the best training. . . . [W]e ought to do the same with regard to the Negro. We ought to regard the men who represent the brains and scholarship, the moral stamina and manliness of the Negro race, as the real leaders."[49] The view that holds that Black folk have no need for letters and philosophical thought is abhorrent to Ferris. Ferris believes, "It so happens that the vast majority of colored people get their knowledge through their eyes and ears. The sights and sounds of Nature enrich their knowledge. They learn to do things by seeing other people do things and by having other people tell them how to do things."[50] Because the vast majority of Negroes learn from the instruction of others, their knowledge of the world "is largely imitative and that is why the Negro is largely an imitative being."[51] Ferris is reacting against a dogmatism of his time that

47. Ibid., 365.

48. See Tommy J. Curry, "Concerning the Under-specialization of Race Theory in American Philosophy: An Essay Outlining Ignored Bibliographic Sources Addressing the Aforementioned Problem," *Pluralist* 5, no. 1 (2010): 44–64.

49. Ferris, *The African Abroad*, 366.

50. Ibid., 175.

51. Ibid.

suggests the Negro, being savage and not human, is unworthy of being the subject of study and unfit for higher learning. By indicting the approach from which Black people are engaged, Ferris is making the case that the art, philosophy, religion, politics, and history of the Negro not only merit study but also constitute the only way by which one can ascertain the true character and the spiritual gifts that the Negro holds for the world. In order to escape the banality of mimicry, Ferris says, "A man must read books and study books and master first principles before he can become creative, constructive and original."[52] This rise of the idea within the breasts of man is the generating force for racial change and social equality.

Ferris is dealing with the seemingly unshakable blindness of the world toward the Negro, where "the current belief is that the teachings of history and sociology can be ignored when we approach the Negro problem, that it doesn't require careful and serious study to understand the race question in its deeper issues,"[53] precisely because the world saw no use in the lives and thoughts of Black people in the world. Negroes had no history, no philosophy, no art; they were simply the excess of other people's history, the labor force to be used for true (white) civilization. Ferris understands that "the Negro problem is a complicated one."[54] "Unless a man is a profound student of psychology, sociology, political economy and history, he cannot begin to comprehend and understand, or grapple with its phases and aspects."[55] The Negro problem will not be solved by knee-jerk solutions that target only one aspect of Black existence in America. Rather than simply believing that the Negro is in need of industrial education or liberal arts training, Ferris demands a comprehensive understanding of what obstacles historically formed the seemingly insurmountable barriers to Negro equality and robbed the race of its desire to strive toward higher spiritual goals. This historical perspective on the race problem is fundamental to Ferris's thinking. It is only in understanding the past, Ferris thinks, that Blacks can adequately determine their course for the future. Ferris insists that the study of history must come first: "So we might take up other political, social or educational problems and find the genetic method of explaining the present by the past—the only satisfactory way of dealing with any problem. The reason is obvious. The present is the outgrowth of the past, and has its roots deeply grounded in the past. Hence, the present can only be understood in the light of the past. And

52. Ibid.
53. Ibid., 366.
54. Ibid.
55. Ibid., 367.

we cannot understand things as they are save as we understand how they came to be."[56]

Understanding history allows the observer to account for the entities and dispositions of the present. Ferris insists that our misunderstanding of history, our inability to discern substance from dogma, rewards piecemeal political reforms that never address the exclusion of Black people in America from humanity. Our focus on equality, or voting, or industrial education does not address the barring of the Negro from mankind. This is why the ideal is so import to Ferris; it transcends the historical taxonomy of the Negro and offers testament to his immortality, the manhood of the race, which is to say, the capacity of the race to affect the flow of history and show to the world its envisioning of civilization. In this moment Ferris shows the reader how the historical is necessarily the sociological, since "you cannot understand history unless you understand man as an ethical, aesthetical and religious being."[57] The observer, the student of the Negro, cannot comprehend his history if said observer does not understand the character from which it was built and the end for which it was designed. We must empirically study the Negro as is, not as the result of some fixed biological essence, to comprehend what he has been and what he shall become. It is in the capacity of Negroes to create beauty, the spirituals, to create resistance through politics, to offer the poetry of Phillis Wheatley as testament to their genius and humanity; it is their ability to create that warrants the study of their creations.

What is the content of resistance? What is the beauty necessary to draw the soul and consciousness beyond the corporeal limits of the flesh? What is it that allows the observer, the patient caretaker of the Black soul, to glimpse its existence within the cursed strife of the body? It is the aesthetic, political, philosophical, and religious synergy of the race that offers proof of ideas that generate moral reform in society. This view is somewhat strange to us in our present-day arrangements of disciplines, which have distinct methods and materials of study, precisely because it views the human and the social environment created by human living to be separate from the spiritual and religious ideals generating a peculiar humanity and a particular society. But Ferris is not of our time and is attending to the sociological as a condition made possible by the spiritual striving of a race-culture aiming to change the established moral milieu of his day. This is part of the heritage Ferris obtains from George Trumball Ladd's religious thought.

In *The Philosophy of Religion*, Ladd argues, "Science and philosophy, art and literature, industrial and political and moral improvements—all the

56. Ibid.
57. Ibid., 25.

concurrent factors of advancing race-culture—are subject to the same considerations,"[58] in part historical and social, but not wholly of the absolute. Race-culture, or civilization, is the principle of group elevation in Ladd's thinking. Ladd explains the operation of this principle as follows: "It may be said that the religious development of the race, or of any particular smaller or larger portion of the race, depends upon the advance of race-culture."[59] By culture Ladd means "man's relation to the world as far as this is determined by his own rational activity."[60] The Negrosaxon, the Black American, is the smaller portion of the larger human race charged with this elevation, and by consequence it is his development which is key to changing history, realizing civilization anew, and inspiring the ideals that will energize the moral demands for social reform. What we now designate as the political and/or social is specifically generated by ideas for Ferris, and it is when an idea is entrenched as race-culture that it captures the grand narrative of a nation or civilization. "In fact, we may say that the greatness of a race or nation is measured by the greatness of the idea that dominates it; by the greatness of the ideal that it endeavors to realize in its national or racial life. The same is true of an individual."[61] It cannot be stressed enough how parallel his thinking is to Ladd's in this regard. Ladd insists,

> Especially is this true of the forces that make for the moral reform of any age or people; whether their forces chiefly express themselves in protest and action against the existing state of public morality, or attempt to supply the needed energy for a positive betterment of the ethical multitude. For it is these ethical forces of reform and amendment which have, both as respects their origin in the soul of man and also as respect to the end they strive to secure, the most intimate kinship with the forces that are active in producing the higher developments of the religious life of humanity. . . . Great ideas are energetic forces in man's religious development. And these great ideas largely spring from the experience and reflection of a few individuals.[62]

This reformulation of Black ideas, the encouragement of learned striving, is the platform from which Ferris launches his philosophy and measures that of others. Perhaps his most controversial and profound articulation of this is his argument for the realization of the Negrosaxon.

58. George Trumball Ladd, *The Philosophy of Religion: A Critical and Speculative Treatise of Man's Religious Experience and Development in the Light of Modern Science and Reflective Thinking* (New York: Charles Scribner's Sons, 1909), 1:230.

59. Ibid., 215.

60. Ibid.

61. Ibid., 167.

62. Ibid., 231.

## RACIAL IDEALISM AND THE BIRTH OF THE NEGROSAXON

It should be obvious to the reader by this point that Ferris's study of history serves more than to unearth the foundations of racial inequity; history is the means through which the Black American transforms and masters the principles of civilization. "What is human history but man's coming to self-knowledge, man realizing his own spiritual birthright, man realizing the moral and spiritual meaning and significance of life, man realizing that the same human soul pulses and throbs in men of all ages and races and colors."[63] Ferris is unrelenting in his idealism and holds it to be the necessary condition from which racial uplift can be had. The idealist—"men of thought rather than the men of action have been the real makers of the world's history"[64]—is the only hope for the Black race in Ferris's view. "Thoughts and ideals rule the world. And men are only great in so far as they realize and embody ideas,"[65] says Ferris. But this is not the path of the colored man in America today. He asks,

> What encouragement does the colored man, who has spent a score of years in school and college, who has delved in philosophy and history and literature, and whose aim and ambition in life is to produce a work in literature, philosophy or history, that shall live after him and cause the youth of his own race to feel that his own race has made some contribution to civilization and wrought something in the world of ideas and the realm of letters, get? The Anglo-Saxon race will regard him as an impractical dreamer, who is wasting his life, while the head of one of the great industrial schools of the South will speak of him as a literary bum and educated tramp and speak in contempt of a rosewood piano in a log cabin or country schoolhouse or a colored youth studying a French grammar in the backwoods. He will be pointed to as an educational failure; even if he has written and had typewritten a work on philosophy, history and literature, he can arouse no interest in the Anglo-Saxon race and no enthusiasm in his own race.[66]

Ferris writes *The African Abroad* in part to address this vitiation of the Black idealist. His aim is to lift the spiritual aspirations of the race and show that it is through ideas that one can address the larger racist obstacles of America. Because the idealist, the lofty thinker, is discouraged from engaging the problems of the race, Ferris hopes to show that this step is necessary, that the opinion of the race should not be reserved for the preacher or the

63. Ferris, *The African Abroad*, 275.
64. Ibid., 102.
65. Ibid.
66. Ibid., 204.

activist but should in fact be shared by the careful thinker and student of Black people. He in many ways argues for the role of the Black intellectual as public figure and leader. He says,

> What Homer did for the heroes of the Trojan War, what Carlyle did for Cromwell and his other heroes, I am going to try to do for the great men of the Negro race. I am going to try to rescue from the dust and dusk of obscurity and oblivion, and surround with the halo of immortality the names of those heroic men and women who braved unpopularity and misrepresentation for asserting their manhood and womanhood. If life and health be spared me, I will endeavor to write the Negro histories that will inspire the colored youth of the land. I hope that the future historians of the race will build upon me and see through my spectacles. I trust that they will accept my point of view and take their cue from me.[67]

Ferris urges Black Americans to rethink the figures given the platform to lead the race. He insists that a formal education in history, sociology, philosophy, and religion forms the basis from which to engage the race problem in America. The popular conceptualization of race leadership and race theory about the problems facing Black Americans is inadequate if it lacks rigor, the comprehensive understanding of the past such that it has conditioned and, in many ways, determined the present and set the course toward the future. Ferris asks Black Americans to consider the message given to the masses of Black folk looking for direction. He says, "People seem to overlook the fact that the ministers, teachers, editors, lawyers, physicians and business men are the leaders of the Negro race, and that upon the kind of education and training that is given them will depend the salvation of the masses."[68] This change in leadership, in the messages offered to the masses, is not as simple as a shift in the representative class placed in front of Black masses; rather, it is a complete shift in the conceptualization of Black Americans and their racial destiny. Black Americans must be trained to "think" themselves differently.

The specificity of Ferris's attention to Black Americans requires some remark at this stage. Ferris believes that Black Americans are a race quite distinct from the Negro. Black Americans, whom he calls Negrosaxons, will lead the revolt against white civilization and introduce into humanity the unfulfilled promises of American civilization: fraternity, justice, religious liberty, and the equality of man.[69] Negrosaxons are God's mortal helpers toward the realization of a more advanced civilization, helpers who take the best of

67. Ibid., 369.
68. Ibid., 354.
69. See William H. Ferris, "The Success of Philosophy," in *The African Abroad*, 167.

the Anglo-Saxon's reign without the vices of such a warlike people content to dominate and exploit the lands and peoples of the world generation after generation. Just as past epochs of civilization ended and rose anew from the triumph of the ideas representing a people, so, too, would Black Americans lead and nourish the failing foundation of Western civilization. Ferris holds that "the twentieth century will witness the application of the ideals of personality, the conception of individuality, to the darker races. It will witness the embracing of the darker races within the brotherhood of the human family. It will mean that the Negro will be regarded as a person and not as a thing."[70]

The Negrosaxon is not a Negro in Ferris's new racial taxonomy. The Negro "ethnologically refers to the full-blooded Negro in Africa, or of African descent living elsewhere."[71] Not only is Ferris adamant that the term "Negro" is inapplicable to the sociological and cultural condition of Black people in America at the dawn of the twentieth century, but he also considers the categorization of Black Americans as Negroes to be derisive.

> The term "Negro" suggests physical and spiritual kinship to the ape, the monkey, the baboon, the chimpanzee, the ourangoutang and gorilla. The term "Negrosaxon" denotes the physical kinship of half of the colored people of America and the spiritual kinship of ninety percent of the colored people of America to the noble Anglo-Saxon race. It is up to the Negrosaxon or Colored man to say which badge he shall wear, the badge of monkeyhood or of manhood, the badge of brutehood and bestiality or the badge of humanity. Calling ourselves "Negrosaxons" or Colored people will not let down the social barriers to us and give us entrance to Anglo-Saxon society; but it will give us the only kind of equality and opportunity that we need and desire—civil and political equality and industrial and economic opportunity.[72]

To Ferris's mind, calling oneself a Negrosaxon is a necessary preparatory consciousness of the distinctness of kind and mission that befalls the Black American.[73] The name conditions the Black American to accept his separation from the savagery of Africa and his embrace of the grand ideals introduced into civilization through the rise of Anglo-Saxon dominance. The

70. Ibid., 198.

71. Ibid., 296.

72. Ibid., 309.

73. Ferris also takes great care to eliminate the use of "Afro-American" and "colored" as labels Black Americans should embrace. "Afro-American" is "a geographical rather than an ethnological term. The Canadians, Indians, Mexicans and Brazilians are just as much Americans as the citizens of the United States. And the Egyptians, Berbers, Arabs, Phoenicians and Carthaginians are just as much natives of Africa as the Negroes" (*The African Abroad*, 296), so the term fails to refer to the racial heritage or capacities of its referent. Similarly, the "colored race is a heterogeneous group of individuals in whose

reader of this passage is probably at wits' end. Our present sentiments have conditioned us to reject prima facia this ethnological account of Black inferiority and racist depiction of Africa, but Ferris, writing at the dawn of the twentieth century, has a different view of the contentions determining civilization and racial progress than the scholars of our time, given only amalgamated fractions of his moment and its precursors.

Ferris is proposing a radical assimilationism, where Black Americans take the useful ideas of Western civilization that themselves are far too grand to be realized by white nations. Ferris aims not to rescue all of Blackness but to claim for Black Americans an American identity that will be the catalyst for a higher twentieth-century racial vision. Black Americans are the authors of not only *their* present but also *the* future—they are the platform upon which civilization advances. Remember that Ferris is arguing for the mastery of the laws of civilization. He is arguing that the knowledge offered to the world under Anglo-Saxon rule, while initially useful, has run its course and now needs Black Prometheans to continue lighting the path of the world toward a higher civilization. This is why Ferris can say, with no hesitancy, "If the Negrosaxon expects to share in the political inheritance of the Anglo-Saxon, he must be made over in the likeness of the Anglo-Saxon. He cannot bleach out his complexion, or straighten his hair, or sharpen his nose, or thin his lips. But in mind and character and disposition he must become a black white man. After the Negrosaxon has been made over into the likeness of the white man he can hope to be made over into the image of God."[74] "The Negrosaxon has high ideals, but he is born and reared in an environment that makes it very difficult for him to live up to his ideals."[75] Ferris aims to provide the manual from which the Negrosaxon can become the master of history and society alike.

Ferris maintains hope. He holds firm to the idea that the Negrosaxon can rescue Anglo-Saxon civilization from itself—its hypocritical tyranny. For example, when challenged by the pessimism of esteemed Black educators who held that "the original barbarity of the Teuton is mildly tempered with

---

veins Negro, Indian, Jewish, Celtic, Teutonic and Latin blood is mingled, rather than a homogeneous race" (ibid.). As Ferris notes, the colored race is also wanting in ethnological character. He says, "The colored race has no ethnological integrity. It does not spring from the same stock, has not similar physical and psychological traits and characteristics, nor common ideals. The force that welds it together does not come from within, but from without. The colored race is held together by adhesion rather than by cohesion" (ibid.).

74. Ibid., 304.

75. Ibid., 229.

Christian hypocrisy"[76] and announced that they had "lost hope for your people,"[77] Ferris reminds his interlocutors that "the Negro race will slowly and surely absorb and assimilate and appropriate the highest elements of the Anglo-Saxon civilization and embed the Anglo-Saxon ideals into the ground roots of its being, into the very fibres of its moral nature."[78] Quoting Ralph Waldo Emerson, Ferris affirms a shared belief: "Though the black man's skin be as dark as midnight, if he has genius, it will shine through and be as transparent as the everlasting stars."[79] This Emersonian sentiment sustains Ferris's unshakable faith in the capacity of the Negrosaxon to change the sentiment of the white American. By controlling the laws of civilization to fulfill the failing ideas birthed in Western civilization, the Black American will be recognized, and once he is seen as worthy of civilization through a demonstration of his worth, society will open itself to the race. Ferris believes that it was God's divine and deliberate will that Black Americans awaken from their slumber and rise toward the ideas that sustained the world and heaven alike. All of history has led to this moment—the awakening of the Negrosaxon and *his* command of the ideal.

## CONCLUSION

It is truly impossible for the introduction of this magnificent text to do any degree of justice to the various debates, historical accounts, and sheer quality of thought in Ferris's *The African Abroad*. Needless to say, *The African Abroad* is a trove of intellectual and historical nuance with far-reaching implications for any number of areas of study. For example, Ferris's discussions of Josiah Royce and Kelly Miller offer invaluable insights into a long-standing debate over Royce's assimilationism and imperialism.[80] His criticism of both Du Bois and Booker T. Washington, his account of Egyptian civilization, his later Pan-Africanism under Garvey, his love of philosophy as the synthesis of the empirical and humanist sciences—all these ideas are present in this text and, if explored, will add a much-needed complexity and

76. Ibid., 191.
77. Ibid.
78. Ibid., 191.
79. Ibid., 192.
80. See Tommy J. Curry, "Royce, Racism and the Colonial Ideal: White Supremacy and the Illusion of Civilization in Josiah Royce's Account of the White Man's Burden," *Pluralist* 4, no. 3 (2009): 10–38.

accuracy to the disciplinary practices of interpretation and the literature on Africana philosophy.

The mark of Ferris's work is historical, of an acute genealogical temperament, that shows no restraint whatsoever in its commentary and evaluation of the scholarship, texts, and opinions of his peers. He marks with compulsiveness the associations, meetings, and events that have sparked and influenced his thought and driven the thinking of his generation. Despite our inclinations to read Ferris as among the moderates of his day due to his uplift politics and idealism, we would do well to remember that Ferris undertakes *The African Abroad* as a staunch critique and radical declaration against the tides of his day. Ferris declared with pen to page that the Black writers of his day were little more than a class of cowards:

> [Because they are] afraid of following the dialectics of their own nature, the genius of their racial psychology, consequently the note of individuality is not heard in their writings. As a rule the colored writers and colored speakers, who have the ear of the country, are more desirous of winning the favor and esteem of the Anglo-Saxon race than in giving utterance and expression to the thoughts that are burning in their own souls. Consequently they sing a song that will catch and please the ears of the Anglo-Saxon instead of speaking in trumpet tones the message that wells up in their souls, and comes to them from the Eternal God.[81]

Throughout his corpus, Ferris articulates poignant and careful analyses of the writings of his contemporaries. He is caustic but fair, clear that his goal is the spiritual elevation of the race, and relentless in his critique of the philosophies that seek to contravene the emergent idealist—Negrosaxon—of the race. His work marks continuity as well as careful division of opinion and fact in the declarations of his opponents. Throughout his work, Ferris comments upon the stake the Negro has in following the programs set forth by Du Bois, Washington, Kelly Miller, and Marcus Garvey. For Ferris, these plans all represent possibilities from which one could view, interpret, and decide the Negro problem; yet he, unlike many in his day and many in ours, saw that they had to be weighed and measured. There was no one panacea for white supremacy or the problem of degradation and segregation plaguing the race. Knowledge then was not exclusive to the prophets of the day; rather, it required the training and ascendency of the Negro beyond its conditions and toward the heavens. While it may seem to some that he merely reiterates the promise of liberal arts training, it would be a mistake to simply encapsulate his work in the highlighted debates offered as the core issues of contention in Black intellectual history.

81. Ferris, *The African Abroad*, 267.

Ferris's text is the first published account of a self-identified Black idealist made available for our study and dissection in philosophy. He is a thinker who places the utmost confidence and faith in Negro(saxon)s' racial inclination to think and imagine themselves, as spiritual entities, beyond the material limitations of the West. Ferris believes, "The Negro is more of a dreamer and an idealist than a doer of deeds. Consequently the contribution that the Negro will make to civilization will be in the realms of music, oratory, literature and art."[82] He thereby builds a philosophy of liberation, his philosophy of history, upon what he takes to be the ultimate purpose of Black American experience in the world. It is my hope that Ferris's text will enable us all to become better dreamers and aspire to grander visions of Black thinking about the world. Ferris offers an idealistic account of Black American identity, one that is more American than African. He offers Black philosophers and race theorists a way to reconcile the seemingly irreconcilable tension between Blackness and Americanness. Perhaps his philosophy is in fact the Black philosophy of the twenty-first century as well—a metaphysical account of why Black American identity is exceptional, why Black Americans have been placed in the belly of empire, so to speak. Ferris provides a lens to think about the racial identity of Black citizens beyond the dichotomies of separation and integration. He offers Black philosophy a historiography rooted in Black Americans' acceptance of their unique duty and divine obligation. As a matter of fact, perhaps it will be the racial idealist who reminds the minds of our day that Black thought is more than the political problems it finds itself amid and its desire for recognition by those who continue to erase our contributions from the annals of history. Perhaps it is the Black American who was chosen to write history.

---

82. Ibid., 268.

*Part One*

# INTRODUCTION TO A PHILOSOPHY OF HISTORY

## *Chapter One*

# A Narragansett Reverie upon the Eternal and the Ephemeral in Human Life and History

As I selected for a task giving to the world an interpretation of the hopes and longings and strivings and aspirations of the Black Man, and a record of his deeds and achievements, I thought of the larger life of mankind, of which the life of the Negro is but an eddy in a stream. I pulled back the curtain of time and saw savage man emerging from the caves thousands of years ago. I saw how he learned the use of fire and mastered the art of writing. I saw him dwelling in communities and developing states. I saw him offering sacrifice to an avenging deity, and then rise to the lofty conception of an Eternal One. I saw nations rise and fall, dynasties come and go, saw great men play their part in the drama of human history and pass on into oblivion. And then I asked, What is the significance of the toil and struggle, of the effort and aspiration of man, of the blood and tears he has shed? What is human history? Is there any meaning to history? Is it a divine poem, epic in its sweep? Is it a world drama? Is there a mighty power, a Master Mind behind the curtains, shifting the scenes? I will relate the experience that led me to reflect upon the meaning of history and man's place in the universe.

Whoever has visited Great Barrington, crossed the Housatonic River and wandered along the street which lies at the foot of East Rock, can never forget the beauty and serenity of the view before him. Great Barrington lies in a valley between two long low ranges of hills. As the eye glances down the hill, it stops for a moment to watch the play of sunlight and shade upon the Housatonic River, flowing so calmly between two rows of trees.

Then the way in which the village is nestled among the trees, the infinite variety and contrast of the scene, the dreamy play of the sunlight on the leaves and branches, and the sense of repose and quiet pervading the whole village cause a serene, rapturous feeling to take possession of the beholder and lift him to realms of the infinite.

Finally the eye rests upon the sloping hillside at the other end of the village, and the large residences built upon it. It observes the mixture of forests and meadows, and the trees on the top of the hillside. I thought of the serenity of nature, of those enduring hills that had stood for ages, and something of the peace and quietness of nature, something of the granite strength of those hills came into my soul. But it was another experience which was to lead me to see in nature the manifestations of a creative spirit and to contrast the eternal life of nature with the ephemeral strivings of man.

It was a beautiful August morning when I started for Tower Hill, one of those days when poets love to sing. As I looked up at the sun shining with all its sky-high splendor, casting its rays here and there, and felt the invigorating breeze as it swept over the Atlantic, I was moved by it. I went up the road and turned into the lane that leads to the woods. I listened to the singing of the birds, to the chirping of the crickets, and saw what variety nature threw around me. I looked at those large fir trees that formed an arch over my head, saw the sun-beams as they peeped through the leaves of the trees and cast a yellow glow on some spots and left a dark shade where they did not alight. Across the fields I could see the cows grazing, the bright, sparkling water and the mountains in the distance. I contrasted the different forms of vegetation from the deepest green to the brightest yellow.

Filled with a poetic thrill, I gave myself up to nature, and, stretched on the banks of that beautiful stream, viewed and studied the wild and enchanting scenery. I went to the top of that pile of rocks on that scenic eminence called Tower Hill and looked toward the Atlantic Ocean. I saw every possible variety of scenery—streams, meadows, forests, gardens, houses nestling among the trees, hotels and cottages low lying along the shores, the waters of the broad Atlantic, and, about ten miles across—a dim view, Newport hid among the trees.

I turned to the left and saw how prettily the river meandered through the meadows and around the hills, to my right I studied the wild grandeur of the scene.

But this was not all; turning in the direction of Kingston, I saw the little village of Wakefield, and that prettiest of all villages, Peacedale, almost concealed from sight by the luxuriant foliage of wide spreading trees which surrounded her. Still looking in the direction of Peacedale, I jumped down from the rock, and ran over the ground to the edge of the hill; there I studied and studied that grand, nay, that heavenly beauty of the scenery. So moved was I by this scenery that I forgot everything but the peace and beauty which enveloped me upon all sides. Could I depict the beauty in nature as Homer or Wordsworth did, I could not express the emotions and thoughts which this scene aroused in me. I hold this as a scene which is remembered a lifetime.

It seemed that I was in some vast cosmical cathedral, built within a still vaster cathedral, whose carpet was the green grass, whose statues were the waving trees and flowing vines, whose stained windows were the gilded and golden clouds which reflected the light of the sun, whose choir was the singing birds and whispering winds, whose choral music was the organ roll of the mighty thunder, whose incense was the vapor rising from the misty sea, whose candles were the evening stars and whose lurid lights were the flashing of the lightning, whose vaulted roof was the blue domed sky.

I felt like taking off my shoes, for I believed that I was on holy ground in the temple of the Most High.

Ten years later I visited the same scene, and lived in that Tower Hill house for several weeks. On an autumn afternoon or Indian summer day, I felt that same heavenly peace come over my troubled spirit and felt the tranquilizing influence of a Sabbath benediction. But this time I contrasted the peace and serenity of nature and the calmly grazing cows and the quiet life of Wakefield and Peacedale with the bustle of the summer life of Narragansett Pier and Newport. The cows need only plenteous grass and bright sunshine to complete their happiness; the farmers of Wakefield and Peacedale, who die unknown to fame, need only good crops and the presence of loved ones to complete their happiness.

But it was different at the Pier and at the fashionable American summer resort. There, people sought pleasure and life and amusement, there people vied with each other in giving entertainments. There social rivalry was keen, and men and women were dominated by the passion for social leadership, social prestige and social preeminence.

I reflected, how evanescent is the fame of social kings and queens! Ten years ago a calm and tranquil Tennessee belle and a bright, vivacious Western belle held regal sway at the Pier. Their wish was law in the circle in which they ruled! Gazing admirers stood silently awed. Ten years ago, a sturdy Oxford oarsman and a brilliant, dashing American athlete were lionized. Ten years ago a wife and daughter of a famous Southern statesman, a Southern Governor and retired Commodore were centers of attraction. To-day their names are barely mentioned. Other stars are in the ascendency, other queens hold their court and other figures hold the center of the stage.

In Newport it is essentially the same. Ten years before Count So and So, Lord Somebody, Duke of Somewhere, Earl of Someplace and Marquis of Abroad, were in everyone's mouth and were followed by envious, admiring eyes, as they rode around the town. Now no one ever mentions their names.

Six years ago a $50,000 dinner, given when mill hands were on a strike and out of work, was the talk of the town. Now it is forgotten. Three years ago a brilliant automobile parade stirred Newport, but now it has passed into oblivion.

To-day two manly English tennis players are in the limelight. To-day the monkey dinner is discussed. But ten years from to-day they will be forgotten. Then I thought of the fate of the favorites at the fashionable resorts, which is ultimately the fate of men and women who dominate things in their day and generation. The thought occurred to me that men prominent a generation or two ago are practically unknown to-day, and even some of the things that should render their names immortal are forgotten. Men who were public figures when I was a schoolboy, twenty years ago, are barely mentioned now, except by their personal friends and descendants. The names of James G. Blaine[1] and Roscoe Conkling were in the air twenty years ago. The present generation is fast forgetting them for new heroes and new issues. They live only in the memory of their friends, and even their greatest achievements are practically unknown.

That they played almost as important a part as Charles Sumner in reconstruction legislation, that Conkling in the United States Senate in 1875 crushed the Louisiana conspiracy to overthrow the Federal Authority, that James G. Blaine in his twenty years in Congress paid a remarkable tribute to the colored men who went to Congress, is practically unknown; and one Connecticut Governor, whose name was in every one's mouth when I was learning my A, B, C's, has dropped completely out of sight and notice.

Sixty years ago the slavery debate held the center of the stage, but the present generation has not only forgotten the names of many of the chief actors then, but has even forgotten the moral issue involved in the contest. In

1. James Gillespie Blaine was a political savant born January 31, 1830, in Pennsylvania. He died in 1893. He served as a speaker in the U.S. House of Representatives, then was elected to the Senate, and ended up serving as secretary of state from 1888 to 1892. He also ran for president several times during the Reconstruction era. It is interesting that Ferris cites James G. Blaine and Roscoe Conkling, given the political feud between the two that some believe ruined Blaine's presidential runs. This is the opinion expressed by James B. Fry in *The Conkling and Blaine-Fry Controversy, in 1866: The Outbreak of a Life-Long Feud between Two Great Statesmen, Roscoe Conkling and James G. Blaine* (New York: A. G. Sherwood and Company Press, 1893). Beyond this feud, Ferris could be pointing to the attitude of these men toward the Negro. For example, James G. Blaine advocated Negro suffrage in a published debate titled "Ought the Negro Be Disfranchised? Ought He to Have Been Enfranchised?," *North American Review* 128, no. 268 (1879): 225–83.

the late forties and early fifties Samuel Ringo Ward,[2] a giant in ebony, electrified English and American audiences on the slavery question, but now his name is forgotten. No one reads his autobiography or cares for the issue that was so dear to him. Very few people know that Gerrit Smith,[3] who educated him, was a philanthropist, who, in 1849, gave an immense tract of land to colored men in the Adirondack Mountains. Also, very few know that George Luther Stearns gave $10,000 to maintain liberty in Kansas, supplied John Brown with arms and equipped a colored regiment in the late Civil War. So I might go on and mention many others.

Fifty years from now some of the living men, whose every movement is chronicled in big headlines, who are constantly sought out by newspaper reporters and have snapshots frequently turned upon them, will be almost forgotten by the popular mind.

The vanity of human life constantly recurred to me in these reflections. In the fourteenth chapter of Job we are told, "Man that is born of a woman is of

---

2. Samuel Ringgold Ward was born a slave in Maryland on October 17, 1817. He was a well-respected and popular abolitionist who rivaled Frederick Douglass not only in prestige and popularity but intellect and character. In *The Black Man: His Antecedents, His Genius, and His Achievements* (New York: Thomas Hamilton, 1863), William Wells Brown says of Ward, "As a speaker, he was justly held up as one of the ablest men, white or black, in the United States" (284). Ward was best known for his book *Autobiography of a Fugitive Negro: His Anti-slavery Labour in the United States, Canada, and England* (London: John Snow, 1855). According to the biographical entry on Samuel R. Ward in Carter G. Woodson's *The Negro in Our History* (Washington, DC: Associated Publishers, 1922), "His greater strength lay in knowing that words and ideas are not inseparable" (151). Ward's work and orations were not restricted to the South but were international in effect, being heard by audiences not only in the North but also in England and Jamaica.

3. Gerrit Smith was a well-known white abolitionist and friend of Frederick Douglass. He was born in Utica, New York, on March 6, 1797, and died in New York City on December 28, 1874. According to Edward J. Renehan's *The Secret Six: The True Tale of the Men Who Conspired with John Brown* (Columbia: University of South Carolina Press, 1997), Gerrit Smith was well aware of and supported John Brown's raid on Harper's Ferry, despite the disapproval of his friend Frederick Douglass. Octavius Brooks Frothingham's *Gerrit Smith: A Biography* (New York: G. P. Putnam's Sons, 1878) is still the definitive historical work on his life. However, while much of the original historical scholarship on Smith focused on his relationship with Douglass and his ambivalence about radicalism (see John R. McKivigan and Madeleine Leveille, "The 'Black Dream' of Gerrit Smith: New York Abolitionist," *Courier* 20, no. 2 [fall 1985], available at http://library.syr.edu/digital/exhibits/g/GerritSmith/dream.htm), John Stauffer's *The Black Hearts of Men: Radical Abolitionists and the Transformation of Race* (Cambridge, MA: Harvard University Press, 2004) highlights the interracial alliance between Smith and James McCune Smith, Frederick Douglass's mentor and teacher.

few days and full of trouble." In the 90th division of Psalms we are told, "In the morning they are like grass, which groweth up. In the morning it flourisheth, and groweth up; in the evening it is cut down, and withereth. . . . We bring our years to an end, as a tale that is told." The cycle of a man's life is soon run. Men die broken-hearted of political hopes and issues that are soon forgotten. Women fret and worry over invitations to social functions that soon pass into oblivion. The world doesn't know who gave and doesn't care who was invited to social functions a decade ago. In school and college days we strive for school and college honors. It seems that our future is bound up with these honors. It seems that without them life would not be worth living. But after we have been out in the world a few years, men will forget them and our record as students, and will ask us, "Can you solve this problem; can you face this situation; can you meet this emergency?" The tragedy in the lives of most men and women is that they fret and worry, pine and grieve over things that will appear trivial and insignificant when they reach the years that bring the philosophic mind.

Nature joys in her floral beauty and her verdant hills, her radiant dawn and sunset tints, her calmness and repose, her peace and serenity, and the splendor of the starry hosts seems to rebuke the feverish, fretful and fitful strivings of man for pomp and honor and fame and glory.

I am glad that when, in the fall of 1902, I began to prepare lectures upon the Negro's religion and focus the light of sociology upon the Negro question, I was living upon Tower Hill.[4]

There is nothing that gives a man perspective in human history, that makes him a spectator of all times and spaces and enables him to see all things subspecie aeternitatis, as a view from a lofty eminence. From the top of that lofty eminence I surveyed four civilizations. Down in Wakefield and Peacedale, I saw the civilization of the New England village; down in Narragansett Pier, I saw the civilization of the South and West; over across Narragansett Bay, I

4. Ferris's pointing out his interest in studying the Negro's religion under the light of sociology is fascinating given his times for several reasons. First, the only sociological studies specifically looking at the lives and condition of Negroes were being conducted by W. E. B. Du Bois at Atlanta University. This is a remarkable coincidence given that Du Bois himself published Atlanta University Publication No. 3, *The Negro Church*, the following year, in 1903. One can only surmise that William H. Ferris's relationship with Du Bois in the American Negro Academy and his reading of Du Bois's *The Souls of Black Folk* had a somewhat profound effect on his sociological thinking through of the race problem and his focus on Black religiosity. As he says in his chapter titled "The American Negro's Contribution to Literature, Music and Oratory," Du Bois's *The Souls of Black Folk* inspired him beyond the words of Ralph Waldo Emerson and Thomas Carlyle—hitting him as "a bolt from the blue."

saw in the distance the civilization of America's metropolis; while in the breeze that swept over the Atlantic, in the mirroring sea, and blossoming fields and forests near me, I saw the joyous life of that Nature which never changes and ever remains the same. And at night, when the lamps of heaven began to send out faint rays from afar, I thought of the eternity of the starry hosts and reflected that those same stars looked down upon the cave men, who endeavored to interpret the universe five hundred thousand years ago. They saw the mighty Ethiopian, Egyptian, Babylonian, Assyrian, Persian, Greek and Roman civilizations rise and fall in their splendor, dominate the world for a few centuries, and then pass away. They saw the conquering Pharaohs and mighty Persian kings ride forth to battle; they saw the life of little Pompeii blotted out in a day; they saw the glory that was Greece's and the grandeur that was Rome's. They now see the triumphal, resistless march of the Anglo-Saxon race. In the next 50,000 years they may witness the rise of the black, brown and yellow races. Men come and go; kingdoms rise and fall; but the stars shine on in their lonely splendor in the immensity of space.

But what of the men who made these ancient civilizations possible, what of the renowned Ethiopian, Egyptian, Babylonian, Assyrian, Persian, Greek and Roman warriors who led vast armies to battle and dragged nations captive at their chariot wheels? They have mostly passed out of the memory of men and have been swallowed up in oblivion.

The queen of Sheba, and Candace, a shadowy Ethiopian queen, are the only ones of the powerful Ethiopian rulers whose names have gone ringing down the ages. Of the famous Egyptian monarchs, who ruled from 5000 to 200 B. C., Khufu, known by the Greeks as Cheops, who built the wonderful pyramid at Gizeh; Tholmes II, Seti I, Rameses II, and Meneptha, the greatest of the Pharaohs; Psammetichus, Necho II, Ptolemy Soter and Ptolemy Philadelphus are the only names that have survived the marks of time. Of the mighty Babylonian kings who held sway from 5000 to 728 B. C., Sargon I and Hammurabi are the only names which shine with splendid lustre.

Of the powerful Assyrian kings who, in 728 and the following years, conquered Babylon and took captive the Ten Tribes of Israel, and who for six centuries, from 1100 to 600 B. C., made Nineveh great, Sargon II, Sennacherib, and Asshur-bani-pal, known to the Greeks as Sardanapalus, are the only names which have survived.

Of the Chaldean kings who made the seventh and sixth centuries, B. C., ring with their glory, Nabopolassar and Nebuchadnezzar II and Nabonidus are the only names which still live in the memory of man. Of the Persian kings who for over two centuries dominated Asia and part of Africa and broke the sway of the Assyrians and Chaldeans, Cyaxares, Cyrus, Kambyses, Darius and Xerxes I are the only names familiar to every schoolboy.

The study of the Greek and Roman classics and the study of the Bible has made the modern mind almost as familiar with the Greek and Roman heroes and Hebrew prophets as with the great modern figures. But twenty thousand years from now, perhaps Homer, Socrates, Plato, Aristotle, Demosthenes, Phidias, Pericles and Alexander the Great will be the only Grecian names, and Scipio, Caesar, Augustus, Constantine, Cicero and Vergil will be the only Roman names, and Abraham, Moses, Jesus and Paul the only Hebrew names familiarly known to posterity. Each succeeding century will make their names more dim and shadowy, until finally a hundred thousand years from now, Homer, Alexander, Abraham, Moses, Jesus, Paul, Hannibal and Cesar may be the only names of antiquity known to man. In another hundred thousand years they may all, with the exception of Jesus of Nazareth, have completely dropped out of memory.

Of the great names and figures of the Middle Ages, it may be that twenty thousand years from now, Mohammed, Peter the Hermit, Charles Martel, Charlemagne, William the Conqueror and Dante may be the only ones who will stand out as beacon lights.

Of the great names of the fifteenth, sixteenth, seventeenth, and eighteenth centuries, Martin Luther, Columbus, Copernicus, Kepler, Galileo, Newton, Shakespeare, Cromwell, Milton, Bacon, Queen Victoria, Rousseau, Kant, Peter the Great, Mirabeau and Chatham may be the only familiar names twenty thousand years from now. Of the famous men of the nineteenth century, the Duke of Wellington, Napoleon, Washington, Lincoln, Emerson, Grant, Darwin, Spencer, Carlyle, Gladstone, Browning, Tennyson, Goethe, Lotze, Bismarck, Hugo, Watts, Roëntgen, Metchnikoff, Marconi, Harvey, Koch and Marquis Ito may alone find a place in a history of civilization written twenty thousand years hence.

One hundred thousand years from now the world may have forgotten who discovered America, who discovered the law of gravitation, who propounded the evolution hypothesis, who discovered the X-ray and who first flashed a message across the sea by wireless telegraphy. Perhaps then Shakespeare and Napoleon will be the only modern men known to mankind. Two hundred thousand years from now they may be mythical and legendary figures, and scholars will be writing books to prove that the only existence they ever had was in the imagination of some poet, orator or novelist. Five hundred thousand years from now the only historic or mythological figure known to mankind, who will be on the lips of men, will be Jesus of Nazareth. He alone will escape oblivion.

Perhaps in that distant time scholars may write books to prove that the world-renowned and world-conquering Anglo-Saxon race never really existed, except in the imagination of rapt poets, and was only a mythical, legendary race. Yes, in the course of time—in the course of five thousand centuries, the races and men now familiar to every schoolboy and girl will be swallowed up in oblivion.

If the great races only dominate the world for a few centuries, and then give way to fresher, stronger races, if even after a few thousand years the great figures in history are forgotten, what is the use of the striving of man?

Though the Egyptians, the Hebrews, the Greeks and Romans have fallen from their high estate, the mathematical, philosophical, religious, and political ideas that they have bequeathed to mankind have been woven into the fibre and texture, into the very web and woof of modern civilization.

Our conception of God, our ideas of the sanctity of life, of the value of virtue, of the sacredness of the marriage tie, our doctrine of property rights and our principles of representative government, our moral maxims, our political and our industrial organizations represent the thoughts, the ideas and the crystallized experience of men who lived and died centuries ago, and whose very names are forgotten.

Back in the dim and distant past, unknown men discovered the use of fire, conceived the ideas of steps on an inclined plane, discovered the arch, conceived the idea of hollowing out the trunk of a tree and setting a sail in it, conceived the idea of wheeled carts, domesticated animals and used the force of running water to turn a mill. They have handed down their discoveries as legacies.

Though nations rise and fall, though they pass off the stage of existence, they yet live in the ideas they have bequeathed to civilization. Though great individuals die and are forgotten, they yet live in the thoughts they have thrown out, which constitutes our intellectual inheritance. Though teachers and preachers are forgotten, they yet live in the lives they inspire, and they kindle a flame that burns in the breasts of countless generations. So our striving is not vain. It ultimately becomes a part of the structure of civilization.

But astronomers tell us that solar systems are constantly being destroyed and other solar systems are constantly being born in the universe. Suns are burning out. Other dead suns are being transformed into fiery, gaseous vapor by the heat generated from collision with other similar bodies. And then begins again the whirling, the cooling, the condensation and throwing off of rings or satellites from the burning, gaseous mass in the center.

Astronomers tell us that, in the course of a few million years, our shining sun will have burned itself out, ceasing to shrink and contract and to radiate light and heat. The earth can then no longer support vegetable or animal life. Then all vegetable and animal life will die out on this planet of ours and the human race will cease to exist.

But before this catastrophe occurs our sun is liable to be transformed into gaseous vapor by collision with a giant sun, the equilibrium of our solar system destroyed and our earth burned up by the heat generated by the collision, or else deorbited. Or our earth is liable to be struck by the head of a rushing comet. The earth would then be enveloped in a fiery, gaseous hood, and every living thing would be burned up or else destroyed by the poisonous gases thrown out. Or, again, our earth may be powdered to dust by collision with a dead star.

The first of these catastrophes will surely occur in the next hundred million years and the second and third and fourth may occur. So there will finally, in the course of a few score million years, come a time when every semblance of vegetable or animal life will have disappeared from the planet, and every trace or vestige of man's civilization will have become completely effaced. Annihilation is the ultimate fate and destiny of the human race on this earth of ours.

And then I asked, was this the end of Nature's strivings, was this the final destiny of man's aspiration, was this the consummation of man's hopes, to be swallowed up in the dark midnight of nothingness and oblivion, to fade away forever out of existence? Was human life a dream? Was human history a farce? Were the ideal dreams which have lured on mankind to higher heights of achievements, illusions? Were the heroic ideals to do and dare and strive and achieve, nothing but hallucinations? Were the mighty hopes which made us men but mirages in the desert? In a word, is our striving to realize and embody ethical ideals in our lives and characters a vain struggle, which will finally end in defeat?

That which is most fundamental and basal in human nature asserts itself, rises in protest and cries out, No! No! No! And yet, if the fate and destiny of this earth on which we live and of the human life it sustains, is to vanish and be blotted out of existence, this would seem to be the nature of man's ideals, and the end of his strivings, unless man were immortal. But if the universe were not the fortuitous play of blind, unthinking atoms and ions, if it were not a chaos but a cosmos, if reason were embedded in the very structure of the universe, if a world drama were being enacted, in which a Master Mind were behind the curtains, shifting the scenes, then it would seem that man is immortal and that his strivings are not in vain. And I asked myself, is there a God, is there a Master Mind behind the mechanism of Nature, who utters his eternal decrees in the immutable laws that regulate the movements of the starry hosts above, and who thunders in trumpet tones in the ideals of man?

Then I paused and thought of the wonderful universe in which I lived, of Nature's abounding life and her daily miracles, when the leaves on the trees become laboratories. Then the principles involved in plant growth were no longer dead, abstract principles to me, but became the living methods by which this wondrous universe robed itself in a garment of verdure and created through the forces that unconsciously work in plants, trees and flowers, this beautiful world in which we live. The living, palpitating world, throbbing with life, which was presented to me by the study of botany, caused it to take on a new meaning and opened my eyes to the beneficent purpose of that Deity whose vesture is this beautiful world, in which we live and move and have our being and who works through the wonderful growth of plant life for man's good. It seems to me, that if a man knew something of this marvelous universe in which we live, if he could but lift the curtain and peep behind the veil, where the mysterious forces of nature are silently working, the world would take on a new meaning and he would see a new glory in meadow and field, forest and stream. The flowers would speak to him a new language. The flowers in the crannied walls would tell him, as they told Tennyson, something about the nature of the world and of the God who created it. Like Wordsworth, he would look through nature to Nature's God and see that "the clouds that gather round the setting sun do take a sober coloring from an eye that keeps watch o'er man's immortality."

And then I thought of the internal structure and of the wonderful mechanism of the atom, so small that it could be contained within the billionth part of a square inch, so small that it could not be seen by a microscope which magnified it a thousand times. Then I reflected that the spectroscope, the cathode ray and radium revealed the fact that this infinitesimal atom was not a single indivisible entity as was supposed twenty years ago; but that it was a wonderful machine, an intricate mechanism, a solar system in miniature, composed of thousands of gyrating and circling and revolving centers of force, whose velocity is almost as great as speed of light and who, by their harmonious gyrations and oscillations, give the little atom its power of effecting chemical changes. Then I thought of how the atoms build up the molecules and the molecules build up the universe of matter. I reflected that what we call solid matter is the result of the gyrations and activity of little ions so small that seventy or eighty thousand of them could be contained in a space smaller than one billionth of an inch square. I thought of these wonderful structures and of the wonderful mechanism of this solar system in miniature. I saw that it was a trillion times more intricate than the mechanism of a watch: I saw that it could not come into existence by chance, that the Mind which planned it, the Mind which could bring law and order into that miniature solar system must be Divine.

As I stood at midnight on Tower Hill and looked at the myriad stars that dot the milky way, and reflected that many of them were immense suns, rushing through space with their revolving planets and satellites whirling about them, as I reflected that some of these faint, twinkling stars were suns several times larger than the sun that illumines this solar system of ours (a few being a million times larger), as I reflected that it takes light traveling at the rate of 186,000 miles a second, fifty years to reach us from the Pole Star and four hundred centuries to reach us from the furthest of these dim specks, and then considered that this immense universe hangs together and is governed by law and order, I was constrained to believe in a God, the source and ground of that law and order. And when I thought that the planetary laws of motion which governed the movements of Halley's comet compelled it, though traveling away from the earth for 3,400 million miles, with a speed greater than that of a cannon ball, to return again every seventy-five years, then I understood how the devout astronomer, Kepler, could say, when he discovered the mathematical laws that regulated the movements of the planetary bodies, "Oh God, I think thy thoughts after Thee." I then saw that God was the great Geometer, that the universe is crystallized mathematics and that nature is the time vesture of the Eternal, the garments we see Him by, which reveals Him to the wise and hides Him from the foolish. Then I understood how the Psalmist, gazing in rapt adoration at the starry hosts, which glorify God, could say, "The heavens declare the glory of God and the firmament sheweth his handiwork."

Such were my reflections, when the stars, the silent sentinels of heaven, came out every night and stood forth in their lonely splendor; but the cynic may say that this was only a dream. We have forever passed beyond the age of atheism, when men could say, "There is no God," and we now are in the age of the Spencerian agnosticism, when men say that knowledge of the cause behind the phenomena, knowledge of the real nature of the Infinite and Eternal Energy which manifests itself in the world of mind and matter transcends the limitation of human knowledge. The human mind is impotent to grapple with transcendental realities.

"There may be a God," the agnostic says, "but we can never know; we cannot see beyond the veil; we cannot look beyond nature to a present God. All is vain surmise. It is a vain hope to think we can know the why, the whence, the whither of our eternal destiny." But is this so? Cannot we trust the guidance of that reason which leads from facts of every class and kind to theories and hypotheses, which from the phenomena of nature carries us to molecules, atoms, ions and ether as the underlying entities.

Can we not trust that reason which created the Copernican astronomy and framed the Newtonian belief in gravitation's universal laws, the nebular hypothesis and the Spencerian theory of universal evolution? Can we not trust the organ which guides us through the labyrinth of life's perplexing problems? We must, we cannot think that our life is vain illusion, our experience a lie. Whatever contradicts the testimony of reason, that we must reject or else confusion and discord will be introduced into the very inmost life of reason—man's divine and regal wings for soaring up beyond the world of sense, up into the ethereal empyrean of thought's luminous realms.

What is the universal testimony of human reason then? Reason asks, "Can a cosmos, vast and orderly, be built by countless millions of minute, invisible, intangible atomic elements of seventy odd different things, each acting, reacting and interacting in ways peculiar to itself alone, unless the atoms are embraced in one Infinite Mind, who expresses his eternal laws and inmost life in the activity and uniform co-working of atoms? Can millions of gyrating, revolving and minute invisible ions build up by their ceaseless activity this vast and orderly cosmos, and, hence the world of matter, unless they express the thought and plan and are the forthputting and energizing of one Infinite Reason?"

Reason again asks, "Can life come from that which is not life; can the mental come from non-mentality? Can mind be conjured up from that which is not mental in its inner structure? Can primordial small elements and germ-like cells develop into the majestic oak, the splendid lion, the graceful dove, the God-like man, without the presence of immanent ideas in plants and animals to guide and control the growth? Do we not here see internal purposiveness bedded in the very nature of things? Can the moral qualities be evoked from sources that are unethical? Can living beings come from a non-living cause? What's conscience but the pleading, warning voice of God? What's the 'I ought' but the embracing grip of the eternal God, forever immanent in finite things and selves, the life and soul of all, upon his sons? What's nature's beauty then, but the divine garment in which God does eternally weave the outward fabric that reveals and expresses his eternal thoughts and inner life?"

Reason again says, "That One who brought us here must ever be as great, as wise, as noble as we finite ones, his creatures. You may point to sin and misery, which hang forever over life, as a dark and gloomy curtain. But we cannot hope to pierce beyond the veil and enter into the deep counsel of the Most High. Forget not that our God has all eternity at his disposal, yea remember that it is in the light of immortality, which can illumine these perplexing doubts and send a luminous ray o'er the speculative mysteries."

Reason again says, "Consider, agnostic, how we build up our sense world out of impressions, caused by excitations of the end organs of our five senses. These shocks and quivers of sensation come to us scattered, but are unified by the mind's activities and categories. How now can the mind of man impose its mental forms upon the world of sense, unless the world were the manifestations of mind, yea a mental being in its inner life. What can this mean save one, who is self-conscious and rational as we are? In the fundamental laws of human thought we see the movements grand of the eternal mind of God. If there is order and law in the universe, if there is reason in the mortal soul it has its source in the Universal Reason who expresses and manifests his mind and will and life in this fair world of ours. Were it not so, would not our lives and thoughts be a mockery?"

Such riddles, questions and puzzles, the human reason puts to the confident and rash agnostic. The mind of man, then, in seeking to understand and interpret the universe, in seeking to strike rock-bottom and give a rational explanation for the ultimate nature of things, is inevitably led to the conclusion that the universe of mind and matter is the expression of the one infinite and eternal Being.

The science of the nineteenth century has borne overwhelming testimony to the unity of the universe. The Newtonian gravitation, or rather Newton's theory of gravitation, has been shown to apply not only to our own solar system but to the entire stellar universe. The entire universe is bound together by the tie of gravitation. The elastic and undulatory, luminiferous ether, the medium for the transmission of light, heat and electric waves, is now shown to pervade all space and to extend from farthest star to farthest star. The spectroscope and spectral analysis have discovered that the farthest star shining in space is composed of the same physical elements that form the constitution of our earth.

Planetary bodies composed of the same physical and chemical elements, luminiferous ether pervading all space, and gravitation the force that knits and ties those bodies together so that they do not fly apart in space, all testify to the unity of the universe. But now this is a unity dominated by law and order, so that we have an orderly totality and a cosmos instead of chaos. The only explanation that satisfies the reason of man, for the law and order that makes the universe an orderly totality and a cosmos, is that the universe is the forthputting of an Infinite Mind who manifests his own ideas in the laws of Nature.

But I am a child of Nature. I have been generated in Nature's womb, and I am an offspring of the universe and an integral part of the universe. Hence, I am the manifestation of the Infinite Being, who manifests himself in the universe. The same Being who wells up in grass and flower, who registers his laws in the movements of the heavenly bodies, also manifests himself in me. Truly has the Apostle said, "In Him we live and move and have our being." And in seeking to understand the Power or Infinite Energy who manifests himself in the universe we must find a being big and brainy enough to beget man.

The philosophy of Dr. Samuel Eugene Stevens, author of "The Great Unconscious,"[5] which maintains that matter is the origin of all things that make unconscious matter the sole origin of conscious mind, that makes "electro-atomic matter" the sole cause of the rational and ethical life of man, refuses to satisfy the reason of man.

We cannot believe that the stream can rise higher than its source. We must believe that there is something in the cause adequate to produce the effect.

That an unconscious world ground could manifest itself in conscious, rational beings, that a universe whose background was blind, formless, unconscious matter, could usher in rational beings, that an irrational, unethical world ground could manifest itself in rational and ethical personalities and impose rational, ethical ideas upon them, as the deepest law of their being, this the mind of man refuses to believe. So, then, the Superhuman and Supersensible Cause and Source of the universe of mind and matter must be a universal life, which is as coextensive as the life of the universe, and a universal self-consciousness which is coextensive with the mental and physical changes in the world of finite mind and finite matter, and embraces them in the totality of its own being, manifesting its mind and its ideas in the orderly sequence which we term the laws of Nature and its will in the force of Nature.

The happenings in the universe of finite minds and finite matter are not only phases and aspects and doings and forthputtings of finite selves and things, but they are also movements in the life of the Absolute, facts in his consciousness. For he is the Immanent and Causal Ground of all the psychic and physical changes in the universe, and of the system of things. He is the Absolute Self of whom all finite things and finite selves are but partial and fragmentary manifestations.

To destroy me, the Absolute must destroy a part of himself and destroy his own offspring. The question then arises, Is the Absolute interested in the ideals and strivings of man? Have the ideals and strivings of man an eternal value and significance for the Absolute? Have our personalities and individualities an eternal meaning and value for the Absolute? On the answer to these questions hangs the immortality of man.

In developing our manhood, we are not only realizing our latent potentialities and developing the germs of divinity that slumber in our natures, but we are developing a bit of the Absolute. If we share in the life of the Absolute, and are partakers of his divine nature, what is more natural than that we should share in and partake of his eternity and immortality? No mother, in her senses, would murder her child, and does it seem natural that a rational

5. Samuel Eugene Stevens, *The Philosophy of the Great Unconscious* (Boston: Old Corner Bookstore, 1908).

and ethical personality would bring into existence rational and moral beings only to destroy them as they began to develop and unfold and express their latent capacities? I am no prophet, but it does not seem reasonable that the Power, not ourselves, which makes for righteousness, who brought us into being, would implant certain ideas as the deepest laws of our nature, would impress certain qualities of mind and heart, as things worth attaining and striving for, only to blot them out of existence forever. We cannot fathom the purposes of the Almighty, but the human reason refuses to believe that the Creative Spirit would impress the moral imperative upon us as the fundamental law of our being and then cut our development short by annihilation.

The Being who shot us through the crucible of his own nature, ran us through certain molds of thinking and feeling, stamped us with the impress of his own personality, and then launched us forth from the shores of eternity out into the sea of time, endowed us with a reason that can fathom the secrets and mysteries of nature, extract the ores from the earth, harness the forces of nature, water, wind, steam and electricity, to run our mills, carry us over land and water and transmit messages across space; with an imagination that can catch and depict, on canvas and in verse, the fleeting glories of sunrise, the passing beauties of sunset when the sky seems bathed in colored seas of lambent light, and can create those flowing melodies and cathedral harmonies that waft the soul upon the wings of faith above the world of sense and light into the realm where the soul catches fleeting glimpses of eternity; with a will that enables a man to chisel and carve and hew out his own career and be the architect of his own fate and destiny; with a will that enables a man to tunnel mountains, bridge chasms, brave dangers and defy obstacles and obstructions; with a will that exultingly cries, "There shall be no Alps, I will find a way or make it,"—this Being will call us back home some day and then he will longingly look to see whether we have preserved or effaced the divine impress. The impression of the Almighty is upon us; a divine spark slumbers in us; divinity stirs within us; we are men, not beasts of the field.

That throbbing, divine life, with which the universe pulses and which transforms the world into a fairyland every spring, breaking into expression in leaf and blade and flower and covering the earth with a garment of verdure, wells up in us as the fountain source of the impulses, the instincts, that lift us above the plane of animal life. It manifests itself in the divine discontent and dissatisfaction with our present mode of life. It utters itself in the stirrings within us that prompts us to transform the actual into the likeness of the ideal. It voices itself in the strivings after the higher life, that are the springs of human progress and of the development of man in history. And while the Negro needs to buy all the land, and get as large a bank account as he can, while he needs to branch out into the mercantile world, and go into business, he must remember that this is not the end and goal of our existence. That end and goal is to realize the mighty hopes which make us men.

Every living thing fulfills the laws of its being and realizes the immanent idea that Nature implants in it. The grass grows; the seed buds and blossoms into fruit and leaf and flower; the acorn develops into the wide-spreading oak; the majestic lion stalks the forests, monarch of all he surveys; the eagle soars aloft on his powerful wings and sights his prey from afar, and man develops from a babbling babe into a Godlike being, in whom reason and conscience are inthroned. The plant and animal do this unconsciously, obeying their instincts. Man does this consciously, through the guidance of reason, and by the power of choice.

The ideals which man consciously sets up before himself and endeavors to realize in his life and character spring from the abysmal depths of a superhuman source. Man wills whether or no to register, incarnate and embody these institutions and ideals in his life and character, but they come from the eternal God. We must remember that this earth is a stage on which a world drama is being enacted and that our little lives not only have significance for our poor finite selves but also for the universe which begat us.

The teleological instinct is basal and fundamental in man. The doctrine of final causes has ever appealed to him. He has always inquired about the final purposes of things. And the man in men asks, "For what final purpose was man created? Why did the universal mind never pause in his struggle and striving, in his manifestation until he begot man? For what reason did the Absolute impose the ethical idea upon man, as the supreme law of his nature?" Unless we believe the universe, with all its vastness and splendor and glory and grandeur and law and order, to be begotten by blind chance, and unless we believe the world ground to be having fun with us, there must be an infinite and eternal meaning and significance to the supremacy of the ethical ideals of man. And I am inclined to believe that the Absolute will preserve whatever is of eternal significance and value in the universe.

But the scientists tell us that the immortality of the mind of man is an impossibility because the mind states are epiphonema thrown off by the brain. The brain secretes thoughts just as the liver secretes bile. A blow on the head will cause unconsciousness and when the brain ceases to function the mind of man dies.

While the brain influences the mind, it is also true that the mind of man, through the brain, influences the body. Worry poisons the secretions of the bile and liver and depresses the entire physical organism. Joy accelerates the entire physical organism. Anger excites and fear paralyzes the heart. The worry, fear and stage-fright of Jim Jeffries made a physical weakling of that giant on July 4, 1910, at Reno, Nevada. Doctors had pronounced him physically sound and perfect; but his mental collapse, caused by worrying over the outcome of his fight with Jack Johnson, the black champion, completely upset and threw his physical organism out of tune. Yes, the mental states have a powerful effect upon the nervous systems of men. The mind influences the brain just as much as the brain influences the mind.[6]

The mind and brain, then, are two separate things, which are causally related to and reciprocally influence each other during the temporal life of man. But the mind of man has a life and nature that is peculiarly its own, that is sui generis, that behaves in ways peculiar to itself alone, and that transcends the functioning of the brain.

There is a great gulf between the movements in the molecules, atoms, nerve cells and nerve tracts in the brain of a Plato, Aristotle, Kant, Hegel, Shakespeare, Emerson, Wagner and Beethoven and the wonderful mental creations of these gifted souls. How translate the commotion in the nerve centers of their brains into the grand thoughts of lofty sentiments that surge in them?

It may be true, as the late Professor William James of Harvard has said, that the brain is the medium for the transmission of thought as well as for the production of thought. And it certainly seems clear that the brain, instead of producing the mind, is the occasion for the mind's manifesting its own peculiar nature and activities.[7]

---

6. It is of special importance that Ferris uses the infamous "Fight of the Century," or the "Fight of Giants," to speak about the relationship between the mental states of the mind and the physiology of the brain. The battle between Jack Johnson and James Jeffries was waged to redeem the fighting superiority of the white race. In December 1908, Jack Johnson won the world championship title from Tommy Burns. However, many white critics claimed that Burns was an inadequate champion and that Jack Johnson could not beat the "Great White Hope," James Jeffries, who had retired in 1905. Historically, Black athletes have been at the forefront of refuting racist pseudoscientific theories of Black inferiority and have been the symbols of racial progressivism. Both Thomas R. Hietala's *The Fight of the Century: Jack Johnson, Joe Louis, and the Struggle for Racial Equality* (Armonk, NY: M. E. Sharpe, Inc., 2002) and Randy Roberts's *Papa Jack: Jack Johnson and the Era of White Hopes* (New York: Free Press, 1985) show that sports and Black athletes were of intellectual and political concern for the race organizations and popular racial consciousness (pride) of the day.

7. It is highly likely that Ferris is drawing from William James's *Human Immortality: Two Supposed Objections to the Doctrine* (New York: Houghton, Mifflin, 1899). Given Ferris's description of the brain's transmissive function, a description James used to argue that the brain functioned beyond its productive capacity of ideas rooted in its physiological makeup, it seems likely that Ferris was inspired to make this connection through William James's 1899 introduction to the second edition of his 1898 lecture. In the 1899 introduction, James claims to be a "pantheist of the monistic pattern" (vi) and provides ample room for being interpreted as claiming that the transmission function of

How, then, could two such separate and distinct beings as the brain and mind reciprocally influence each other and be causally related to each other? Only on the hypothesis that they are the manifestations of the same Infinite Mind, who manifests himself in the world of mind and matter and whose self-consciousness is coextensive with and inclusive of the psychical and physical changes in the universe. The mind of man is the manifestation of the mind of God. And if God so wills, the conscious, rational life of man will survive the death of the body and the destruction of the brain. God has the whole universe at his command.

The mind develops in constant and ceaseless dependence upon the protoplasmic molecules of the brain; but in its growth and development it evolves an ego, a unity of personality, a center of self-consciousness that persists and endures during the modifications in the substance of the brain and changes in psychic states. Nerve cells in the brain wear out and are replaced by new nerve cells; psychic states come and go, and succeed each other in the stream of consciousness like the waves of the sea. But the self, the ego, the unity of personality, the center of self-consciousness, the permanent subject of the psychic states, the "I" who thinks, perceives, imagines, remembers, feels, and wills, remains. And, is it strange that this unity of personality, this center of self-consciousness should survive the destruction of the body, should persist during the physical change of death and be clothed in a new garment and raiment and be attached to a new medium and organ of expression? If God wills it, the rational life of man will survive the death of the body and the destruction of the brain.

I know that this is the age of practical atheism, of agnosticism, the age when men say, "We don't know whether there is any God!" But when I reflect that I am living in a universe which is built up out of millions of some seventy odd different kinds of atoms, of millions of minute gyrating and revolving ions, in which law and order reign, when I reflect that certain fundamental laws of reason govern my thinking and the constitutional mode of the operation of my mind, when I reflect that from the depths of my nature, beneath the subsoil of my conscious life, rises the impulse of instincts that make me a moral personality, I cannot believe that this vast universe, and myself a mental and moral being, were formed by the fortuitous concourse of blind and unthinking atoms.

The universe needs a God back of it to explain it. I need a God back of myself to explain myself to myself. No wanderer who has ever set sail on the dreaded sea that laves these terrestrial shores, has ever returned to tell of the

---

the brain is in fact tied to a singular spiritual cognition (mind), or what Ferris freely interprets as God.

sights he saw, the sounds he heard, or what beautiful visions greeted his eye on yonder shore; no one has ever returned to tell of the strange land and countries beyond the sea. But when I must shuffle off this earthly coil, leave this bright, beautiful land I love so well, this pleasant sunshine, and the friends whose presence to me is so sweet and dear, and trust myself to a stream that will bear me, I know not whither, I must believe that the unknown ocean currents, urged on by unseen forces, will bear my bark to the region that the Author and Maker of my being and of the universe in which I live, has prepared for me. And when the imprisoned soul has escaped from the cage of the flesh, and has left behind its prison bars, it may be that the noble spirits who have spent their lives doing something to lighten the sins, sufferings, miseries and wretchedness of the world will realize the words of the Apostle when he said, "Beloved, now are we the sons of God, and it doth not yet appear what we shall be; but we know that when he shall appear, we shall be like him, for we shall see him as he is." And who can tell but what the powers, strengthened by battling with evil and sin in this world, will there find an ampler field of exercise, a broader sphere of activity and a larger arena?

And how can we do better than to act well our part in this life, and then when the hour comes for us to face the mystery of Death, leave the shores of time and venture forth upon the ocean of eternity—how, I say, can we do better than to trust the power that brought us into being in a world that breaks into expression and bursts into a thousand forms of beauty, in leaves and flowers, in grass and foliage every spring, unfolding in beauty and grandeur, in glory and splendor and putting on the robe of beauty which has ever delighted the eye of man?

## *Chapter Two*

# God Revealed in the Course of Human History, in the Movements of the Human Spirit in Its Historical Development—The Meaning of History

As I have studied history, two questions have constantly forced themselves upon me, What is the meaning of history? Is the hand of God revealed in the movement of human history? Does the way in which man has moved along in his historical development, does the influence of great men upon history, does the moral order that is revealed in history, does the fact that history shows that religion is the deepest thing about man prove anything with regard to the nature of the world ground? I think so. I will endeavor in this chapter to give a brief survey of the course of human history; to show the part that great men have played in history and the secret of their influence; to show how the immoral nations have gone to destruction; to show how religion is the life blood of humanity; to show how ethical ideals and moral instincts have been the dynamos which have whirled the car of civilization on its onward way; to show that the conscience of man has been the mainspring of his activity; to show that his instinctive morality and capacity for moral development has determined and dominated his movements in history. And then I think that the following conclusion will be forced upon it.

All human history is inexplicable and incapable of being explained if human history is not the manifestation of the self-revealing life of an Immanent God, who is the center and source of all human progress, because he is the Immanent Source and Ground of the ideals and instincts which have been the propelling cause of human progress. If this universe is not rational to the core,—and by rational to the core we mean that the universe is the manifestation of a self-conscious mind; if moral principles are not interwoven in the very web and woof of the universe, imbedded in the structure and nature of the universe itself; if this universe is but the result of the accidental and fortuitous play of diverse atoms; if human history is but an accidental result of the play of blind mechanical forces, then is not only all human history, all ethics, art and religion an illusory dream, but life itself is an illusion, a monstrous farce. If history is to be understood, if human history is to be interpreted, it can only be so as we recognize, in a dim way though it may be, the presence of God in human nature and history.

There is one set of students of history who regards man as a product of physical conditions, the resultant of physical forces. In their estimation he is a child of Nature. They say that "History is accounted for by the action and interaction of physical and psychical forces. The interaction of known physical laws accounts for the development of history; and by a study of those laws we can predict with a probability approaching to certainty the course of history." This is the biological, the mechanical and anthropological view of history. It is a materialistic view of human character, human life, human history.

Now it is no doubt true that men can develop in history only by constant and ceaseless dependence upon physical and psychological laws. Such are the laws of the physical and natural sciences. Heat and cold, the change of the seasons, the physiological laws of one's bodily organism—these are laws to which a man must conform. Then, too, the geographical distribution of land and water, the fertility and barrenness of the soil, the healthiness of the climate, all of these things determine the movement of men in masses. Again, the fact whether men live on the seashore or in a tropical climate where little exertion is required to get a living and where consequent indolence and idleness result, or whether men live in a rugged mountainous climate where they must get their living by the sweat of the brow, and where sturdy, manly qualities of soul are developed, where self-reliance and thrift and energy are developed, these things profoundly influence men's lives and the movements of history. Then, too, consider what effect the fact that the country of Greece was broken up into deep valleys by the mountain ranges had upon the history of Greece and upon the history of mankind. One writer says, "It resulted in the autonomy of the commonwealth." It divided Greece into many little states instead of into one state. "Large armies could neither be trained nor supported; nor could they be transported so that they could come down over the mountains and despoil those in the plain." It prevented Greece from being a United Greece. And if the several Greek states had been united into one large state, what effect would it have had upon the future history of mankind?

Then, too, the physiological and psychical differences of the sexes, the universal laws of family life, must be recognized. But while we must admit that man is acted on by his environment, is influenced and modified by his environment, still it is true that man reacts upon his environment and changes it. He does this in ways peculiar to himself alone. He forms tools out of the elements of nature, he builds houses, he shoots game, he raises crops, he invents machinery and makes the forces of heat, water, electricity and other forces of nature drive his mill, run his cars and administer to his physical wants and necessities, to his comforts and to his luxury and ease. The dog or the horse or the ape does not develop machinery or utilize the forces of nature to the extent that they can feed and clothe and shelter the increasing multitudes of their kind; but man reacts upon his physical environment in ways that are peculiar to himself alone. There you must recognize in man a mind and a will of his own that changes the aspects and facts of nature.

Professor Ladd truly says, "Human history is an extremely complex affair in which the whole human nature, aesthetical, moral and religious as well as the physical and sensuous side, reacts in extremely complicated ways upon the changing condition of the environment." The peculiar and inexplicable fact about man's reacting upon his environment is not so much that he shows more intelligence in providing for his daily wants, for that would only make him a superior animal, but that man has intellectual ideals and a love of truth for its own sake; has ethical, aesthetical ideals and sentiments of awe and reverence, from which he reacts upon his environment in a way to get his philosophy, science, art, ethics and religion—this is what can't be explained on biological or mechanical or anthropological grounds. You cannot understand history unless you understand man as an ethical, aesthetical and religious being. All degrees of civilization, all eras and epochs of history show that the love and appreciation of beauty is an essential part of man's progress.[1]

---

1. While the specific passage cited by Ferris of George Trumball Ladd's work has not been found in my exploration of Ladd's expansive corpus, the passage above, likely paraphrased by Ferris, does accurately capture Ladd's view of religious experience and his philosophy of religion. Take, for example, Ladd's thoughts in a chapter titled "The Moral Attributes," in the second volume of *The Philosophy of Religion* (New York: Charles Scribner's Sons), published in 1909, where he says, "God is in the World, the indwelling and controlling Power which is shaping human history toward the progressive realization of ethical ideals" (360). In a subsequent chapter titled "God as Moral Ruler and Providence," Ladd continues, "Religion answers the problem with its conception of God as perfect Ethical Spirit, immanent in human history as man's moral Ruler and Redeemer, and operating in the totality of human experience and in the form of revelation and inspiration" (347). Given Ferris's time at Yale, it is not beyond the realm of possibility that he was privy to some of Ladd's reflections before their official publication.

Professor Ladd again says, "It is the soul of man which makes history what it is. History is a study of the development of the free spirit of man. It cannot be explained on biological, anthropological and statistical grounds alone. Some of the most important economical changes have been due to the fact that man is a religious being. History is the resultant of the entire complex development of man considered as body and mind and determining his own development." That view of history which makes it a matter of biological mechanism ignores the most important class of facts.

Professor Ladd again truly says, "If you confine your handling of it to mere external and mechanical considerations, objective details, you can't get at the heart of the matter. If you deal with the history of Europe from the time of Christ to the present era as a purely economic and political affair, you leave out of the account the greater whole. The politics and history of Europe have been profoundly modified and influenced by moral and religious ideas. The history of political institutions and the history of economic changes is an important but small part of history. The history of domestic and private institutions is an important part of history. The history of art is just as much a necessary part of historical institutions as the political and economic history. Man's philosophy, his science, his art, his ethics and religion are not caused by mechanical forces external to himself; but they arise out of the depth of the human soul. The intellectual, moral and spiritual characteristics of the human soul are what is of main account in history. Then, again, we cannot explain the psychological genius of the Greeks, the genius of Beethoven, the monotheistic and ethical genius of the Israelites, the political genius of the Indo-Germanic races on biological and anthropological grounds. Neither can you explain the great racial characteristics, psychological peculiarities of the different races on biological and anthropological grounds. The race, reacting in a different way on its environment, determines the course of development the race will take. The inexplicable soul life of the Germanic nations is the thing of main account that will explain what the Germanic nations have done and will do in history." How account for the psychical and psychological differences between races, that one has a genius for religion, another for art, and another for politics, how account for the psychical differences between men of genius of different kinds? You can't do it in terms of mechanism.

You cannot explain on physiological and biological grounds how Moses, Jesus, Paul and Luther became such powers in history. You can't account for the genius and personality of Christ on the ground of enlarged brain area. It is his inexplicable soul life that explains him as a religious genius. His wonderful spiritual insight was the resultant of his spiritual hopes and longings and aspirations; it arose from the inner experience of the man. We cannot leave out of account human individuality and human personality in history.

Then, too, certain sociologists and political economists regard society as an organism; they speak of the social forces which work in this organism, and of the laws which reign and hold sway in this organism. This view of human society is a biological and mechanical view and leaves out of account human individuality and human personality. This view of human society does not consider individuality to be the making force in history. But it sees in human society nothing but the blind, mechanical working of "social laws" and "social forces." It is interested only in the mechanics of society.

There is a very erroneous school in sociology which regards society as a mechanism or as a blind unconscious organism. It looks upon human history as a product of social forces and inexorable laws. Indeed, one hears of the laws to which society is subjected, of the forces that work in human history. But Professor George Trumbull Ladd of Yale University, a philosopher possessing a mind of wonderful depth, subtlety and comprehensiveness, has completely refuted that school of sociology when he says in his "Philosophy of Knowledge," one of the most profound and comprehensive philosophical works ever written: "When one turns to face the concrete and life-like picture of the multitudes of men in the present world and in the course of history, then, too, one inclines to believe that these souls are themselves the forces and that their ever varying and self-chosen relations to the world of things and to each other are the laws which constitute the figuratively so-called social organism. Social forces are not existent, so far as the science of sociology goes, until the souls are existent. They are no more uniform than are the souls from which the forces spring. And as to the laws of a 'social organism' there are none except those which are made by the action and interaction of the souls themselves. But these are not ready-made laws, as it were; they are only the actually ceaselessly varying and, as we hope, improving modes of the behavior of the individual members of the so-called organism."[2] There is one set of students of history who regard man as a product of physical conditions, the resultant of physical forces, a child of nature. But this is a materialistic view and it ignores the spiritual side, ignores the influence that man is capable of producing upon events. Some men say that events of the past would have happened no matter what men lived. But is it so?

---

2. William H. Ferris is quoting from George Trumball Ladd's *Philosophy of Knowledge: An Inquiry into the Nature, Limits, and Validity of Human Cognitive Faculty* (New York: Charles Scribner and Sons, 1897), 313–14. This could be considered one of Ladd's earlier works in philosophy proper, given his extensive writings on the Bible, religion, and psychology previous to this 1897 publication.

There are two great sets of facts that this way of looking at human history overlooks. There are the enormous influence of great men upon human history. If a few military geniuses, a few political geniuses, a few speculative thinkers had not lived, the entire course of human history would have been different. They are Jesus Christ, Paul, Augustine, Luther, Moses, Abraham, Buddha and Mohammed, Socrates, Plato, Aristotle, Kant, Alexander, Caesar, Charlemagne, Columbus, and a few others. Take them out of history and no one can tell what the course of human history would have been. I know that the essential elements of human nature—its hopes, longings and aspirations—are facts to be reckoned with. I know that the prevailing social, moral and spiritual conditions and tendencies of the time are also facts to be reckoned with and facts which the great man must take account of. But it was the peculiar genius of the individual men that was the most important factor.

But while history is to be primarily accounted for by the development of a rational and free human nature, we must remember that the structure of physical nature, the fact that there are rivers in certain places and mountains in certain other places, are facts to be reckoned with also. But someone will object that there are certain great men who were the mere product of circumstances. Circumstances made the man, emergency called him forth and placed him on the top of a swelling tide. But there are two classes of great men; there are men who possess intrinsic greatness, and there are other great men whose greatness is purely the greatness of opportunity. But it is no doubt true that even the men of intrinsic greatness are partly dependent upon opportunity. They require that they shall live in circumstances which will develop and quicken the latent germ. They require that they shall be given a chance or opportunity to exercise and display their wonderful powers. The political and social genius, and even the speculative and religious genius, is assisted if he casts his seed upon fruitful and fertile soil.

Still the men of intrinsic greatness are distinguished in two ways from the men whose greatness is the greatness of opportunity. The partly great men are carried along by the events, swept along by the advancing tide of public opinion and aroused feeling. They are merely figureheads, who happen to represent the advancing tide or give expression to the aroused sentiment. But the truly great man determines the course of events, guides and directs affairs. The partially great man could be taken out of the situation and he would not be missed; another man could step in and fill his place just as well. But a truly great man is a man who cannot be easily duplicated. It is very hard or impossible to find a man who can fill his place. He is unique. He possesses a penetrating insight, an iron will and a self-possessed nature.

A human ideal has been slowly and progressively realized in the development of human society. Some pessimists have only seen strife and carnage in nature, the survival of the fittest, and they have remarked that nature is red in tooth and claw. But self-sacrifice is as noticeable in animal life as is selfishness, self-assertion and cruelty. As Dr. Gordon has said, "Parental love is the tie that binds the whole brute creation to God." Love is the emotion that binds the generation of the brutes together. Were it not for the facts that mothers of animals cared for their offspring, were willing to sacrifice their lives for their offspring, the young animals could not live. The emotion of love is even found in a lion's den.

But it is not until we reach human nature that the emotion of love passes from a blind, unconscious, natural instinct to an ethical sentiment. The entire history of humanity has consisted in broadening the sphere for the emotion of love. At first we see man in a savage and wild state. Every man was an Ishmaelite, with his hand against his neighbor. Then there was a crude family love, caused by the family being knit together in caring for and protecting the young. Then the ties of blood relationship widened, until the family love extended itself, until the clan was but another name for a larger family. Then the emotion of love broadened its scope until it took in the tribe, then the nation or race, and, finally, the growth of commerce, the spread of Christianity, the missionary movement and the hope of international arbitration have so expanded that men are beginning to realize what the brotherhood of man means. The family life is the source from which the nation sprang and it is also the source from which the emotion of love took its rise. We can see that the whole of the higher spiritual qualities of man and the whole tendency of history has moved towards the triumph of moral principles and towards the enthronement of love. Not only has a moral ideal been slowly and progressively realized in the life of the individual, but a moral order has been slowly and progressively realized in the course of human history. This clearly indicates the thought and plan of God which is being realized in human history. I know that there has been a great waste of material and life. I know that there has been many a regression. I know that the element of luck and chance has played a prominent part in human history. I know that there is no special providence in the sense that God directs every movement. But still an immanent idea has been realized in human history and there has been a movement towards some goal; namely, the ideal social community.

And in the course of human history we can see the method of the movement of the Divine Mind. We see first that the method of history has been one of evolution rather than of revolution, of slow and gradual growth rather than of sudden transition. Secondly, we see that the great advances of history have been made by a few men being faithful to an ideal. Thirdly, we see the law of the survival of the fittest prevailing in history.

When Christianity first made its entrance into the world slavery was embedded in the very structure and life of the Roman Empire. Indeed half of the population of Italy were slaves. Christianity advocated a sentiment and embodied a spirit (namely, the intrinsic worth of every individual soul) that was at war with human slavery. Christianity finally conquered, but the process was a long and slow one. The despised plebeians finally obtained full civil and political rights and intermarriage; but the process was a long and slow one. The Jews had been persecuted for centuries; but at last a Jew became prime minister of England, and now the Jews are beginning to breathe freely. About twelve hundred years ago all Europe was groaning in serfdom, but finally the French Revolution broke forth upon astonished Europe and indicated that the time was at hand when the peasant would secure his rights and privileges. The Saxon peasants, under William the Conqueror, were serfs, and serfdom for a long while held sway in England, yet slowly and gradually the striving Anglo-Saxon spirit burst its fetters, until the Magna Carta was secured and until the constitutional form of self-government prevailed in England. The whole course of human history indicates the terrible patience of God and the fact that he has all eternity at his disposal.

Then, too, when we look at the heroic spirit of the Hebrew prophets; at the heroism of Paul and the other Apostles; at the dauntless courage of Luther, Knox, Wesley and their disciples; at the heroism of the Pilgrim Fathers and the Abolitionists, we can see that human history would not have been what it now is were it not for those little bands of heroic souls, were it not for those rugged adamantine spirits who stood against the world for principles. All human history is a witness and testimony to the psychological fact that a little band of faithful souls, who will not flinch, can shape and cause to totter the confidence of the guilty and can rouse the conscience and stir the spirit of the indifferent.

The entire cycle of history is replete with instances of a rich, luxurious but effeminate nation falling before a hardier and stronger one. Persia became rich, powerful, immoral and degenerate only to fall before the hardy Greeks. The Greeks became powerful, but immorality sapped their manhood and vitality and they fell before the hardy Romans. The little city of Rome ruled the world; but licentiousness and debauchery weakened her and she was unable to resist the tide of barbarian invasion that swept in continuous hordes over the barriers of her empire, until it overwhelmed her. Similarly the fall of Constantinople in the fifteenth century was caused by degeneracy, consequent upon dissipation.

Fifteen hundred years ago the hardy Norseman and fierce, fearless Vikings made their presence known and felt in Europe. They laughed at the perils of the deep, courted danger, burned villages and pillaged houses. The Anglo-Saxon race ever since has stood forth as the perfect embodiment of daring courage and adventurous aggressiveness. By its bold, daring, adventurous and aggressive spirit the Anglo-Saxon race has conquered every race that it has come into contact with. It has taken up Christianity and has shown its aggressive spirit in carrying forward civilization into the very heart of Africa and in carrying forward the missionary movement. That race, with its progressive spirit, is now developing and carrying still higher the twentieth century civilization. But just look at the facts: Israel, Greece, Rome, the Germanic and Saxon races are the five great races that have thus far made important contributions to civilization. Each race developed a peculiar genius along one line and perfected it in an organized and national life. Israel, as an ethical and religious genius, left her impress upon civilization; Greece, as a philosophic and artistic genius; Rome, as a military, practical and political genius; the Germanic races, as the embodiment of a free and independent spirit; the Anglo-Saxon race, as the manifestation of an adventurous and progressive spirit. After Christianity appeared in the world, each of these five great race stocks not only was influenced and modified by Christianity, but each left its own impress upon Christianity and contributed its own distinctive genius to it. Thus it was from the Hebrew mind and spirit that Christianity derived its conception of the ethical perfection of God and of the reality of sin as an alienation from God. It was from the Greek mind that Christianity obtained its conception of the immanence of the Divine mind in nature, obtained its notion that every visible thing was but the symbol and manifestation of an invisible thought. And here it is that Julius Caesar made his indelible impress upon human history. He conquered the Britons, the Gauls and Germans; he cleared the Mediterranean Sea of pirates, enlarged and strengthened the Roman Empire in the far East, united and centralized the political life of Rome. Had it not been for the political and military genius of Rome, and especially of Julius Caesar, which conquered the civilized world, built magnificent roads and assimilated the conquered into one State, Christianity would not have been the force that it is to-day. Rome became the purveyor of the Hebrew and Greek mind and so conquered and unified the world that it was possible for Christianity to be disseminated over the entire civilized world. We find the Germanic spirit free and independent during a process which began with the Mediaeval mystics and culminated in the heroic pleas of Luther for the sanctity of inward piety, of the soul's communion with God, and for individual freedom in studying and interpreting the Bible. Inward piety, philosophical and theological freedom have been the distinctive contribution of the Germanic race to Christianity, and it was from the Mediaeval mystics and the German Reformation that Germany received its impulse.

But someone may say, What has the Anglo-Saxon race contributed in philosophy, theology and inward piety? Nothing. But what Rome did for the Hebrew and Greek mind the Anglo-Saxon race has done for the German mind. The Anglo-Saxon race has assimilated the results of the Hebrew, Greek and German genius and is aggressively carrying forward to all parts of civilization the indestructible elements contributed by the Hebrew, Greek and Roman mind. The Anglo-Saxon race is the advance guard of civilization and it is the source from which the great missionary movements have sprung. It is the embodiment of a progressively aggressive missionary spirit.

So the Negro race will never achieve much if it scatters its energy and attempts to blot out the precious traits of the race. We are a race possessing a lovable nature, a spiritual earnestness and a musical genius. The nineteenth century civilization, the nineteenth century Christianity, and especially the American civilization and American Christianity is absorbed in a gross materialism which takes away the spirit of love and depreciates the spiritual side of human nature. There is a felt want and need in our modern civilization and Christianity. The Negro possesses those spiritual and emotional qualities which can soften human nature and spiritualize religion and music. Here is his sphere. He must shake off the infirmities of the Negro race; he must cease imitating the vices of the Anglo-Saxon race; he must acquire the aggressiveness and tenacity of purpose of the Anglo-Saxon race and develop all that is precious in the Negro genius.[3] But the Negro poet, musician, artist and philosopher must remember that, if he is to accomplish something that will live forever and go down the ages, he must rise above the limitations of a Negro

3. Even here Ferris's reading of Ladd's *Philosophy of Religion* comes through. Ladd believed that "genius," the ideals and sentiment of representative men, emerged from religious and ethical experience, a kind of revelation within the currents of human history. Ladd actually argues a similar point about racial genius: "It has been in the virtual possession of this faith that the best of the race, the noblest thinkers and actors in human history, have with an increasing confidence, and often with a passionate and undying enthusiasm, proclaimed the ultimate triumph of righteousness. Their optimism has not been economic or anthropological; it has been ethical and religious. They do not now believe that commerce, or science, or art, without righteousness, can regenerate humanity, or elevate the race to its highest attainable, much less to an ideally perfect, social" (376). Ferris reads Ladd earlier in the chapter as stating, "It is the soul of man which makes history what it is. History is a study of the development of the free spirit of man," and this "soul" cannot be captured economically, biologically, or anthropologically. This is the reason for Ferris's rejection of the rising environmentalist accounts of Negro development in the first

environment, touch the common heart of humanity, rise to the Universal and strike the Universal chord in the harp of God's world. Genius of whatever kind is an inborn quality of the human soul. It enables the possessor of it to constructively and creatively deal with the material at his disposal in unique ways, in ways that cannot be taught or learned. This is true of every kind of genius. It is the peculiar, the inexplicable psychical and psychological differences between men which causes one man to be a political genius, another man to be a military genius and another man to be a religious genius. The environment doesn't make the man, the environment only quickens the latent germ, only develops and brings out what already exists in the man, though perhaps only in embryonic forms. The environment may develop some qualities in a man, may modify others, may repress others. But it can never put into a man what is not in the man. The ideals and fundamental instincts which impel a man of genius or any great man are not imposed upon him from without. They come from within. They grow from within. They are the results of the innate tendencies of the man and they burst forth with the irrepressible vehemence of pent-up energy. The possibilities of every man's personality, the peculiarities of his genius exist, in a dormant state though it may be, in the man and are independent of the man's environment.

While environment may modify a man's original endowment, still the way that a man shall choose or decide at the crises of his career, at the critical moments of his life, moments in which the character is formed or changed, when a man chooses his calling or decides upon any line of action, this is something that is not determined by circumstances, but is accounted for by his inexplicable soul life and by his freedom of mind in choosing and willing. Caesar's decision on the banks of the Rubicon was not caused by mechanical forces external to himself, but arose out of the depth of the experience of the man. The righteous indignation of Luther at the sale of indulgences was not caused by the physical forces which acted upon his sensuous organs, but arose out of the spiritual nature of the man.

The other central fact is that if the soil was fertile and the sower had not come and cast his seed the spiritual life of mankind would not be what it is now. If the conditions were all right for a political revolution or religious

---

decade of the twentieth century. This cultural and physical environment, or what would be more accurately termed "milieu," in Ferris's time did not fully explain the capacity or full potentiality of Negro genius; he, in the language of Ferris, could rise above it.

This idea of rising above the basic imitation of whites was also mentioned by Ferris specifically in his essay "Typical Negro Traits," published in the *American Missionary* 62, no. 4 (1908): 99–102.

awakening, but if the great man had not come and set the forces and tendencies into operation and roused men, the course of human history would have been far different. As to whether, if Christ or Mohammed or Buddha or Caesar or Alexander had not lived, other men of genius would have taken their places and done their work, we do not and cannot know. But we know of no other men of their age who could have done the work they did. And if these other men of genius had lived, we do not know whether the conditions would be the same. But the positive fact that we do know is this: a few unique individuals, coming at the time they did, exerted a tremendous influence upon human history and determined its course, destroyed empires, founded new ones, and were the founders of religion.

Each one of the three great religions, Buddhism, Mohammedanism and Christianity, some one of which influences almost every tribe and nation upon the earth, has been the fruit of the thought and inspiration of a single individual. We must take account of the general condition and civilization of the people at the time that Siddartha, Mohammed and Christ arose, as we must also of the general characteristics of human nature as modified by its environment. We must consider the spiritual needs and longings and hopes and aspirations of man. But the dominating force and essence of each one of these three movements was the genius and personal power of the man who gave his thoughts and life to the world to meet its needs.

Before Mohammed's time, the Saracens were men of a narrow iconoclastic spirit and were scattered into a few Bedouin tribes.[4] But what did Mohammed do? In the brilliant words of Professor George Burton Adams: "Putting into definite and striking form the unconscious ideas and aspirations of his people, and adding a central and unifying teaching, and inspiring and elevating notions from various sources, he had transformed a few scattered tribes into a great nation and sent them forth under a blazing enthusiasm upon a career of conquest entirely unparalleled in motive force and extent."[5]

Mohammed starts out with a few Bedouin tribes and a territory six thousand miles in diameter was occupied and conquered within a hundred years. True it is that the tendencies towards Mohammed's results existed before Mohammed was born. True it is that Mohammed did not build out of chaos. True it is that the Semitic race was an intensely religious race. 'Tis a fact, also, that the conquests of the Mohammedans were easily made because the

4. The term "Saracens" is an ethnicization of Muslims utilized by many Christian writers during the Middle Ages. See John Victor Tolan, *Saracens: Islam in the Medieval European Imagination* (New York: Columbia University Press, 2002).

5. Ferris is citing George Burton Adams, *Civilization during the Middle Ages: Especially in Relation to Modern Civilization* (New York: Charles Scribner, 1898), 259–60.

races which they overthrew were old, weak races and that when the Arabs met the young and vigorous Franks they were turned back. These three causes partly account for the rise of Mohammedanism, but they do not wholly explain it. A psychological cause remains to be explained, namely, the influence of the personality of Mohammed upon the minds and hearts of the Arabs. The tendencies of the tribe and the intensely religious nature of the Semitic race needed the powerful personality of a Mohammed to put the vague, floating desires and tendencies to unity in religion, language and government, into a definite and clear shape. The creative genius and powerful personality of a Mohammed gave the people a deep channel to work in. If Mohammed had not come and unified the tendencies and desires of his race, no one can tell what the history of those Bedouin tribes would have been.

And with regard to Luther. The fact that there were a religious movement in Switzerland by Zwingli, a movement in France led by LaFevre, a movement in Spain, a desire for reform in Italy, which were independent of each other and of Luther, the fact that some of these movements were before the time of Luther, have led some historians to believe that the Reformation would have come if Luther had not lived, although it might have come later and perhaps in some other country. And some see in the Reformation nothing but the bursting forth of forces working unseen beneath the surface. But these men lose sight of the central fact. No one questions that for a moral and spiritual reformer to exert great influence the times must be ripe and the conditions favorable. He must come at the proper time. But suppose a Luther had not come along and applied the match? Who can tell but the combustible material might never have burst into a conflagration? Who can tell but what the volcanic fires might have continued to smoulder and ferment instead of belching forth in a stream of hot lava that blazed and burned its fiery path to the sea, if Luther's rugged and heroic personality had not come in the nick of time, as it were, and set the forces and tendencies into operation.

The influence of the truly great in every form of development, in every line of activity, is enormous. But important in the history of the race as is the influence of a great discoverer, explorer, inventor, military leader, statesman or thinker, more important still is the influence of great individuals and a few rare personalities in the religious development of the race. The reason is obvious; the discoverer, explorer, inventor, military leader and statesman makes a change in the external structure of life which reacts upon the individual; but the founder of a religion or prophetic seer works directly upon the hearts and characters and minds of men. A Christopher Columbus, a Julius Caesar, an Alexander, a Charlemagne, a Napoleon Bonaparte, ceases to exert a personal influence upon men after his death, but the life, the words and writing of a Buddha, a Mohammed, a Newman, a Luther, a Paul, a Christ, continue to inspire and awake the spiritual nature centuries after he is dead.

But it may be asked, Why is it that whereas a great thinker or inventor or discoverer can only hasten the onward march of civilization, yet to a few religious geniuses, often men of narrow views, but possessed of indomitable will, energetic natures and a burning enthusiasm, it has been given to change the course history, to create history and to found religions and empires? Can we explain it by saying that mankind loves to follow illusions and mirages and hence will follow those men who embody its dreams and illusions? No. No religion has its hold upon the world and upon human nature by reason of the error that is in it or the illusions that it contains, but by reason of the truth that is in it. And Buddha became such a spiritual force and factor in history and founded such a world-embracing religion, because his religion met the spiritual needs of the Eastern mind, which desired an escape from the ills and misery and sin of this life.

Mohammed, Buddha, Luther and Newman or any narrow fanatic or enthusiastic reformer sways men as a speculative thinker and scholar never can, not because of the illusions which they follow, but because the ideals which they embody and their own intense and powerful personalities are able to appeal to and stir the deep-lying ethical and religious impulses of the human soul. It is because they can liberate the heroic in men and touch and vivify human nature in its inmost depths.

But how account for the magical spell which is wielded by a great man? How account for the secret of the enchantment of his magnetic presence over the hearts and minds of men? Mankind is ruled by kings, because hero worship is an instinct of the human soul. We see Roman soldiers blindly following Caesar. We see a Richelieu, a Calvin, a Bismarck erecting a liberty-crushing despotism and ruling with a rod of iron. Nay, from the French soldiers who instinctively bowed before Napoleon and obeyed his every nod and call, as though he were a frowning Zeus hurling his dreaded thunderbolts from the rugged heights of Mount Olympus, up to the noble Oxford youths who eagerly hung upon the lofty words of Newman, so strangely fascinated and overawed by the moral sublimity and spiritual transcendency of the man, we see all men dominated by the man of superior intellect and stronger personality. There are certain instincts as fundamental as the distinction between right and wrong. There is an instinct about that sense of reverence, that sense of yielding ourselves to that which is above us, and it is this that partly explains the superlative influence of a great man. For it explains the influence of the personality of a great man upon the minds and hearts of his contemporaries, and this influence of one personality upon other personalities is an important element in the effect which any great man produces upon his own and following ages. But as to whether that man's word, when it has been spoken, or deed, when it has been done, will be taken up by a tide that no one can control and swept onward, no one can predict, as that belongs to conditions that lie beyond the ken of finite mortals. The conclusion of our study of history would seem to be that it is great men with the breath of the Almighty upon them, great men inspired by ideals, who are the making forces in history.

When one looks at the magnificent civilization of Babylon and Assyria, at the still grander civilization of Greece and Rome, one notices a striking similarity in the causes which led to the overthrow of these nations. The same sad story is told of all. By reason of their heroic character, simple way of living and sturdy virtues these four nations acquired vast riches and great power. Babylon became rich, luxurious and corrupt, and fell an easy victim to the hardy and sturdy Persians. Then the Persians gave themselves up to fast and loose pleasures and dissipation. They then became physically weak and cowardly. On the plains of Marathon and Salamis the vast hosts of the Persians were routed by the small but valiant bands of the Greeks. And then followed that tale that causes cultured men to look back with saddened eyes to Greece. Greece, the land of beauty, culture and art, became the home of corrupt and degenerate sons of the old heroes; weakened by their dissipation they became an easy prey to Philip of Macedon, to Rome. We next see Rome rising in her might, gaining control of Italy, annihilating the Carthaginians, clearing the Mediterranean Sea of pirates, subduing the Gauls, Germans and Britons, extending her conquest to the far East and binding the whole civilized world into a unified kingdom, whose center and source of power was Rome—Mighty Rome. The power that Rome, that single city, showed in aggressively enlarging her boundaries and in assimilating the conquered nations into Romans and building up a strongly centralized state, challenges our admiration. But with the increase of wealth and power, luxury, cruelty, corruption, dissipation, physical weakness followed. Virtue and chastity became lost; family life became corrupt. The very plain and sturdy virtues by which the Romans gained power were lost, and the effeminate and degenerated Romans were not able to resist the tide of barbarian invasion which rolled over Europe. Mighty Rome was turned over to the barbarians. These four nations of antiquity serve us as a terrible reminder. But let us look a moment at the modern nations and see if immorality and atheism is a cause of their weakness and downfall. The fall of Constantinople in the fifteenth century was due to the corruption, dissipation and consequent physical degeneracy and weakness resulting therefrom. The partition of Poland was caused by the luxury, injustice, cruelty, fast and high living of the Polish nobles. Someone may here object that "Poland was overthrown by the greed of stronger nations." That is true, but the life of the nobles sapped their physical energy and their unjust government and caste system took the patriotism and lofty spirit out of the middle class of Poland.

France is the best example in modern times of the full results of atheism. France, in the eighteenth century, forgot God and became atheistic. Then, when they believed that there was no future life in which virtue would be rewarded and vice punished, the Frenchmen lived solely for pleasure, sensuality. All Europe in the eighteenth century showed how scepticism and atheism are necessarily followed by crime and vice. But nowhere did there a worse atheism exist than in France and nowhere were licentiousness, sensuality, crime and vice of every description more rampant. And the most central causes of the French Revolution were the atheism of France and the corruption which resulted from it. The licentiousness, luxury, sensuality and love of pleasure of the nobles prevented them from regarding the rights of the people and made them grind every last cent out of the peasants. Then, when the French peasants were aroused, there was no fear of God, no belief in God and the future life to restrain them from the terrible crimes and wholesale murders that even now cause a shudder to come over us, whenever the French Revolution is mentioned. It is a fact of life and history that cannot be denied, that men and nations cannot live a perfect, ethical and moral life, when they think there is no God; as soon as men think there is no God, no future life, they invariably say with Greek and Roman atheists, with the Epicureans, "What is the use of all our striving, of all our suffering, of all our self-denial if there is no God, no life after this life? What is the use of our building up a perfect character and making lofty our whole nature, what is the use of building such a fine edifice of heroic manhood and noble womanhood only to see this fine manhood and womanhood destroyed and perish? Let us eat, drink and be merry, for to-morrow we die. Let us live solely for pleasure and let us gratify our animal passions." That is the state of mind that atheism brings a man into; that is the state of mind that ruined Babylon, Persia, Greece, Rome, Poland, France; that is the state of mind that will sap the strength of and ruin any nation.

Someone may object here that "some atheists are good men, nay, even are heroic and noble men." A few atheists are, but very few. For it is a matter of biography that almost all of the atheistic philosophers, the great men of whom atheism boasts, are immoral men. Voltaire is one of a great number of them.

Very few men have that iron will, that herculean strength of character that, without belief in "an Eternal Power not ourselves that makes for righteousness," without a belief that righteousness will finally conquer in this world and that somewhere in the universe, somehow or other, virtue will be rewarded—I say that very few men have that strength of character and iron will that, without a belief in God and immortality, they can suffer unpopularity and hatred and death for right's sake, can calmly face seeming defeat, through all disappointments and failures can be courageous or cheerful, can be proof against every temptation. Parnell and Mark Antony are only representatives of that class of strong men, not guided by religious motives, who have succumbed to temptations. Parnell was a Catholic, and a church member I think, but God and religion did not mean much to Parnell. His religion was not the reality of his life.

I will only glance for a moment at the transcendent heroism of those who had a living faith in the ever-present and living God. Look at the old Hebrew Prophets, who sternly rebuked the Jewish multitudes and suffered persecutions, telling the truth and uttering the thoughts God inspired them with. Look at the Apostle Paul and all the other Christian martyrs, who, with singing and rejoicing, suffered persecutions and went to be torn into pieces by the lions in the Roman Amphitheatre or to be burned alive at the stake. Look at the intrepid Luther, fearlessly speaking the truth about religion; and when dissuaded by his friends from going to the Diet of Worms and to seeming suffering and death, boldy said, "If there were as many devils in Worms are there are tiles on the house roofs I would still go there!" Look at the old Pilgrim Fathers, who, in order to worship God in their own way, left their happy homes in England, came to bleak and barren New England, heroically endured the frosts, famine and attacks of the Indians, and founded a commonwealth. That old, stern, heroic Puritan blood still courses in the veins of their descendants. That blood caused Wendell Phillips, Charles Sumner, William Lloyd Garrison and other abolitionists to agitate the slavery question and to suffer for so doing. That old Puritan blood and faith in God caused John Brown to cheerfully die. Look at Chinese Gordon, the Christian soldier, the hero of the nineteenth century, sustained by his faith in God, accomplishing seeming impossibilities, calmly overwhelming odds and so cheerfully bearing the terrible strain at Khartoum and so heroically dying there. Look at the long list of Christian missionaries and martyrs of the nineteenth century, Henry Martyn, Percy Alden, Livingston, Armstrong and others, who have given up personal comfort and selfish ambition, lived for others and been happy in their heroic self-renunciation and self-sacrificing love. Consider that the backbone and strength of England rests in her religious faith and moral stamina.

I know that my proof has not been a strictly logical one. I know that I have barely touched upon some important points. But the subject with which I have to deal is so complex and so wide that it can only be illumined by flashing sidelights upon it from different positions, by looking at it from different points of view.

## *Chapter Three*

# Teleology in Reality; or, in What Sense Is There a Teleological Movement in the World? Is Man One of the Final Purposes of the Universe?

There is one sentence in Hamilton Wright Mabie's essays in literary criticism which equals the best of Emerson's epigrammatic sentences, which could condense a whole system of philosophy into a single phrase. And this sentence will form the text of this chapter.

"Through personality the universe reveals itself, and in the high and final development of personality the universe accomplishes the immortal work for which the shining march of its suns and the ebb and flow of its vital tides were ordained."[1]

I shall endeavor to unfold the meaning of that sentence in this chapter and to throw the illumination of its light upon the great problem of man's immortality.

But, before we proceed, it will be well to glance for a moment at the line of thought already traversed. I have endeavored in the two preceding chapters

1. The phrasing is somewhat awkward in the text. Ferris is citing Hamilton Wright Mabie, *Essays in Literary Interpretation* (New York: Dodd and Mead, [1892]), 170. The specific lines are from Mabie's reading of Robert Browning. This citing of Mabie is not as random as one might think. Mabie specifically argues "that Browning is a philosopher as well as a poet, and that his verse, instead of lending itself to the lyric utterance of isolated emotion, becomes the medium through which the universal harmony of things is translated into song" (ibid.). As seen in the previous chapter and Ferris's "Typical Race Traits," this is the duality, the complementarian aspect of poetic imagination and philosophy, that he believes resides in the Negro soul.

to show that the universe and man are only to be understood upon the hypothesis that they are the expressions and forthputtings of an immanent, rational, ethical and benevolent world spirit. Then we took up the objection raised by the pessimist, that the sin and suffering and misery and moral evil in the world introduces a discord in the world ground and indicates some imperfection in his nature.

But in those chapters we saw that altruism was as universal a principle as egoism, both in the animal and human world; we saw also that from the time when the nebula began to condense and contract into revolving fluid balls, up to the present time, the whole process of evolution has tended to the producing and perfecting of the spiritual nature of man. This looks as if the universe were ethical to the core and that love and benevolence were imbedded in the very structure of the universe. Then we saw that the hypothesis of man's immortality would resolve the difficulties involved in the problem of evil.

Now, the pessimist may say that I am arguing in a circle; for we cannot prove that God is love unless man is immortal, and we cannot prove that man is immortal unless God is love. But our adversary does not distinguish between positive arguments and negative objections. It is by our positive argument that we prove that God is love. On the hypothesis that God is love we prove that man is immortal. And upon the supposition that man is immortal we can show that the sin and suffering in the world does not invalidate our positive proof that the world is the eternal expression of a rational and ethical Personality.

Thus far, instead of arguing in a circle, there has been a steady progression in our argument. Now we will try to discover what is the destiny of man; but, before we do that, we must see what is man's place in the cosmos. And that will be the burden of this chapter.

The old Ptolemaic astronomy placed the earth in the center of the solar system, around which all the other planets revolved. In the eyes of the old theology man was the lord of the earth; the entire solar universe was created for him and his comforts and he was the center of cosmic space. The earth in this conception was not only the center of the solar system, but was the largest and most important planetary body in that system.

The earth and its revolving planets were formed but for one purpose, to be the terrestrial stage and scene of action in which man would perform his part in the drama of life. Man was a monarch, whose throne was the earth, whose canopy was heaven and whose kingdom was the universe. And this view was given classic expression in Pope's beautiful Essay on Man:

> Ask for what end the heavenly bodies shine,
> Earth for whose use? Pride answers, "'Tis for mine;

> For me kind nature wakes her genial power,
> Suckles each herb and spreads out every flower; Annual for me, the grape, the rose, renew
> The juice nectareous and the balmy dew;
> For me the mine a thousand treasures bring,
> For me, health gushes from a thousand springs;
> Seas roll to waft me, suns to light me rise,
> My footstool earth, my canopy the skies."

But this childlike naive belief in the special creation of nature and her forces for man's use and comfort vanished, like the mists before the rising sun, when Copernicus revealed the fact that the sun was the center of our solar system, around which the earth as well as Mercury, Venus, Mars, Jupiter and Saturn revolved. Then, with the invention of the telescope, the new astronomy disclosed the truth that those dim, fixed stars, which twinkle faintly in the distance, are light-shedding suns and centers of other solar systems with their revolving planets. Our sun is at least a million times larger than our earth. Julia McNair Wright in her fascinating book on astronomy says that, "Most of the fixed stars are larger than our sun. Sirius is supposed to be as large as eight suns like ours. Vega is as large as thirty-eight suns."

Think of that, Vega, a star-sun, is forty million times larger than our earth. And when we reflect that some astronomers declare that in space there are nine thousand millions of star-suns, with their wheeling planets, we can form some idea of the insignificance of our earth in the solar system. But when we remember in the words of the same author that, "As to distance, one tries in vain to realize it. The nearest fixed star is trillions of miles away. Light travels at the rate of one hundred and eight-six thousand miles a second, yet so far off are the stars that it takes their light from three and a half to many thousand years to reach us. If to-day one such star suddenly perished, for a thousand years the light that has already left it would be streaming to us,"—we are appalled by the size and vastness of this universe.

But when we reflect that there are nine thousand millions of shining suns with revolving planets in space; that most of these are more than a million times larger than our earth, and that some of them are ten million times larger than our earth and one of them forty million times larger; when we reflect that Canopus, Rigel and Betelguese are a million times larger than our sun, which is a million times larger than our earth; when we reflect that it takes light, traveling at the rate of one hundred and eighty-six thousand miles a second, over thirty thousand years to reach us from the farthest star-suns and three and a half years from the nearest star-sun, we see that our earth is to the universe as a mere drop in the ocean; compared to the whole system of light-giving suns and gravitating satellites, our earth is but a tiny speck in the universe. It becomes the height of absurdity for man to say: "For me those shining suns in the infinite spaces shine and sparkle and are set like diamond studs in the dark heavens." Then man seems dwarfed into insignificance.

But another line of reflection takes man down from his self-erected pedestal or egoistic pride. This thought is expressed by Pope when he says:

> But errs not nature from this gracious end,
> From burning suns when livid deaths descend,
> When earthquakes swallow, or when tempests sweep
> Towns to one grave, whole nations to the deep?

It is a fact that Nature seems to pay no regard to the life and comfort and happiness of man. The dreaded lightning, the raging cyclone, devastating fire, and flaming and smoking volcanoes spare no human being that is athwart their destructive paths. The ocean engulfs the helpless souls who jump from a burning ship, summer's heat and winter's cold spare neither saint nor sinner. Nature seeks not to please man. She does not ask what he desires. And if man is to survive he must step in line and adjust himself to Nature and her moods.

The principle of the survival of the fittest holds universal sway in nature. And by the survival of the fit, Nature does not mean the intellectually, aesthetically and ethically fit, but those who can best adapt themselves to their physical environment. In the desert, the Bedouin Arab will survive where the Christian saint will perish. In the wilds of Africa, the Hottentot stands a better chance of living than the Caucasian philosopher. Nature says to man: "I don't care whether you are wise or foolish, honest or dishonest, pure or impure, brave or cowardly, adjust yourself to my conditions and you will live." Nature does not wait on man. You must conform yourself to her ways, or else you will suffer, starve or perish. Nature takes no account of your ignorance. You may not know that your next step may plunge you down a precipice to instant death; you may not know that the mode of life you are living will injure your health and bring you to premature death; but you must pay the penalty just the same. Nature punishes you as much for your ignorance as for your perversity and willfulness and wickedness. In vain do you pray for Nature to yield and spare your life or that of your loved one.

But not only is Nature thus careless about the individual welfare and happiness, but she ruthlessly cuts off the most sensitive and highly organized souls just as they are beginning to bud. Those who have read the "Studies in Mediaeval Life and Literature" and the introductory essay, "Brief Introduction and Notes to Literary Criticism," by Edward Tompkins McLaughlin, and seen the memorial volume published soon after his death, will say that his prose and poetic writings reveal rare gifts for a man just turned thirty. He had just been appointed full professor of Belles Lettres at Yale, had spent years of study of Dante and mediaeval and modern literature, had begun essays upon Dante and other forms of mediaeval and modern literature, and had just begun to give the world the fruits of his study and reflection when he was cut down by typhoid fever at the age of thirty-three.[2]

I well remember, when a freshman in Yale University, twenty-one years ago, while assembled one Tuesday afternoon in Linonian Hall for our exercise in English composition, a rather small, black-haired man, of somewhat feminine appearance and manner, strode nervously into the room. He began in a pleasing, delicate, conversational voice to talk about literature in general, restlessly twirling his slight mustache or twisting his watch chain. There was something about his ardent way of speaking that riveted my attention. I soon forgot his dainty appearance, his feminine voice, his seeming embarrassment and nervous mannerisms and became fascinated by the noble thoughts and beautiful sentiments that easily and naturally flowed in a limpid stream of delightful sentences from the inspired lips of the speaker as he spoke of the literary traditions of dear old Yale and the refining and ennobling influence of the study of literature.

I went out of the place a changed man. I saw that there was an indefinable something about this delicate and sensitive man that I lacked and wanted to possess. Such was my first impression of Professor Edward Tompkins McLaughlin, a man who opened up before my eyes and the eyes of many other undergraduates the vista of the aesthetical and spiritual beauties to be found in literature.

Professor McLaughlin was one of those rare spirits who represent the happy blending of philosophical and practical gifts with the poetic temperament. He was an Emerson, but an Emerson in whom the poet predominated over the philosopher, in whom the philosopher was lost in the poet. He combined the broad and profound scholarship, the sound sense and fine literary taste of a Lowell with the rare imaginative and poetic gifts, the delicate humor and deep spirituality of a Newman. I do not know whether he had that perfect ear for music which would place one in the front rank of lyric poets, although he wrote some short poems that were gems. But if ever a man had the creative imagination, the dainty, fancy and literary feeling and spiritual sensibility of a true poet, McLaughlin was that man. He had a sure and unerring literary sense. His poetic intuition, aided by his spiritual sympathy with and responsiveness to all that was noble in sentiment or beautiful in expression, would

2. See Edward Tompkins McLaughlin, *Studies in Mediaeval Life and Literature* (New York: G. P. Putnam's Sons, 1894).

penetrate to the heart of the matter in a way that a profound literary scholar or keen critic never could. He instinctively discerned the secret of the magic beauty of a phrase, or the haunting music of a line.

Had he lived, he would have given to the world essays which would have combined the insight of a Carlyle with the delicate fancy and quaint humor of a Lamb. Indeed, he might have sent forth books like Mabie's "Essays in Literary Interpretation" and Santayana's "Poetry and Religion," essays which register the high-water mark of American literary criticism, and are fit to be placed alongside of Matthew Arnold's essays in Criticism and on translating Homer.[3] But McLaughlin's essays would have been more imaginative in quality, more poetic in feeling. A delicate vein of sentiment and humor would have run through and pervaded them. They would have been characterized, too, by a quaint fancy and been bathed in a dreamy atmosphere. His "Studies in Mediaeval Life and Literature," which had not received his final touch, and his other writings which I have mentioned, showed his genius in its budding stages. He was one of those sensitive and strenuous souls, like Emerson, who felt an inner prompting to preach the gospel and carry the glad tidings of great joy, but his broad faith could not be confined within the limits of any definite religious creed, so he chose literature as his pulpit. Had he lived, he would have delivered his message to the world. It might not have been as philosophical as were those of Carlyle and Emerson, but it would probably have been the message of Mabie, touched with the sentiment of Ik Marvel's "Dream Life" and Curtis's "Prue and I."

Like Newman in his famous St. Mary's sermons, he would have searched the human soul and lured it back to the forgotten dreams and forsaken ideals of its youth in language that would have charmed men with its beauty.

What sane gardener would cut off a rose just as it is beginning to blossom forth into a glorious flower and distil its delicious odors? And yet that is what Nature does when she cuts off, before its prime, the budding genius of gifted and noble souls like Charles Ray Palmer, Edward Tompkins McLaughlin and John Keats. These, and other rare spirits, have been cut off before they could do their life work, before they could reveal their powers to the full. And humanity is the poorer for their loss and suffers for their premature death.

If, then, Nature goes on her way regardless of the fact whether she crushes or bruises men, either physically or spiritually, how then can man be so presumptuous as to say that this earth was only created for man's use and comfort, and the forces of the universe to run man's errands and perform his

3. See Mathew Arnold, *Essays by Matthew Arnold Including Essays in Criticism, 1865, on Translating Homer and Five Other Essays*, ed. Francis William Newman (Oxford: Oxford University Press, 1914).

bidding? Does it not look as if Nature had purposes of her own to fulfill and that man is only one of the many instead of the only final purpose that is being realized in the universe?

But while man is not the only final purpose in the world, yet the adaptation of the earth to man, the part the mystery of sex has played in the evolution and development of life and the evolution of man in history, clearly show that man is one of the final ends for which the creation of the world was planned. And in the morning of creation God saw that his divine process would culminate in the evolution of and development of man's spiritual qualities.

Whether the earth was purposely designed and consciously fashioned for man's uses, the fact remains that the earth is especially adapted to man and his comforts. If the forces of wind and water and fire and electricity are destructive of man, yet, when they are mastered and harnessed by man, they do his work for him, carry him over land and sea, run his errands and carry his messages. Even the deadliest poisons, like iodoform, carbolic acid and corrosive sublimate of mercury and creosote, are useful to man as germicides and disinfectants. Even poisons like arsenic, strychnine and phosphorus are useful in the animal economy for retarding tissue waste, repairing tissue waste, and stimulating the formation of new cells.

From the most poisonous herbs man has distilled a balsam for his wounds. The bark and roots can be made to discover their hygienic properties and given as medicine to purify our blood and tone up our stomachs. Indeed, Nature has, in the curative properties of her roots and herbs and fruits and acids, remedies for every conceivable ailment of man. But, though these forces and powers are at the disposal of man, they are not given him gratuitously, but must be wrested from Nature by his brain and sweat. And, though the elements of Nature and the animals which are so terrible and destructive of man can be made to work for him, they must first be harnessed and bridled and curbed. This earth furnishes food for man, protects him against summer's heat and winter's cold, and shelters him against the storms and cold, chill blasts of winter. She furnishes him with wool and cotton with which to clothe his body, with coal and wood with which to cook and warm his house; with candle, kerosene, gas, electricity, with which to light his streets and houses. Nay, she furnishes him with implements with which to work and subdue his environment, both vegetable and animal, to his needs.

But man must work hard and wrest Nature's secrets from her, either by force or cunning. The earth, with her pathless woods, trackless forests, fertile soil, with her copper, coal, oil, gold, silver and diamond mines, is lying a rich prize for her conqueror, man. But she waits for pioneers like Vasco Da Gama, Christopher Columbus, Daniel Boone to pierce her unexplored depths. And she needs a genius like Eli Whitney, Robert Fulton, Watts, Stevenson, Edison, Tesla and Bell to bring her boundless wealth within the use of their fellow men.

But besides these powers and forces of nature, which man must bend to his purposes in order to utilize them, it is true that Nature, silently and unsought, ministers to man's wants. The winter's frost breaks the shell and husk of seeds in the earth, and purifies the atmosphere. The bracing wind causes the blood to circulate in our veins and sets our nerves tingling. The cold freezes our ponds and gives us ice to preserve our meats and cool our drinks on warm days. Springtime comes, when all nature wakes to life; the rain moistens and fertilizes the soil; the light and heat of the sun warms and vivifies the seed, and this combined play of sun and rain on the soil and seed gives us the profuse growth of vegetable life, the ultimate basis of all animal existence, and that divine beauty that intoxicates our eyes with joy. The wood and the vegetation that decays in rivers are metamorphosed into coal which cooks for us, warms our houses and runs our engines, thus propelling our boats through the water, our railroad cars over the land, and furnishing the motive power in our machine shops and manufacturing industries. The lightning purifies the atmosphere of noxious odors; that same electricity serves man in numberless ways. The vapor is absorbed from the ocean and it wends its way heavenward. In the skies, it is condensed into rain and comes down in those cooling and refreshing showers which put an end to the drought and prevents us from dying of thirst. Thus we see that Nature bountifully satisfies our need for food, drink, clothing and shelter.

Then, too, the beneficent change of the seasons, the beneficent variety of day and night appeals to us. It is not so cold in winter that we freeze to death, nor so hot in summer that we die of heat prostration. Thus we see that there is a nice adjustment between the temperature of man's body and the outside heat. If man lives in the frigid zone, Nature protects him with fur against the bitter cold; in the torrid zone, she gives him wide-spreading trees. If it were perpetual day, man could not get his adequate amount of sleep and nervous and mental recuperation, as witness those persons who turn night into day, who work or sport at night and sleep in the daytime. If it were perpetual night, vegetables and plants and fruits and flowers could not grow, man would grope about in darkness, and plant and animal life could not grow and develop as it has. Indeed man would neither be physically nor mentally the being that he is now.

Man is the right size and has the proper organs for utilizing his environment. Suppose man were six inches or sixty feet, instead of six feet high; suppose he lived five hundred or a thousand years, instead of seventy years; suppose he were not an erect being, but walked on all fours; suppose his hands and fingers were not fitted for grasping, man's life on earth and his development in its history would be totally different from what it is.

The whole significance of the evolutionary hypothesis is beautifully brought out on page 307 of Royce's "Spirit of Modern Philosophy." Professor Royce says: "It is only after a patient scrutiny has revealed, as is the case with the doctrine of evolution, a vast unity in a long series of phenomena; a growth like this which links civilized to savage men and savage man to an animal ancestry; and the animal ancestry to unicellular organisms and these to the inorganic matter of a primitive earth crust, and this crust to an antecedent fluid earth ball, glowing, and parting with its bulky satellite, the moon; and this glowing ball to a primitive nebula; and perhaps this nebula to a previous manifold streaming of multitudinously clashing meteors,—it is only then, I say, when such a book as this splendid history of life lies open before us, only partly deciphered, daily more clearly read by science, that we have a right to ask: 'Who, then, is this self, and what manner of life is this he writes in this book, itself merely a waif from the last tales of endless time, just as the endless time also is merely an illusory form wherein the self is pleased to embody and manifest this truth? Its illusory form is not wholly an illusion. For the Self is all that is and his world is the chosen outcome of his eternal reality. Beyond all these illusions must lie a meaning deeper than we have ever yet comprehended, higher than our thought will soon reach. What fragment, then, of the meaning does the story of evolution convey?' "[4]

Professor Henry Jones in his "Browning as a Philosophical and Religious Teacher" gives the best answer to these questions that I have yet seen. He says on pages 209–211 of that book: "Granting the hypothesis of evolution, there can be no quarrel with the view that the crude beginnings of things, matter in its most nebulous state, contains potentially all the rich variety of both natural and spiritual life."[5] [Professor Jones continues:]

> If out of crass matter is evolved all animal and spiritual life, does that prove life to be nothing but matter; or does it not rather show that what we in our ignorance took to be mere matter was really something much greater? If "crass matter" contains all

4. Ferris has a very interesting and strong intellectual affinity for Josiah Royce's work. This will come up later in the text especially in regard to Royce's views on the Negro, but for now he introduces the reader to Royce's work on religious experience and evolution. A key aspect of ethnological thinking and development during this time had to do with the concept of God embraced by a people or race. See Josiah Royce, *The Spirit of Modern Philosophy: An Essay in the Form of Lectures* (Boston: Houghton Mifflin, 1892).

5. See Sir Henry Jones, *Browning as a Philosophical and Religious Teacher* (New York: MacMillan, 1891).

this promise and potency, by what right do we still call it "crass"? It is manifestly impossible to treat the potencies assumed to lie in a thing that grows, as if they were of no significance; first to assert that such potencies exist, in saying that the object develops, and then to neglect them and to regard the result as constituted merely of the simplest elements. Either these potencies are not in the object, or else the object has them in it, and is, at the first, more than it appears to be. Either the object does not grow, or the lowest stage of its being is no explanation of its true nature.

If we wish to know what any particular living thing means, we look in vain to its primary state. We must watch the evolution and revelation of the secret hid in natural life, as it moves through the ascending cycles of the biological kingdom. The idea of evolution, when it is not muddled, is synthetic—not analytic; it explains the simplest in the light of the complex, the beginning in the light of the end, and not vice versa. In a word, it follows the ways of nature, the footsteps of fact, instead of inventing a willful backward path of its own. And Nature explains by gradually expanding. If we harken to Nature and not to the voice of illusory preconceptions, we shall hear her proclaim at the last stage, "Here is the meaning of the seedling; now it is clear what it really was, for the power which lay dormant has pushed itself into light, through bed and flower and leaf and fruit." The reality of a growing thing is its highest form of being. The last explains the first but not the first the last. The first is abstract, incomplete, not yet actual but mere potency; and we could never know even the potency, except in the light of its own actualization.[6]

"From this correction of the abstract view of development momentous consequences follow. If the universe is, as science pronounces, an organic totality, which is ever converting its promise and potency into actuality, then we must add with Edward Caird, that the ultimate interpretation even of the lowest existence in the world cannot be given except on principles which are adequate to explain the highest.[7] We must 'level up and not level down'; we must not only deny that matter can explain spirit, but we must even say that matter itself cannot be fully understood, except as an element in a spiritual world."[8]

[Henry Jones concludes:] "Thus the movement of science is towards idealism. Instead of lowering man, it elevates nature into a potency of that which is highest and best in man."[9] "When Nature is thus looked upon from the point of view of its final attainment in the light of the self-consciousness into which it ultimately breaks, a new dignity is added to every preceding phase. The lowest ceases to be the lowest except in the sense that its promise is not fulfilled and its potency not actualized, for, throughout the whole process the

6. Ibid., 197.

7. Henry Jones is citing Edward Caird's *The Critical Philosophy of Immanuel Kant* (Glasgow: James Maclehose and Sons, [1889]), 1:35.

8. Jones, *Browning as a Philosophical and Religious Teacher*, 210.

9. Ibid., 211.

activity streams from the highest. It is that which is about to be which guides the growing thing and gives it unity. The final cause is the efficient cause; the distant purpose is the ever present energy; the last is always first."[10]

That is what we mean by evolution, and before I examine the theory in detail, I desire to make three remarks with reference to it:

1. The evolutionary hypothesis is not an established fact or truth. It is merely a working hypothesis with a high degree of probability.
2. If the evolutionary hypothesis be true, so far from its being contradictory to a philosophical conception of human history, it cannot be understood save upon such a view. For how could seventy different kinds of atoms build up one world, an orderly and harmonious cosmos? How could life come from non-life? How could mind come from the non-mental, consciousness from the unconscious, human reason from blind instinct, ethical sentiments from animal instincts? Only if matter were the manifestation of mind and contained the promise and potency of the higher spiritual life.
3. If evolution be true, it only indicates that the whole creation has been groaning and travailing to evolve the higher spiritual qualities of man.

Dean Everett has so many wise and profound things to say with such lucidity and beauty of style about evolution that I must quote him once or twice more. He says evolutionists say "That these results have been produced by the play of external forces acting upon these organisms. But there was a tendency from the beginning to produce the harmonious and complex universe. And if the organisms and environments were cooperative in working together, why they were the correlative and harmonious elements which were bound up in the world from the beginning. The play of the germ and the environment isn't an accidental play, because they are bound together. We must recognize this organic tendency and organic unity in the universe as the movement of the world ground. There is an inherent tendency in the organisms to produce the higher forms of life. The result of excessive forms of aggregation is the cosmos as we find it. It is idle to say that something must have come together and why not in this form as well as in another? It must strike somewhere in the series and it is not remarkable that it should strike in one place rather than in another. The integration of which Herbert Spencer speaks is that which would result from differentiation. It is impossible to draw an absolute fixed line where chance stops. The original atoms must have been endowed with the possibilities of producing this universe, or else it is a mere chance

10. Ibid., 214.

by which this harmonious world was produced. In the general structure of the world we have geometrical results, we have movements in an ellipse, etc. The world is continually producing a condition in which it can support life, and when life appears, it moves to ever higher and higher forms. The principle of natural selection is supposed to produce organic beings. Could it produce this result, unless it was the working of teleological principles moving in and through the world process?" I think Dean Everett is right.

Now, how can we account for the wide leap from inorganic compounds to organic life, from plant to animal life; from animal life to man? We can't do it, save upon the hypothesis of the forthputting and energizing of an Absolute Mind, immanent in the world and realizing through the method of evolution his own divine purposes.

Thus all through the millions of years, we find an upward movement from undifferentiated star dust to differentiated worlds; from inorganic compounds to simple plant life; from simple plant life to complex plant life; from complex plant life to lower forms of animal life; from lower forms of animal life up to higher forms of animal life; from higher forms of animal life up to primitive man; from primitive man, controlled by passions and instincts, to civilized man, dominated by conscience. Doesn't this upward trend through millions of years, culminating in man, look as if a divine plan, a divine idea was being realized through evolution? Must we not say, that evolution cannot create anything new; but can only evolve what has already been evolved? Must we not interpret the process of evolution in the light of the highest products? If the atoms produced man, they must contain man's intellectual, aesthetical and moral faculties in embryo in the germ. But the truth of the matter is, that we cannot understand evolution, save as it is the method of the world ground in creating beings and manifesting himself.

And now to sum up what I have been saying. When we consider how this world is adapted to the wants and needs of man, how important and necessary a part the differentiation of the sexes has played in the development of organic life, it is hard to believe that a process, which in an upward movement culminated in man, did not have in mind, in the very beginning, the production of rational self-conscious, ethical spirits. The scientist may say that man is a legitimate child of Nature, springing from Nature by a natural process, according to natural organic and biological laws. Natural laws of organic and biological evolution account for man.

I do not deny this, but what I affirm is this: man emerges at the end of this process of organic evolution because these natural laws, these biological laws, are nothing but the modes of operation of the Divine Mind and Will—God's method for realizing his ideas and manifesting himself in temporal forms.

As we go back in thought to the time when God evolved the world out of primeval mist and chaos and sent five hundred million suns, with their revolving planets, whirling into space to chant the song, "The hand that made us is divine," we behold the unfolding of a mighty cosmical drama. The primitive star dust in the form of a hot, gaseous vapor began to contract, whirl and throw out rings, which cooled off and condensed into planets, revolving around a central sun. Our solar system was one of the countless myriads thus formed. The earth was at first swallowed up in water. Then the dry land appeared. Somehow protoplasm, a germ-like cell, containing wonderful potencies and possibilities of development, found a lodgment upon this planet and started a cycle of development that reached its culmination in the evolution of man, a rational self-conscious spirit. It looks as if the whole creation were groaning and travailing for the advent of man. Seventy odd kinds of atoms, composed of whirling and revolving ions, could never have accidentally gotten together and built up this cosmos. The blind play and fortuitous concourse of atoms could never have produced this wonderful universe. Some Guiding Mind is needed to account for it.

But the question arises, could not man have been evolved and developed as a spiritual being without carnage in nature, without this ruthless destruction of animals, without animals tearing and rending each other in their slime, without such waste of material? Could not the same end have been obtained without such a bloodthirsty and painful process? These are the real questions involved in this vexed problem.

But, if it is true that selfishness and cruelty have played such a great part in the evolving of life, altruistic forces have been at work in the universe from the first. The love of mate for mate, the love of the mother for her offspring,—without this animal life could not have been preserved. In this love of the female animal for her child, we see a divine spark that unites the animal to God. And especially, when we come to human life, we see that love in some form or other, whether low or lustful or high and spiritual, is the ruling passion in men and women. If this principle of love holds such universal sway in nature, does it not indicate something as to the nature of the World Ground? Again, if the whole course and trend of history and evolution has tended to a higher and richer and nobler expression of the same passion, doesn't it show that the World Ground is a loving personality, rather than a cold, pitiless Absolute? We have not the undoubtable proofs that God is a loving father, as we have that the World Ground is rational, aesthetical and moral to the core; but we may have a rational hope with a high degree of probability attached to it.

*The method of God's procedure in evolving and developing life.* It is because God is operating in and through the laws of organic life that man comes into being. Man is finally produced on this earth because God had him in mind from the beginning.

The scientist may again say that God did not consciously design this earth for man; but that man is the natural offspring of the earth, springing from biological germs that have been generated by the parent organisms.

That is no doubt true, but the parent offspring has the power to throw off seed germs, and these seed germs, in a certain peculiar manner, develop into human beings, only because God's plan and will is immanent in the organism and germ from the start.

The question, is there a teleological movement in the world, admits of but one answer. That man is one of the final purposes that this universe was intended to realize, does not admit of a doubtful answer. But when we ask, is man the only final purpose that this universe was intended to serve, or is he the supreme final purpose that this universe was intended to serve, we are asking far different questions. The fact that Nature, in her obedience to inexorable laws, never swerves from her path to please man, that she frustrates his most cherished hopes and dearest wishes, ruthlessly and permanently destroys the fairest flowers of human blossom when her laws are disobeyed or man happens to stand athwart the path of her titanic forces, such as the cyclone, volcano, lightning or angry waves, forbids us believing that the only purpose this earth exists for is to produce man. Nor again can we ever know whether the creation and eternal preservation of finite moral personality was the supreme and most important final purpose God had in mind when he manifested himself through this universe.

I cannot do better than close this discussion by quoting from the chapter, Light Thrown upon the Problem of Immortality, in my work, "The Agnostic Tendency of Modern Thought," which I hope to publish sometime in the near future:[11]

"Now with such a theory of the presence of Absolute Mind in finite minds as their immanent source and ground, immortality is not only possible but probable. For we share in the life of the Absolute Life, as the Apostle says: 'In him we live, and move, and have our being.' But if our spiritual and mental life has no abiding and permanent ground in an Absolute Self-Conscious Life, which is in touch with it all the while, why, then, with the decay of the brain tissues, immortality is an impossibility.

"Unless there is an Infinite Self-Conscious Life, an infinite spiritual life, with whose life our spiritual life shares, why, then, the only consistent theory

11. This is a very interesting moment in the text. So little is known about William H. Ferris, but this passage suggests to us that there must be papers or a manuscript being prepared simultaneously with this work. This is an exciting prospect for future researchers interested in the actual archives of his intellectual production.

is that thought and all mental life is a product of the brain. But if the mental life is not a product of the brain or has no source in an Absolute Life, whence does it derive its life and its varied complexity? It is only because our mental life shares in the life of absolute mind, that the mind, while in reciprocal influence with the brain, can transcend the brain and live in a mental and spiritual kingdom, which is not translatable in terms of matter or physical unconscious life?"

## CONCLUSION

Herbert Spencer says that the Absolute is unknowable.[12] Some scientists claim that the universe was formed by chance as the result of the blind and fortuitous concourse of atoms. Some philosophers say that the universe was formed by blind necessity, that unconscious reason created the universe.

How do we know man? We know him through the works that he does,—so we can know God. In daytime, the city streets and buildings, the works of man, so absorb our time and thoughts that we don't get out into the country and think of budding and blossoming nature, as the life, the forthputting and manifestation of a creative spirit. In the nighttime, the glare and glitter of the city lights, man's creation, so dazzle us that we don't have time to think of the far-off stars, the flaming and whirling chandeliers of heaven, that are held in their places by the laws of gravitation, in the blue-domed vault of God's vast cosmical cathedral—a cathedral whose immensity, complexity, grandeur and sublimity dazzles the imagination, in its highest flight.

The law and order reigning in the heavens above, the law and order reigning in the atomic world, show that God does not work by chance. Then the geological study of the earth, the study of astronomy and the long and slow process of biological and historical evolution show that God does not hurry, but takes his time.

We have found out four things about the Author of the Universe, the Architect of the cosmical cathedral, and the Geometer of the Heavens. He puts on a robe and garment of beauty every spring. He has created a vast cosmical cathedral in which the laws of mathematics are crystallized into blazing suns, with their revolving satellites. Then He works by law and not by chance. His method seems to be that of slow evolution of forces, residing within the

12. Ferris was most likely referring to Herbert Spencer's *First Principles* (London: Williams and Norgate, 1870). For a great discussion of Herbert Spencer's position on the Absolute and the "unknowable," see Michael Taylor, *The Philosophy of Herbert Spencer* (New York: Continuum International Publishing Group, 2007), 135–38.

organisms and atoms rather than of interference from the outside. Our first thought is that God is a being of vast worlds—embracing intelligence, and of wonderful power.

Then, too, we really know that we are the children of Nature, the offspring of the Universe. The moral imperative is the deepest law of our being. It wells up in us spontaneously. It rises from the abysmal depths of our being. It speaks with a more than human authority. It seems to come from a superhuman source and to issue out of the life of the Eternal One. To seek and will the morally good is a law of our being, as it is a law of water to flow down hill, for incense to rise or for fire to burn.

These facts ought to give us some insight into the basic nature of the Being who brought us onto the stage of existence, onto the scene of action. The offspring gives some token of the nature of the parent. The structure gives some indication of the mind of the architect. If the universe were not ethical to the core, how could the moral imperative be implanted in us as the fundamental law of our being? Is not the wisdom of the ages crystallized in the thought, "the voice of conscience is the voice of God."

Every reflective mind has contrasted the reign of God in nature and the reign of human ideas in the mind. We find necessity in nature and freedom in the human personality. The same God who created matter with its laws also created mind with its ideals. And in this resides the tragedy and pathos of human life. The unchanging laws of matter frustrate our desires at every turn, prostrate us on a bed of sickness and finally destroy us, as a sentient personality. Nature seems to pay no regard to the wishes of man and brings to naught his choicest plans. The laws of matter decree that the cycle of our existence as sentient beings will be sooner or later brought to an end. Our physical bodies are made of perishable materials and will sooner or later crumble and decay and mingle with the material elements, from which they came.

On the theory that the production of the physical happiness of sentient beings was the final purpose of the universe, we find ourselves confronted by difficulties that we cannot surmount. But on the theory that one of the final purposes of the universe was the development of man as a spiritual being, his unfolding as an ethical personality, we can have a philosophy of life that is not set at naught by the facts of experience. On the assumption that the divine spark survives the dissolution of the body, we can see the rationale of the World Spirit's mode of procedure. On the assumption that the grave ends all, the universe is an enigma, a sphinx riddle and an unsolved problem. The human mind demands an explanation of the universe. Only one explanation will satisfy it. Nothing short of the immortality of the human personality will satisfy human reason, in seeking for a rational explanation of the meaning of the universe and the meaning of the creation of man.

But the "how" eludes human analysis and defies human speculation. And the "why" of God's mode of procedure also escapes our observation. It is verily true that we see through a glass darkly. At the best, we only have vague hints, intimations, guesses and surmises. We but see the unfolding of a colossal cosmical drama, whose inner forces escape our ken, and whose final outcome escapes our finite vision. But we have a clue to the secret of the universe, to the mystery of existence, a pillar of cloud by day and of fire by night, that may lead us through the wilderness of doubt, a key that may guide us through the labyrinth of speculative inquiry.

That man, as a rational and ethical personality, was finally evolved, after long eons, after the groaning and travailing of ages, as the highest product and fairest flower of the universe, ought to give some token and indication of the purpose and plans of the creative spirit, who didn't stop in his creative forthputting, in his historical unfolding and terrestrial manifestations, when he had flung millions of huge, flaming balls of fire with revolving planets into the distant spaces, but called on the whirling ions that form the atoms, upon the circling atoms that form the molecules, upon the molecules that build up matter, to do something more than form whirling and blazing rings and worlds out of gaseous vapor and primeval mist, until the growth forces, inherent and latent in matter, finally evolved life, then sentient life, then rational, ethical spirits.

We whose life rarely exceeds four score years, and whose period of productive activity rarely exceeds two score years, have not sane perspective, as a God who has all eternity at his disposal, for whom centuries are but a moment of time, whose omniscience embraces past, present and future. But we must believe that God has some purpose in manifesting himself in the world of mind and matter and in creating the universe, and us as a part of the universe.

May not the Hebrew sages have been right when they said that man was made in the Divine image and that the purpose and end of his existence was to grow into the likeness of his Maker? May not the Presbyterian Catechism have been right when it said man's first duty was to glorify God and that he could glorify God by making his body the temple and dwelling place of the Holy Ghost. The desire to have spiritual children, to reproduce himself in his creatures, may be one of the ideas that the Creative Spirit is endeavoring to realize in this vast cosmos.

Necker, sometimes profound, oftentime eloquent, uttered a profound truth when he said: "There is some magnificent secret concealed behind this superb proscenium which the drama of the world gives utterance to. We will never believe that our imagination only outsoars the limits of time to furnish us with a simple plaything. It is not worth while deceiving us if we have but an ephemeral existence."[13]

I cannot better close this hovering around the porches of philosophy than by quoting the words of one of the men who has stood for the best in Yale life. When I was an undergraduate at Yale there were three men on the faculty whose academic position enabled them to mould the lives of the students. I refer to ex-President Timothy Dwight, a New Testament Greek scholar, a sagacious administrator, whose wisdom, grandeur of soul, and kindliness of nature, made him a beloved president; to Dean Henry P. Wright, a man of remarkable poise, balance, sweetness, and serenity, with ability to call out the highest and best in a student's nature, whose worth the University recognized by erecting Wright Hall in his honor; and to Dean Andrew W. Phillips, who irradiated the dry subject of mathematics with his keen wit and genial personality, whose services to the University have been eloquently referred to in Professor William Lyon Phelps's article in the *Yale Alumni Weekly*. Dean Phillips has penned a few lines on the Shadows on the White Mountains; they contain the philosophy of a mathematician who has the Browning optimism; and I cannot better close this discussion than by quoting these lines:

THE SHADOWS ON THE MOUNTAINS.
The floating shadows in the Great White Hills
Fill me with rapture, and my whole soul thrills,
For, on the ground, I have before my eyes
The image of the clouds that deck the skies, Shadows ourselves; what shadows we pursue
Of substances beyond our own purview.
The Universe, yes, all that we find here
Is but the shadow of some vaster sphere,
And man, created in God's image, he
A shadow, truly of that God, must be.

13. This quote credited to French author Jacques Necker (1732–1804) seems somewhat misplaced.

## *Chapter Four*

# The Success of Philosophy

It may be objected by these critical Afro-Americans that it is all very well to philosophize and speculate and write dissertations, disputations and treatises; but the nineteenth century calls for men who will not talk and write, but who can do things. They say, "Philosophy and philosophizing is all right, but this modern age demands action. It calls for men who can act, not for men who can talk."

But it may be well to inquire into the respective parts played in history by great men of thought and great men of action. I will compare the four greatest men of action with the six greatest men of thought. Oliver Cromwell was the greatest ruler and soldier produced in the Reformation or post-Reformation period. He towered above Gustavus Adolphus, Wallenstein, Tilly, Charles XII of Sweden, the white-plumed Henry of Navarre and the Duke of Marlborough as a military and political genius. Indeed he is the greatest man of action that the Anglo-Saxon race has produced. He was a colossal figure, fit to have coped with Hannibal, Alexander, Caesar, Charlemagne and Napoleon.

And John Calvin was the greatest intellectual and moral force, the greatest man of thought produced in the Reformation or post-Reformation period. It might be well to inquire into the permanent influence of the greatest man of thought and the greatest man of action produced by the Protestant Revolution, that tremendous upheaval that shook Europe from center to circumference, changed the character of Sweden, Holland, Germany, Switzerland, Scotland and England, affected France, Spain and Austria, became the dominant influence in the history of America and was almost as widespread in its results as the rise and spread of Christianity.

I presume that John Morley, who rose to eminence both in the realm of politics and statesmanship on the one hand and in the realm of philosophical, historical and literary criticism on the other hand, would be as safe a man to quote from as any other; for in him the practical was blended with the literary and philosophical.

On page 124 of Volume IV of his Miscellanies, John Morley says: "To omit Calvin from the forces of Western evolution is to read history with one eye shut." Hobbes and Cromwell were giants in their several ways; but if we consider their powers of binding men together by stable association and organization, their permanent influence over the moral convictions and conduct of vast masses of men for generation after generation, the marks that they have set on social and political institutions, wherever the Protestant faith prevails from the country of Knox to the country of Jonathan Edwards, can we fail to see that compared with Calvin not in capacity of intellect but in power of giving formal shape to a world, Hobbes and Cromwell are hardly more than names written in water. And what was Calvin's propaganda? Mark Pattison has said, "It was a rude attempt, indeed, but then it was the first which the modern times had seen to combine individual and equal freedom with strict self-imposed law; to found society on the common endeavor after moral perfection. The scheme of policy which he contrived, however, mixed with the erroneous notions of his day embrace at least the two cardinal laws of human society, self-control as the foundation of virtue, self-sacrifice as the condition of the common weal."

Then there was Alexander the Great. Every school boy knows that he tamed the horse Bucephalus, that he cut the Gordian knot, and at thirty-three, before Cromwell or Caesar really started on their careers, wept because there were no more worlds to conquer, and yet the dynasties that he founded crumbled into pieces in a couple of centuries; while Aristotle, the intellectual light of Greece, ruled the intellect and thought of Europe for two thousand years. The only permanent result of Alexander's conquest was that by disseminating the Greek culture and language over the East, he made it possible for the Greek New Testament to be widely read and understood in the East. He but prepared the way for the spread of the ideas of a greater individuality, whose shoe latchets he was unworthy to unloose.

Then there was the great Julius Caesar, the master of Rome, whom Ferrero, Mommsen, Hegel, Shakespeare, DeQuincey, Froude and Frederic Harrison unite in proclaiming the greatest figure in human history, the foremost citizen of the world, the man who gave his name to succeeding Roman emperors, who made his name stand for imperialism in government, and whose name translated in Russian is Czar and in German is Kaiser. As Cassius said, "He doth bestride this narrow world like a colossus." And yet, compared to the work of Jesus of Nazareth, whether you call him the Son of Man or the God-Man or the God-like Man, his work was as the reflected light of the moon to the steady shining of the burning ball that lights up our solar system.

The empire that the great Julius founded was overthrown and broken into fragments within three centuries of his death by the surging tides of barbarian invasion; but the kingdom that Christ founded has survived for nearly twenty centuries. Of Him it may well be sung:

> Jesus shall reign where'er the sun,
> Does his successive journeys run,
> His kingdom stretch from shore to shore
> Till moons shall wax and wane no more.

The only permanent result of the great Caesar's work was that by welding the Roman Empire from Britain to Asia, from Germany to Africa, into a unit, by integrating it and centralizing its power in Rome, he paved the way for the spread of Christianity and prepared the way for the spread of the ideas of a more powerful personality. Like Alexander's work, his work was that of a pioneer and pathfinder. Alexander the Great gave Christianity a language in which it could speak to the East; while Julius Caesar gave it a road on which it could travel throughout the known world.

Had it not been for the rise and spread of Christianity, the beneficent results of the Greek and Roman civilization would have been lost to the world. The savage hordes from the north poured in like a mighty flood and overwhelmed and toppled over the corrupt and decrepit Rome, a ghost of the Rome of the Republic. She lay at the mercy of the sturdy and savage Goths. But one thing overawed and impressed the victorious German tribes, and that was the Roman civilization as expressed in the Roman Catholic Church. The Goths conquered Rome; but they were conquered by the Christian religion. It was not Roman law, Roman jurisprudence, and Roman civil government that tamed the fierce Germanic tribes, taught them to restrain their passions and held society together during the ten silent centuries which have been termed the Dark Ages; but it was the Christian religion as embodied and incarnated in the Roman Catholic Church. Rome gave the Christian religion an ecclesiastical organization in which to shelter the precious seed of divine truth. But it was not the ecclesiastical organization that revolutionized ancient civilization; but the fructifying and germinating ideas that Jesus threw out and that the Christian missionaries carried to the forests of Germany and the British Isles. The Rome that Julius Caesar built gave Christianity a scabbard; but Jesus Christ gave it a sword.

And then there was Napoleon Bonaparte, whose rise was even more remarkable than that of Julius Caesar. Caesar was born great, but Napoleon rose from the ranks; Caesar was of aristocratic birth, the nephew of Marius, the famous conqueror of the Cimbri and Teutons and the son-in-law of Cima;

while Napoleon started life as a charity student and became such a potent figure that he dominated most all of Europe, changed the map of Europe, made and unmade kings, and had kings and queens waiting in his antechambers and trembling with fear upon his frown.

And yet he went down to crushing and final defeat at Waterloo and vanished completely as the star performer in European history. Henceforth an exile at St. Helena, he could only helplessly watch the wheel of fortune and the turn of events. The France whose glory he strove to make shine like the sun in the skies, is to-day weaker as a nation and power than England, Germany, and Russia, whose strength he strove to break and whose spirit to crush. As a political force, Napoleon left France no stronger or vaster than he found it. He cannot be called a great moral force, when all Europe rose in rebellion against his tyrannical despotism. Indeed it might seem that Napoleon's chief service to Europe was by his ruthless policy to rouse the spirit and manhood and self-respect of Germany and the other European States which he trampled upon.

A champion of liberty at first, he afterwards became the king of despots. While his Napoleonic code was valuable, it was not the dominating influence in European history. Napoleon's work, which was to impress Europe with the ideas of the French Revolution, was like an avalanche, a cyclone or a mountain freshet, which sweeps everything before it at first and changes the face of nature; but whose work of destruction and change can hardly be noticed a century later.

Brilliant, creative, constructive and magnetic as he was, the conquests of Napoleon Bonaparte pale into insignificance before the conquests of the followers of the prophet Mohammed.

Mohammed welded a few Bedouin tribes into a unity through the idea of monotheism and sent them out under the flaming banner of his blazing faith and burning enthusiasm to conquer the world. In less than a century the fanatical and zealous Arabs had conquered territory four times as great as the United States. Like a tidal wave, Mohammedanism swept over Asia, Africa and Europe. It rolled into Constantinople, Italy, Spain and France. That wave rolled triumphantly along, threatening to overwhelm Europe, until it was turned back by Charles Martel and his Franks at the battle of Tours. Even the combined strength of Europe could not wrest the Holy Land from the Infidels. And to-day the followers of the Prophet Mohammed are as numerous in Asia and Africa as the sands of the sea. Napoleon shook Europe as no man since Martin Luther has done. He plunged all Europe into a series of wars as Luther did. But he was the matchless champion of the ideas of Rousseau, while Luther was the creator of an epoch.

Martin Luther broke the fetters of medaeval superstition and unfettered the human intellect. The political and religious and intellectual liberty of modern times dates its birth from his nailing his ninety-five theses to the church door at Erfurt. He applied the match and the combustible material burst into the flame of the Protestant Reformation. That flame swept over Europe and Great Britain. It kindled the torches of Calvin, Zwingli, Gustavus Adolphus, William of Orange, Knox, Hampden, Cromwell, Milton and the Pilgrim Fathers. He made half of Europe and half of America Protestant. The armies of five nations rose to defend with the sword the principles that Luther preached. Scholars crossed the seas to plant his principles in a new world. And he scattered like a spark the germs of scientific, philosophic, religious and political progress over Europe and America, which bore fruit a thousand fold. Just as Caesar's crossing the Rubicon and the birth of Christ were the epochal moments of ancient history, so Columbus's discovery of America and Luther's nailing his theses, burning the pope's bull, and confronting the dignitaries of the Roman Catholic Church at the Diet of Worms were the turning points in modern history. Columbus discovered a new world, and Luther extended indefinitely the horizon and boundaries of men's thought.

And it may even be questioned whether Napoleon changed the course of events more than Immanuel Kant, the lonely thinker of Königsburg, the Copernicus of modern philosophy, who said that two things filled him with awe, the starry heavens above him and the moral law within him, who started the wave of German transcendentalism, which through Fichte, Schelling, Hegel, Lotze and Paulsen swept over Germany; and then crossing the seas, influenced England and Scotland through Carlyle, Coleridge, Green and the Caird brothers, and America through Emerson, Royce, Ladd and Harris, and who also set in motion that wave of agnosticism which spoke in Hamilton, Mansel and Spencer, and that wave of religious fervor which uttered itself in Schleiermacher, Ritschl, Kaftan and Hermann. It has been said by an historian that the influence of Kant upon the nineteenth century thought was equal to that of the French Revolution. Compared to the work of Mohammed, Luther and Immanuel Kant the work of Napoleon was as the passing of the comet or brilliant meteor to the steady light of a fixed star of the first magnitude.

We might go further and show that all of the great movements of men, which have changed the course of human history, Christianity, Mohammedanism, Buddhism, Confucianism, the Crusades, the Protestant Reformation, the American Revolution, the French Revolution and the anti-slavery movement, were caused by a few thinkers propagating, disseminating and scattering broadcast a few germ ideas.

Nothing is so powerful as ideas. They have toppled over thrones, overthrown monarchies, destroyed cities, changed dynasties and decided the fate of nations. Stone and brick and marble decay and cities rise and fall and pass away; but ideas are indestructible. They are planted in the minds of the young of each generation and live on forever. The Parthenon on the Acropolis and the Gothic cathedral are crumbling and decaying. The Coliseum is a mass of ruins and the temple of Solomon is no more; but the imperishable works of Homer, Pindar, Sappho, Sophocles, Aeschyles, Euripides, Aristophanes, Plato, Aristotle, Demosthenes, Vergil, Cicero, Dante and the inspired Hebrew prophets still live in the hearts and minds of men. Carthage, Babylon and Nineveh are no more. Rome, Athens, Jerusalem, Alexandria, Venice, Florence and Constantinople are but names that conjure up a greatness that has vanished and a glory that has passed away. But through the literature they have left behind, some of the ideas underlying the Hebrew, Greek and Roman civilization still rule the intellect and thought of men.

Great philosophers like Socrates, Plato, Aristotle, Newton, Bacon, Kant, Hegel, Spencer, Carlyle and Emerson with comprehensive world-embracing intellects only come once in a while, like wandering stars or visitors from other stellar worlds. Sometimes one does not appear in a century; but when it does step upon the shores of time it creates an epoch.

Verily it is true of thinkers like Jesus, the God-man, Abraham, Moses, Elijah, Amos, Isaiah, Paul, Athanasius, Mohammed, Peter the Hermit, Wyckliffe, Luther, Calvin, Knox, Zwingli, Milton, Wesley, Rousseau, Voltaire, Samuel Adams, Benjamin Franklin, Thomas Jefferson, Alexander Hamilton, Daniel Webster, Sumner, Garrison and Phillips and of martyrs like Savonarola, Bruno, Huss, Latimer, Ridley, and John Brown, who launch great ideas on the sea of thought, that one shall chase a thousand and two shall put ten thousand to flight. While their work was not as dazzling to the eye or as appealing to the imagination as the work of Miltiades, Themistocles, Alexander, Caesar, Charles Martel, Charlemagne, William the Conqueror, Columbus, Cromwell, Richelieu, Peter the Great, Frederick the Great, Chatham, Wellington, Washington, Lincoln, Grant, Napoleon and Bismarck, it was perhaps more basal and elemental, for it affected the forces that work unseen beneath the surface, the springs of human conduct, which sometimes burst forth in a volcanic eruption, which at other times well up as a fountain or an artesian well, and at other times pour forth like a mountain torrent or flow like a river or again silently lift themselves as do the forces which build up the magnificent oak.

Ideas plus personality make human history. The difference between Rome of the days of Nero, when Christian maidens were thrown to the lions, and

Boston of to-day, the stronghold of woman suffrage, is not so much a difference in material splendor, for Rome had her Coliseum, her Appian way, her aqueducts, baths and splendid buildings and statues; but it is a difference in the ideas underlying the two civilizations. The fusing of the Christian conception of the worth and value and sacredness of the human soul, in the presence of the Almighty, with the Teutonic reverence for personality and individuality, has transformed the Graeco-Roman civilization of the Caesars into the twentieth century civilization of the Anglo-Saxon race.

The American civilization of the twentieth century is built and erected upon four ideas—the brotherhood of man, fraternity; the Anglo-Saxon idea of representative government or right to have a voice in one's government—justice; the Lutheran idea of the right of each person to interpret the Scripture for himself and make his peace himself with his God—religious liberty; and the Rousseau idea of the equality of man. In the framework of these four basal ideas, the superstructure of our splendid American civilization has been based. So ideas are not so impotent and resultless after all.

In fact we may say that the greatness of a race or nation is measured by the greatness of the idea that dominates it; by the greatness of the ideal that it endeavors to realize in its national or racial life. The same is true of an individual. Caesar, Alexander and Napoleon were dominated by the love of glory, by personal power and military conquests. That idea possessed them and it shaped and moulded their lives. President Eliot of Harvard was dominated by the idea of personality, by the idea of self-mastery, by the idea of the intrinsic worth and grandeur of the human soul, and the dignity of the human personality. The result was that he developed into a man of iron character and commanding personality. An idea is more durable than hammered brass or monuments of bronze. The pioneers of freedom have not worked or labored in vain. The greatest battles have been fought and the greatest victories won, not by generals on the battlefield, by ministers in the council chambers, by statesmen in legislative halls, or by the barons of Wall Street; but by the lonely thinkers, who in their studies by the seaside, on the country roadside, in the desert, or on the mountain tops evolved the ideas that roused a nation or a race to arms and to action and changed the course of human history. The Crusades, the Thirty Years' War in Germany, the heroic struggle of the Netherlanders and the victories of Gustavus Adolphus were prompted by the desire to vindicate with a sword a few ideas. The Crusades were probably the most titanic series of struggles the world has ever witnessed. They were characterized by deeds of heroism that put to shame the achievements of the Macedonian Phalanx, Caesar's Tenth Legion and Napoleon's Old Guard. They are only matched by the valor and process of the Homeric heroes and Leonidas' three hundred. It was the West against the East, the

Crescent against the Cross. Europe was endeavoring to wrest the Holy Land from Asia.

Did ever a general lead such a mighty army as surged out of Europe to vindicate the Cross? Did the followers of any general fight with such fiery zeal and resistless ardor as the followers of Mohammed and Christ, when the two rival faiths clashed under the walls of the Holy City. The Christians were fighting for the ideas of Christ, the Mohammedans for the ideas of Mohammed. The Crusades were not wars of conquest; but a struggle for the supremacy of ideas. How often is the general on the battlefield, and the leader of a political party, but an instrument to realize and actualize the ideas of a thinker like Christ, Luther, Rousseau, Chatham and Samuel Adams?

But why have I written at length of the philosophy of success, defined philosophy as the interpretation of life, and spoken of the dynamic force of ideas?

There is a colored clique and coterie in Washington, D. C., whose hobby is to belittle and make light of colored men of New England birth, breeding and culture. They mean well; but they don't understand the forces that work in history. They don't know that ideas are motive forces and they don't understand the dynamic power of ideas. They don't know that men of thought have moved the world to action in the past and direct affairs of to-day. They don't know that ideas have revolutionized human society and rule the world to-day. They don't know that great men, with the breath of the Almighty upon them, are the making forces in history.

They evidently have not read the "clothes philosophy" of Carlyle's "Sartor Resartus" and believe that the history of civilization consists in the evolution of dress, when in reality it consists in the evolution of ideas and application of ideas to life. Beau Brummel, the king of dandies and arbiter of dress and fashion, is their patron saint. And I presume that they rank him as greater than the God-man, Christ, greater than Moses, Paul, Luther, Wesley, Carlyle, Emerson, Caesar, Alexander, Cromwell, Napoleon, Columbus, Washington, Grant and Lincoln.

They don't understand the nature of things and they don't understand the world in which they are living. They have no appreciation of those colored scholars who in their poverty and adversity uphold their dignity, their manhood and their ideals. The situation is that colored men, who are not intellectually abreast of the times, who are ignorant of these fundamental and basal ideas, which are the common property and stock in trade of every graduate of Leipsic, Berlin, Heidelberg, Göttingen, Oxford, Cambridge, Edinburgh, Glasgow, Yale and Harvard, and which are in current use and circulation in university circles everywhere, by pull and influence get important positions on the faculty and trustee boards of our leading Negro colleges and universities and sit in judgment upon and pronounce as successes or failures Yale and Harvard graduates, who transcend them as much in range of information, comprehensive grasp of mind and philosophical and psychological insight as Socrates, Roger Bacon, Bruno and Galileo transcended their accusers and judges.

But the breed of carping critics, of scoffers and mockers is of ancient lineage. We hear of Thersites in Homer's "Iliad," of the Greek sophists, and of the Pharisees and Sadducees in Christ's time. We must be careful to differentiate between the scoffers and mockers and the real critics. Montaigne, Lessing, Matthew Arnold, Carlyle, Emerson, Professor Charles Eliot Norton, Professor George T. Ladd, and Professor William Graham Sumner are real critics. They have ideals of life, standards of value, by which they estimate men; and points of view by which they look at life and literature and art.

But the scoffers and mockers are not serious and earnest thinkers like the real thinkers. They are not men of solid learning and ripe scholarship, but they are shallow, superficial dilettantes, who possess a thin veneer of culture, a smattering of learning, and who are more smart than wise, and possess more flippancy than brains. Their method is to ridicule and belittle a man and speak of him in contemptuous tones. Their method is not to take him seriously, but to laugh him out of court. They jeer and mock at him. They mockingly put the crown of thorns on the head of the Saviour and the purple robes upon him. They jeeringly called upon him, who had saved others, to come down from the cross and save himself.

The Greek sophists laughed at Socrates and made fun of him. The Greek Stoics and Epicureans in Athens also called Paul a babbler. And these same scoffers and mockers ridiculed the maiden speeches of Demosthenes and Disraeli and called Christopher Columbus and Robert Fulton crazy. Thus we see that the first characteristics of the scoffers and mockers is never to take a man seriously but to take him as a huge joke.

The second characteristic of these scoffers and mockers is that they invariably prophecy failure. They asked, "Can any good thing come out of Nazareth?"

The third characteristic of these scoffers and mockers is that they called names. The names Christians, Protestants, Quakers, Methodists, Yankees and Abolitionists were originally coined by scoffers and mockers in derision. But those who were ridiculed and jeered at, at first, made those opprobious epithets names to be proud of and banners under which to enroll followers.

A fourth characteristic of these scoffers and mockers is that they are as barren as the proverbial fig tree. They found no cities, build no institutions of learning, propagate no religion and produce no great works in literature, art, philosophy and science. They are not constructive and creative geniuses. They are not profound students of anything, but are mere dabblers, dilettantes and surface skimmers. They never stamp the impress of their individuality upon history. The only record they have left behind them is that of having railed at men who were climbing the ladder of fame and mounting the steps of human achievement. Take Beau Brummel, the prince of dandies and mockers and scoffers. What do we know about him? Two things stand out in his life. He was faultless in his attire, critical about the set of a coat, or style of a hat; and when he was snubbed, made fun of Prince George for being fat. Such is the fame of the master of railery.

Thersites of Homer's "Iliad," the Scribes and Pharisees, who mocked Christ, the Greek sophists who railed at Socrates, the Greek Stoics and Epicureans who called the Apostle Paul a babbler, the shallow critics who ridiculed the maiden speech of Demosthenes and Disraeli, who regarded Columbus as an impractical and visionary dreamer, who spoke of Fulton's steamer as "Fulton's Folly" and who predicted failure for Lincoln's statesmanship and Grant's campaign, are dead; but their mantles have fallen upon the shoulders of some American Negroes, and through a succession, that is by no means an Apostolic succession, a double portion of their spirit has descended upon a few Washington Negroes. Yes, the Scribes and Pharisees, the Greek sophists and the historic mockers and scoffers are dead but they live in the spirit. They live in critical Afro-Americans, who speak with scorn and contempt of Negro authors, scholars, thinkers and philosophers. They live in prominent colored educators in Washington, D. C., who refer to colored men who are struggling and making personal sacrifices to publish works on philosophy, sociology, history and literature as educated loafers, Harvard tramps and literary bums. These beraters of Yale and Harvard graduates live in Washington, D. C., and are men of executive and administrative ability and mean well, but lack the psychological and literary insight, the comprehensive grasp of mind and power of philosophical analysis which a critic of other men should possess.

Pope, the inimitable coiner of matchless phrases and inimitable distiller of the world's wisdom in choice lines, has immortalized this breed of men in his much quoted lines.

> A little learning is a dangerous thing,
> Drink deep or touch not the Pierian Spring,
> For shallow drops intoxicate the brain,
> But drinking deeply sobers it again.

This is the class that Christ and Socrates routed, and put to flight so often. They think they know it all, when in reality they know but little. They imagine that the wisdom of the ages is contained within the narrow confines of their brains, when in reality but a mere fragment and segment of the world's knowledge has been grasped by them. And the object of this chapter is to do to men of their ilk what Socrates did to the Greek sophists, disillusion them, teach them that they know nothing and teach them that humility, which sends a disciple to sit at the feet of the masters of them that know.

But there is a difference between the Greek sophists, the Scribes and Pharisees and the Negro critics of cultured men. The Greek sophists, the Scribes and Pharisees had an intellectual pride and arrogance. They did not know as much as they thought they knew, and overrated and overestimated themselves; but they still revered learning and respected culture, nevertheless. But the critical Afro-Americans dwell in that happy state of which the poet has said,

> Where ignorance is bliss 'Tis folly to be wise.
> and they exemplify the maxim,
> Fools rush in where angels fear to tread.

For the colored sophists, Scribes and Pharisees differ from the Greek sophists and Hebrew Scribes and Pharisees in that they despise culture and learning and scholarship. They speak contemptuously of book learning and of men who have mastered books and philosophy. And they contemptuously refer to men who have devoted their lives to the pursuit of literature, science and philosophy as failures. Now it seems to me that no race needs the wisdom and culture and knowledge that may be derived from books more than the Negro race. When I reflect that no Negro scholar has yet made a distinct or positive contribution to philosophy, theology, science, philology, sociology and political economy; when I reflect that only five colored writers, Crummell, DuBois, Kelly Miller, Archibald Grimke and C. C. Cook, have won recognition for sociological treatment of the race question; when I reflect that only two Negro theologians, Blyden and Grimke, have really mastered philosophy, and that only one colored orator, Professor William H. H. Hart, has risen to the sublimity of Burke and the dignity and majesty of Webster; when I reflect that on great occasions when colored educators, clergymen and politicians address white audiences, they constantly fail to rise to the dignity of the occasion or utter only meaningless platitudes, truisms and commonplaces,—I feel that the very thing so many Negro leaders despise, books, scholarships, learning and culture, are the very things that they need. I always tremble when I see a half-educated Negro educator, bishop, clergyman or politician rise before a white audience.

It is often said that a college or university education is not absolutely necessary for a colored man, as so many colored men of great natural ability, like Frederick Douglass, Governor Pinchbeck, Robert Smalls, B. K. Bruce, Booker T. Washington and some of the Methodist bishops and Baptist clergymen and heads of southern schools, who were either born slaves or received little or no scholastic training, rose to eminence and became men of national reputation. But the greatness of most of these men is relative rather than a real greatness. Compared with the mass of Negroes, they tower as giants and titans. But when measured with the intellectual giants of the white race like Burke, Gladstone, Alexander Hamilton, Daniel Webster, Charles Sumner, Wendell Phillips, Elihu Root, Professor Willard Gibbs, E. H. Harriman and J. J. Hill, these colored colossi shrink to the common size of man. They are great men when measured by the tape with which men size up white men. We frequently hear white men say, "He is smart for a Negro."

And we frequently have the spectacle of distinguished Negro divines preaching sermons on "De sun do move and de earph am square," and tracing the genealogy of races from the descendants of Noah. Now the Bible is a fountain and storehouse of moral and spiritual wisdom and divine truth; but a white clergyman or theologian, who would base his geology, astronomy and anthropology upon a literal interpretation of the Pentateuch would lose caste and standing as a thinker and a scholar. Then we have presidents of Negro State and denominational colleges and principals of colored high and normal schools, who could not prepare an address that was fit for publication or worthy of being delivered before a body of learned men, without pressing some literary men into service. And yet such men are held up before colored students as examples of self-made Negroes, who rose to prominence without the aid of a college education, when in reality these intellectual giants of the Negro race are intellectual pigmies when compared with the great men of the white race.

Why are they thus rated and estimated? The immortal Frederick Douglass answered this question by saying, "Measure us not by the heights to which we have attained but by the depths from which we have come," and by saying of a friend, "Like myself he started from the lowest rounds of life's ladder, a slave." It is because the prominent Negroes are members of a proscribed, ostracised, oppressed and persecuted race; it is because they did not have the advantages of a college or university training; it is because opportunities and advantages offered to white men were withheld from them; it is because they started from the foot of the ladder and the bottom of the mountain and forced their way up in the face of obstacles and disadvantages; it is because of all these things that allowances are made for the intellectual shortcoming of prominent Negroes. But such allowances will not be made for the generation of Negroes who are now entering upon manhood and womanhood. The hour is at hand when colored men of free birth will be measured by the same intellectual and moral standard by which we estimate white men.[1]

I do not mean to undervalue the marvellous achievements of self-made colored men and the miraculous progress of the Negro race. Frequently I have seen colored men who could barely read and write accumulate considerable wealth as farmers, contractors, caterers and storekeepers. And then I have heard Negro preachers and orators speak who have hardly spent a day in school, and yet they have dazzled me by the richness of their thought, the splendor and sweep of their imagination and the beauty of their diction. And then I think of the remarkable careers of Frederick Douglass, who received no academic training whatever, and of partly self-made men like Booker T. Washington and Thomas Walker, who only received a partial academic training. The world knows the phenomenal record of Douglass as an orator and business man and Booker T. Washington's success as an educator and manipulator of men. But the world does not know that Thomas Walker is a remarkably successful lawyer and business man, a high-toned gentleman who has an appreciation for Buckle, Scott, Carlyle, Macaulay, Dickens, Thackeray, Gray and Goldsmith. But consider to what heights these men might have arisen had they been blessed with a University education. The untutored Negro preacher might have developed into a Henry Ward Beecher, a Frederick Douglass, a Burke or a Webster. Booker T. Washington might have developed into a President Eliot and Thomas Walker into a Gladstone.

It so happens that the vast majority of colored people get their knowledge through their eyes and ears. The sights and sounds of Nature enrich their knowledge. They learn to do things by seeing other people do things and by having other people tell them how to do things. That is how a man learns to plough, to prune trees, to cook, to wait on table, to make shoes or clothes, to lay bricks, to build a house, to harness and curry a horse, to sail a boat and do the thousand and one things incidental to domestic, farm and industrial work. That is what one means by serving an apprenticeship. The man learns by watching other people or by having other people tell him how to do things. The vast majority of colored people learn that way, but such knowledge is largely imitative and that is why the Negro is largely an imitative being.

A man must read books and study books and master first principles before he can become creative, constructive and original. Before an architect could design the Congressional Library or the skyscrapers of New York, before a

1. Here Ferris reiterates the phrases and sentiment expressed in an essay titled "Douglass as Orator." For that short piece, see Werner Sollors et al., eds., *Blacks at Harvard: A Documentary History of African-American Experience at Harvard and Radcliffe* (New York: New York University Press, 1993), 113–22.

shipbuilder could build the *Lusitania*, before a bridgebuilder could build the Brooklyn Bridge or an engineer could drive the underground tube under the East River, he must read and study books and master the mathematical, mechanical and architectural principles which underlie the building of ships, houses, bridges and tunnels. They need not servilely imitate their predecessors, but can work along original lines, for they have mastered the principles of construction. Now if the Negro is to become a creative and constructive instead of an imitative individual he must read books and study and master basal and fundamental principles, which are universal in their application.

Those critical Afro-Americans who despise men of letters are lamentably ignorant of the history of civilization. The four men back in the dawn of the world's history who made civilization possible were the man who discovered the use of fire, the man who conceived the idea of navigating the waters by hollowing out the trunk of a tree, the man who first conceived the idea of a wheel revolving on an axle and the man who invented the art of writing. History, science, mathematics, philosophy, in a word civilization, first begins with the invention of the art of writing. The inventor of the art of writing made it possible for man to record his fleeting thoughts and emotions, to preserve the experience and knowledge that he has acquired in his lifetime and to pass it on and transmit it to posterity. Books are the storehouses of human experience, human wisdom and human knowledge. Without books, the steps of human progress would be lost and each generation would have to begin all over again. The world is startled with the discoveries of a Newton, a Harvey, and a Metchnikoff, a Darwin, a Roentgen, and a Marconi, and with the aerial feats of Curtiss, the Wrights and Grahame-White. But their discoveries and exploits are the last link in a chain of causes which has stretched through centuries. Osborn in his book, "From the Greeks to Darwin," has shown Darwin's indebtedness to his predecessors.

Then take Marconi's wireless telegraphy. Clerk Maxwell proved that electric waves exist; Hertz discovered electric waves. Then other men invented the ball oscillator, the coherer and the decoherer whereby the electric waves were transmitted through space, received, and the connection broken off. Someone invented the Morse alphabet. Someone conceived the idea of utilizing the Morse alphabet in wireless telegraphy. Another man conceived the idea of similarly tuned instruments. Then Marconi came along, utilized the knowledge of his forerunners and sent his message.

Peary could not alone and unaided reach the North Pole, but he studied polar exploration and profited by the triumphs and failures of his predecessors. He made the dash in winter and started further west than his predecessors and finally reached the goal.

A dozen steps and stages intervened between Fulton's steamer and the *Lusitania*; between the rude huts of the cave dwellers and the skyscrapers of New York; between the chariots of Homer's "Iliad" and the record-breaking automobile. Thus it has ever been. Man progresses by possessing himself of the knowledge, wisdom and experience of his ancestors and predecessors and of making one or two steps beyond. And it is the mission of books to prevent the intellectual acquisitions of mankind from being lost. Books store up the accumulated knowledge and wisdom of mankind. Thus it has ever been.

The dark night of the Middle Ages did not recede before the dawn of modern civilization, until after the revival of learning, the rediscovery of the Greek world and the founding of universities. Without the translation of the Bible into the German and English language; without the invention of the printing press, which disseminates and spreads broadcast the wealth of modern knowledge, the Protestant Reformation and Calvinism could not have affected the world as they did. So when a Negro leader speaks contemptuously of books and book-learning, he is speaking contemptuously of the treasure vaults of civilization. And the man who never reads and never masters elemental and basal principles never can be a creative, constructive and original force in civilization.

The great philosophers were not day-dreamers, star-gazers, recluses and bookworms, but they were men who took all of human knowledge for their province. Plato wrote over the door of his temple of philosophy, "Let no one enter here until he has studied Geometry." And he studied profoundly literature and art and wrote his "Republic," in which he built his ideal state. Aristotle mastered the science and politics and literature and art of his day. Men still read his *Politics* and *Poetics*. Kant mastered mathematics and unfolded a theory of the nebular hypothesis before Laplace. Lotze and Ladd mastered science, history, literature and art. And the great philosophers but sought to harmonize the truths of science and mathematics with the truths of politics, literature, art and religion.

Then, too, the great philosophers were men of affairs. Anaxagoras, the inspirer of Socrates and the real father of the Athenian philosophy, was the friend and counsellor of Pericles. Socrates, in a battle, took a wounded soldier upon his shoulder and cut and cleaved his way through the enemy. Plato was a wrestler and an athlete. Aristotle was a tutor and friend of Alexander the Great. Leibnitz played a part in the affairs of his day. Fichte roused the German nation to arms. Hegel wrote his "Philosophy of Rights" and was interested in the political affairs of his day. Professor Josiah Royce of Harvard has given the world the best analytical study of race prejudice. Professor William James of Harvard has been a very live and vital man; while Professor G. T. Ladd of Yale went on a diplomatic mission for Marquis Ito and wrote an illuminating book upon the Eastern question. Thus it will be seen that philosophers of both ancient and modern times kept their feet firmly planted on the earth, while they soared heavenward in thought.

Now for the mission of philosophy. What Professor A. Young, the famous astronomer of Princeton University, said of astronomy in the *Saturday Evening Post* of October 31, 1903, might be said of philosophy, which harmonizes the generalizations, fundamental postulates and underlying assumptions of all the sciences and embraces them in the life and plans of the Absolute. The Princeton astronomer said: "In closing we can assure our readers that any home student of astronomy will find the pursuit delightful; the universe will seem to him to grow and broaden with it. The ancient heavens will shine with new glories and the earth will partake of the celestial character. If he makes no money by the study he will gain something better in the development of his manhood and his recognition of its kinship to the Divine."

This eloquent tribute to astronomy is similar to Novalis's famous justification of philosophy. A materialistic philosopher insolently asked, "Can Philosophy bake any bread?" Novalis replied, "Philosophy can bake no bread, but it can give us God, Freedom and Immortality." In other words, philosophy will not teach a man how to make a living, but it will teach him those things which give value to life, which are worthwhile and which alone make life worth living.

This thought was powerfully expressed by James Hutchinson Sterling in his "The Secret of Hegel" when he said, "These interests constitute what is essential to humanity as humanity. We shall have no difficulty in discerning that man, deprived of any interest in the questions concerned, would at once sink into no higher a place than that of the human beaver, who knew only and valued only what contributed to his merely animal commodity.

"What is peculiarly human is not to live in towns with soldiers and police, etc., safely to masticate his victuals; what is peculiarly human is to perceive the apparition of the Universe; what is peculiarly human is to interrogate this apparition, is to ask in its regard, what?—whence ?—why?—whither?

"In a word, had there been no such questions, there could never have been this formed world, this system of civilized life, this deposit of an objective life. On no less a stipulation than eternal life will a man consent to live at all; so it is that philosophy and morality and religion are his vital air, without which his own resultant madness would presently dissipate him into vacancy. . . .

"What does Science seek in all her inquiries? Is it not explanation? Is not explanation the assigning of reasons? Are not these reasons in the form of principles? And when will explanation be complete, when will all reasons be assigned? When—but when we have seen the ultimate principles; and the ultimate principles whether in the parts or in the whole may surely be named the Absolute. To tell us we cannot reach the Absolute, is to tell us not to think; and we must think, for we are sent to think. To live is to think, and to think is to seek an ultimate principle and that is the Absolute."

While it is all very well to linger in these tablelands of inspiration and dwell upon these sun-kissed heights and cloud-capped mountaintops, it might be asked, "What relation has all this speculation to the black workman, who is toiling on the farms, in the mines and on the street, endeavoring to make money to feed, clothe and shelter himself and his family?" It might also be asked, what relation had Moses, writing the ten commandments on graven stone, amid the thunders and lightning of Mt. Sinai, to the Israelites, in the valley below, who longed for the fleshpots of Egypt and were bowing before the brazen calf?

This is the materialistic age. The puritanical ideals and traditions are struggling with the lust for gold, pleasure and luxury.

And the young Negro has been caught in the whirlpool and vortex of this struggle. He is no longer frightened by the hell-fire, brimstone, and damnation doctrine of preachers of the type of venerable John Jasper, who taught that "De sun do move and de earph am square." The young Negro is losing the faith of his fathers. He is imbibing the doctrine, "Let us eat, drink and be merry, for to-morrow we die." What he needs is a philosophy of life that will inculcate in him the ideals of chivalry, manliness and honor, that will put iron in his blood, fire him with the ambition to do and dare and strive and achieve.

But just as actors disport themselves differently, according as it is a farce, a comedy, a tragedy or a melodrama that they are playing; so in the drama of life, the black man will shape his part according as he believes the universe to be a godless mechanism, the soul of man the by-product of the brain, and morality merely the conventional standards of society; or according as he believes the universe to issue from the life of the Absolute, the moral imperative to well up from the inmost depths of our being, and the Eternal to express his inmost nature in the ideals and aspirations of man as he struggles toward righteousness.

It is the soul of man that makes history. And the deeds of a man flow from his ideals, which are not imposed upon him from without, but which are the resultant of and spring spontaneously from his hopes and longings and strivings and aspirations. Then the belief or lack of belief in the fundamental verities is the central thing about a man. All else flows from that. If the Negro race is to be lifted, then it must be lifted through those great beliefs which Professor George Trumbull Ladd has termed "The Psychic Uplift of the Human Race."

It is true that the forces of heredity and environment could fashion a sensitive, refined nature, which would realize in its life the highest ideals of manliness, chivalry and Corinthian honor without believing that the system of things is the divine reason in its self-development, without believing that the law and order and harmony in the heavens proclaim that the universe is a unity which is instinct with purpose and informed with intelligence, without believing that what is best, truest, and deepest in human nature is not foreign to the nature of God, who is manifested in the universe of mind and matter.

But such a man can never be a world leader of men. For all world leaders of men have been optimists. And how can a man be an optimist if he believes that he is a lone, chivalrous knight, donning the plumed helmet, and setting his lance in rest, to battle for human rights? How can he be an optimist if he does not believe in the ultimate success of his cause and the ultimate triumph of the principles for which he is contending? And how can he believe in the success of his cause and triumph of his principles if he does not believe in a just and righteous God, who is operating in the consciences of men? But when a man believes in a Power not himself that makes for righteousness; when he believes that there is a moral order revealed in human history; when he believes that the universe is ethical to the core; when he believes that righteousness is embedded in the very structure and woven in the very web and woof of the universe; when he believes that the very stars in their courses are on the side of the good man; when he believes that his ideals are not strangers in the universe, but at home here and are rooted and grounded in the very nature of the Spirit, in whom we live and move and have our being,—then the man has the faith of a Jesus, an Abraham, a Moses, a Paul, a Lutheran, an Athanasius, a Calvin—the faith that can move mountains.

And it is the goal and mission of philosophy to give a man such a faith, a faith in the "mighty hopes that make us men."

## *Chapter Five*

# The Epical Meaning and Historic Significance of the Black Man's Spiritual Strivings and Higher Aspirations

There are three attitudes which intelligent and thoughtful colored men assume towards the all-embracing and all-encompassing fact of American caste prejudice. Professor William H. H. Hart of the Law Department of Howard University says that we must ignore caste prejudice and live and act as if it did not exist; we must forget that we are colored men and live and work on the assumption that we are men the same as other human beings.[1] Dr. Booker T. Washington, the founder of Tuskeegee Institute, says that we must recognize American caste prejudice as a fact that cannot be striven against; but to which we must adjust and adapt ourselves just as we recognize the fact of gravitation as one of the immutable facts and laws of nature. To disregard it and jump from a tower or leap over a precipice is to court and

1. William Henry Harrison Hart (1857–1934) was an attorney and professor of law at Howard University from 1887 to 1922. In 1897, the year the American Negro Academy was founded, Hart started the Hart Farm School and Junior Republic for Dependent Colored Boys. In 1905, Hart was a founding member of the Niagara Movement alongside W. E. B. Du Bois. An interesting aspect of Hart's life outside the legal academy was his political activism. In 1904, Hart challenged the *Plessy v. Ferguson* ruling by "protesting a railroad conductor's order to sit in a Blacks only car" (C. Fraser Smith, *Here Lies Jim Crow: Civil Rights in Maryland* [Baltimore: John Hopkins University Press, 2008], 65). According to Fraser, "Professor Hart thereupon became a Maryland version of Alabama's Rosa Parks, fifty years before Park's refusal to move to the rear of a bus triggered a bus boycott and the official start of what has been called the modern civil rights movement" (ibid.).

meet certain death. So the colored man who clamors for his civil and political rights, who does not lie down, keep still and remain quiet when the white man of the South tells him to, is as wise as the man who butts his head against a stone wall or as the bull who charges into a locomotive that is coming towards it at full speed, with steam up and throttle valves thrown back. Dr. DuBois differs from Professor Hart and agrees with Dr. Washington in that he recognizes caste prejudice as a basic and fundamental fact of the black man's existence, which cannot be ignored or passed by, by our closing our eyes to it, just as the ostrich does not elude its pursuers by burying its head in the sand and thinking that because it does not see its pursuers, its pursuers cannot see it. On the other hand, Dr. DuBois differs from Dr. Washington and agrees with Professor Hart in holding that American caste prejudice can be overcome by the colored man's endeavoring to think and feel and act and live like a human being and an American citizen clothed in the full panoply of his constitutional rights.

## PROFESSOR HART'S IDEA

There is an element of truth in each of these three attitudes Professor Hart holds that the Negro is an imprisoned group, that he is confined on an island, as it were, and prevented by American caste prejudice from getting out into the sea of humanity that surrounds him upon all sides. He holds that it may be, confined and ostracised as he is, isolated in a group with a separate social and church life to himself, and developing within that group different social classes and building up an aristocracy of his own, the Negro may develop valuable race traits. But he also holds that if the Negro goes through life branding and libeling himself as a Negro, and thinking, feeling, acting as if he were a Negro, the country will take him at his own estimate and treat him as if he were a peculiar being. But if he regards himself as an American citizen and acts accordingly, the country will so treat him. Caesar saw that the only way to conquer the barbarians was to make incursions into Gaul. Hart holds that the Negro must accordingly transcend his Negro environment and participate in the national life. Hence he refused to go into a Jim Crow car in Maryland, refused to allow himself or wife to be written down colored or Negro on the marriage register, or his child to be written down colored or Negro on the birth register. As Hart's father was a white man of aristocratic lineage and his mother a refined mulatto, he is theoretically justified in his attitude. It is the only way to overcome race prejudice in the North or West; but if Hart were to carry out his principles South of the Mason and Dixon's line, he would suffer the experience of Bishop Phillips and wife and Dr. R. R.

Ransom; the former were ejected from a sleeping, the latter from a Pullman palace car for refusing to remain in a Jim Crow car. So Hart's theory to ignore race prejudice and act as if it did not exist is the ideal attitude. But it cannot be lived out to the letter in the South.

## THE BOOKER T. WASHINGTON IDEA

Dr. Washington's policy is to recognize race prejudice as a fundamental fact, just as one recognizes the law of gravitation as the basic law of nature. His advice is to buckle down to hard work, don't make any fuss, and everything will come out right in the long run. It is a rash man who bombards Mr. Washington's theories with criticisms, for he has entrenched himself behind the impregnable walls of Tuskeegee. Dr. Washington is something like Alcibiades. During the civic turmoils in Athens, Alcibiades would retire to the temple, where none would dare disturb him and molest him within those sacred walls and he would there carry on his work. Now the sanctuary within whose sacred precincts Mr. Washington is safe against criticism is Tuskeegee. He and his work are so indissolubly connected that to criticise his theories seems an attack upon his work. But we must distinguish between the vulnerability of his social and political philosophy and the utility of his work at Tuskeegee; just as we do not accept Mr. Carnegie as an authority in orthography because he has been a successful financier and amassed a colossal fortune and has dotted the land with libraries. In the other parts of the book, I analyze and discuss Mr. Washington's view at length and will only say one thing here.

In his "Gospel of Work," Mr. Washington has emphasized a basic law of human progress. But it has not been true in the past history of the race that all a man has to do is to toil and labor and save his money, and civic and political recognition will come to him. It has been true in the past history of Greece, Rome, England, America, Germany and France that in order for men to secure civic rights, social and political privileges, they have usually been compelled to clamour and cry for them and sometimes strive and fight for them.[2]

2. I find it interesting that most of our knowledge about Booker T. Washington comes from his 1901 publication of *Up from Slavery*; yet the most explicit articulations of his philosophy of work are actually presented in his first autobiography written to Black Americans, titled *The Story of My Life and Work* (Cincinnati: W. H. Ferguson Company, 1900). The focus on institution building and an economic program of self-determination is much clearer in this first work than in the most circulated text of his views on industrial education.

Men do not often give us the recognition that we deserve. They usually withhold that gift from cowards and bestow it on those who possess the courage to demand it. Then, too, in attempting to solve the race question with the Negrosaxon eliminated from politics, in solving the race question on the basis of the Negrosaxon being a hopeless and helpless social and political unit, Mr. Washington is running counter to the teachings of history. The race problem is practically the Negrosaxon's place in American politics. Everything hinges upon the ballot. It is the door which ushers one into the blessings of justice in the court room, educational opportunities and civic privileges. It is the gate through which one enters the paradise of equality of rights and liberty of opportunity. Without the ballot the Negrosaxon is a helpless and hopeless pariah in society, absolutely at the mercy of a dominant prejudiced race. He is a member of a doomed race. He cannot demand anything like a man. He can only beg and plead, and weep and wail, and whine and cry for his rights.

## THE DUBOIS IDEA

Professor W. E. B. DuBois sees that a man is not the slave of circumstances, but transforms his environment after the pattern of his ideals. He recognizes with Professor Hart that a man by his own attitude may transform the world's estimate of him. Whether DuBois is right or wrong, he is following in the footsteps of Paul, Athanasius, Luther, Knox, Calvin, Cromwell, Milton, Hampden, Samuel Adams, Benjamin Franklin, Thomas Jefferson, Sumner, Garrison and Phillips. What is human history but the attempt of man to reach out after the highest that he knows of and to struggle to express the deepest that is within him? Hence DuBois is following after the saints and heroes, the sages and seers of all ages.

The same principle for which Martin Luther contended, when he nailed his ninety-five theses to the church door at Erfurt and burned the Pope's bull; the same principle for which the Pilgrim Fathers contended, when they crossed the Atlantic in a frail bark and faced starvation and attacks by Indians and bore the rigors of a New England winter; the same principle for which Roger Williams contended, when he left the Massachusetts Colony; the same principle for which the Boston patriots contended when they threw the tea overboard; these are the same principles for which the critics of Booker Washington contend, and that principle is the right of private judgment, the right of an individual to think for himself and to express his deepest thoughts and fundamental convictions. The critics of Booker T. Washington are the twentieth century champions of freedom of thought and liberty of conscience; they are the spiritual descendants of Martin Luther and the brave men and women who crossed, the Atlantic in the Mayflower. The mantles of Samuel Adams and Wendell Phillips have fallen upon our shoulders.

## THE TREND OF HISTORY

Yes, all the ancient world sacrificed the individual to the State and in Japan, which is the modern representative of Oriental ideals, it is not regarded as a terrible thing for a girl to prostitute herself to support a family. Education in the ancient world has to produce a certain type rather than develop the individual.

But in the spread of Christianity, which regarded the soul of everyone as of value in God's sight, and in the ascendency of the noble Teutonic peoples, who reverenced their own personality as something sacred and divine, who craved for personal recognition, we see the emergence of the idea that the individual was supreme and of value for himself alone. For nearly a thousand years these ideas smouldered during the so-called Dark Ages. They undermined Roman slavery and mediaeval serfdom. Then came the renaissance, which emancipated the intellect of Europe from the domain of the mediaeval schoolmen; the Protestant Reformation, which emancipated the conscience of the individual believer from the authority of the infallible Pope; the French Revolution, which toppled over the doctrine of the divine right of kings and the democracy of the nineteenth and twentieth centuries. And I believe that the grand Anglo-Saxon has been the modern champion of the doctrine of liberty and independence, and of the worth and sacredness of human personality. The fact that Napoleon, the son of a revolution, could elect himself as emperor over a republic which had dethroned and beheaded a king; the fact that Louis Napoleon, his nephew, could, in December, 1851, transform the second republic into a second empire; the fact that the French people lean to socialism, shows that for them the state idea is more supreme than the idea of individual development. The German believes in method. Bismarck welded the army into a perfect fighting machine. He understood the German nature and made the soldier a part of a machine. But in England and America we see the aggressiveness of the Anglo-Saxon.

So we may say that the meaning of human history is the growth and spread of the conception of personal freedom; freedom to express one's personality and manifest one's individuality; freedom to think one's thoughts and utter one's deepest longings and cravings; freedom of thought, speech and action in religion, politics and civil life.

The difference between ancient and modern history is that in the ancient Oriental world the individual was ignored, while in the modern Occidental world he is recognized. In China and Japan the family was supreme; the individual was nothing. In Hindoo philosophy the individual was lost and swallowed up and absorbed in the absolute. In Persia, Egypt and Babylon, the individual was nothing; the monarch was supreme. Even in Greece, where the individual expressed his freedom in the realm of art and literature; and in Rome, where the right of private property and freedom in willing such property was recognized, the individual existed for the sake of the State, and not the State for the sake of the individual. That was the dream of Plato's republic. Aristotle was the first ancient thinker who clearly recognized the importance of the individual.

The Athenian democracy and the Roman republic meant that the development of personality and the assertion of individuality applied to all free citizens but not to the slaves. The growth and dissemination of Christianity, the rise of the Teutonic races, the abolition of serfdom in the middle ages, the revival of learning and the rediscovery of the Greek world, the Protestant and Puritan reformations, the American and French revolutions, meant that the development of human personality, the assertion of human individuality applied to all white men and women. And the twentieth century will witness the application of the ideals of personality, the conception of individuality, to the darker races. It will witness the embracing of the darker races within the brotherhood of the human family. It will mean that the Negro will be regarded as a person and not as a thing. It will see the sons and daughters of Ham attaining to selfhood. As DuBois, the Emerson and Thucydides of the Negro race, says, "The problem of the twentieth century will be the problem of the color line." I wonder if the Anglo-Saxon will ever realize that deep in the soul of the Negro divine impulses are stirring and are longing to break into expression in song and story and eloquent speech; that his revolt against some of the teachings of the Tuskeegee sage express his desire to enter into the spiritual inheritance of the human race.

The most pathetic spectacle about the attitude of the American mind towards the Negro is not the facts of lynching, disfranchisement and the enacting of Jim Crow laws, for there are some vicious and boisterous Negroes who ought to be Jim-Crowed and disfranchised, but the fact that the higher courses have been eliminated from the State colleges and the higher schools for Negroes in the South; the fact that the Northern philanthropists are now refusing to aid the schools and colleges for the higher education of the Negro; the fact that the self-reliant, the self-supporting class of colored people are Jim-Crowed. As I read the daily press, the weekly and monthly magazines, I discover it is not the illiterate, vicious Negro who is the recipient of the most abuse and vituperation and vilification; but it is the colored man who desires to become cultured and strives also for the bread of spiritual life. And the Niagara movement is a protest against this low estimate of the Negro. It says Booker Washington is right in urging the Negroes to become an agricultural, industrial and economic factor in the country; but the colored man needs to aspire after the highest things in the American civilization, needs the ballot, whose possession exalts an individual and makes him a man. The Niagara movement is but the world impulses of thought and feeling manifesting themselves in the Negro consciences. It is but the zeitgeist affecting Negro minds, it is but the stirring within the Negro's soul of the Immanent World Ground, the welling up within human nature of the Immanent World Spirit. It shows that the Negro is human and sensitive to slights and insults.

The Niagara movement is but the surging up into the soul of the Negro of that Immanent World Spirit, who has been weaving at the loom of time for centuries, of whom the Apostle Paul said, "In him we live and move and have our being." It will be victorious, because it is in harmony with the tendencies of this democratic age and the genius of Christianity. It will become true of it that the stone that the builder rejected will someday become the head of the column; it will galvanize the Negro with the electricity of hope. From the Great Lakes to the Gulf, it will send the thrill of life throughout the Negro race. It will start a tidal wave of sentiment that will move mountain-high from the Atlantic to the Pacific, lifting the Negro out of the valley of the Shadow of Death to the Mount Ararat of Hope.

What William Roscoe Thayer, in his "Dawn of the Italian Independence," says of Italy may well be said of the American Negro: "We must look for signs of progress in the aspirations rather than in the achievements of anything conspicuous. For this movement was inward and subtle; and its outward expression in deeds was stubbornly repressed. For no man can speak the truth that is in him when the hand of the oppressor is on his throat."

This being true, an epical grandeur is attached to the forces working unseen beneath the surface, which like the forces of nature, asserting themselves in budding spring, are slowly transforming the thought, life and character of the Negro. And that is why the Niagara movement has an epical significance and why DuBois is the hero in the battle for spiritual freedom and Negro manhood.

There is one thing in the attitude of the American mind toward the Negrosaxon that I question and that is the leveling tendency, which acts upon the principle "all coons look alike to me," and which links all Negrosaxons indiscriminately together, good, bad and indifferent, in a mass. President Roosevelt erred this way, when he in his annual message of December, 1906, intimated that the good Negrosaxons sympathized with and shielded Negro criminals. He erred again when he took it for granted that a whole battalion of the Twenty-fifth Infantry entered into a conspiracy of silence to shield the dozen who are said to have shot up Brownsville. New England philanthropists erred again when they intimated that the colored graduate of Yale and Harvard ought to go South to be a missionary and apostle of culture to his people, instead of hovering around Boston, New York, Philadelphia, Washington and Chicago.

The mass of Southern Negroes are so densely ignorant, and so averse to learning and so hostile to scholarship and culture, that it will be at least twenty-five years before a colored scholar will be appreciated at his face value in the South. At present, the attitude of the Southern Negro to the Northern-born colored graduate of Yale and Harvard is one of hostility, distrust and suspicion, of cynical, carping criticism rather than one of sympathetic appreciation. They will inspect him for the purpose of detecting his minor faults rather than discovering his splendid qualities. Woe unto him, if he is not, in addition to being scholarly, an Apollo in appearance, a Beau Brummel in dress and a Lord Chesterfield in manners. This is perhaps as true of New York City and Washington, D. C., as of the South. If a colored scholar is interested in Pythagorus, Socrates, Plato, Aristotle, Kant, Fichte, Schelling, Hegel, Lotze, Spencer, Carlyle, Emerson and Matthew Arnold, he is cut off by the fact that he is colored from contact and association with the scholars of the country and compelled to live amongst those of his own race, who have no sympathy with nor appreciation of his idealistic dreams. The reasons why colored graduates, who won scholarships, prizes and literary honors and oratorical honors in Yale and Harvard, do not grow and develop into scholars of fame and distinction, after they leave the classic walls of their Alma Mater, is because their environment does not give them a stimulus.

One may ask why is it that in the period of the renaissance, in the age of Pericles, in the Kantian and post-Kantian period of philosophy in Germany, in the Elizabethan age of literature, in the Victorian age of English literature, and in New England transcendentalism, there was such a plentiful crop of distinguished scholars and brilliant writers? How account for it, that in a town of only moderate size and population, almost within a span of one human life, there could be produced such remarkable geniuses as Miltiades and Alcibiades in war; Themistocles and Pericles in statesmanship; Aeschylus, Socrates and Euripides in tragedy; Aristophanes in comedy; Thucydides and Herodotus in history; Socrates, Plato and Aristotle in philosophy, and Demosthenes in eloquence? These names, representing the highest heights to which the human intellect has attained in war, statesmanship, tragedy, comedy, art, philosophy and eloquence, were produced in a city which we would regard as small within the space of two generations. Well might Frederick

Harrison say, "It is this sudden blazing up of supreme genius on this mere speck of rock for one short period—and then utter silence—which makes the undying charm of this magic spot on earth." How could this be possible?

Then consider that within one century, from 1450 to 1550, the world witnessed the revival of learning, the invention of the printing press, the discovery of America by Columbus, Copernicus's epoch-making discovery in astronomy, and the Protestant Reformation. How account for it that in art, science, religion, discovery and invention, there was such an intellectual, artistic and moral awakening. For a thousand years the world had been sleeping and then suddenly it burst forth into the greatest quickening of the human spirit along artistic, scientific, exploring and religious lines that the world has yet seen. How account for it? How account for the galaxy of brilliant men?

Then coming down to the close of the eighteenth century and the beginning of the century that has just passed, what do we find? Within fifty years Germany gave the world Lessing, Wieland, Goethe, Schiller and Heine in poetry; Herder, Wilhelm Fredrich Schegel, Jean Paul Richter, Ludwig Tieck, Novalis, Fouque, Arndt, Korner, Ruckert and Nililand in literature, and Kant, Fichte, Schelling, Hegel and Jacobi in philosophy, producing in Goethe a poet who almost equaled Homer, Dante and Shakespeare; in Herder a philosophical student of history, who rivaled Thucydides; in Kant and Hegel philosophers who measured up to the colossal grandeur of Plato and Aristotle. What a galaxy of names we find in England about the middle of the nineteenth century, when Newman was disturbing the peace of Oxford University by the Oxford movement, and when his sonorous voice was being hushed in the retirement of Livermore. Newman, Maurice, Robertson, Stanley and Martineau in religion and theology; Carlyle, Froude, Kingsley, Freeman and Green in history; Pater and Ruskin in art; Browning, Tennyson, Clough, Arnold, Shairp, Rossetti, Fitzgerald and Swinburne in poetry; and Thackeray, Bronte and Eliot in fiction, are the brilliant literary luminaries whose glowing genius lighted up the pages of English history and made the period between 1840 and 1875 fully as fruitful as the Victorian age of English literature, and almost as epoch-making as the golden age of German literature.

It is significant, too, that the immortal names that America has bequeathed to literature—Irving, Cooper, Bryant, Webster, Emerson, Hawthorne, Longfellow, Lowell and Holmes, her great epoch-makers in theology; Bushnell, Channing, Parker and the brilliant group of satellites, Fuller, Thoreau, Alcott, Curtis, Mitchell, Higginson, Hale and Norton, all rose to prominence or received their inspiration during the first half of the nineteenth century; that all of these writers, with the exception of the first three, were the product of New England and that Boston was either the place where they were nurtured or trained or delivered their messages to the world. In a word, almost all of the men who have made Greece, Rome, Florence, Italy, Germany, France, England and America memorable in literature, art, philosophy or religion belonged to groups of thinkers and artists who lived in the same age, so the Periclean age, the Augustan age, the age of Lorenzo the Magnificent; the age of Raphael, the Goethean age, the Victorian age, the Elizabethan age, and the period of New England transcendentalism, and the age of Rousseau, have come to stand for the periods of creative activity in the literary life of the countries and cities we have just mentioned. We might write the life of Pericles, Augustus, Raphael, Lorenzo the Magnificent, Goethe, Rousseau, Shakespeare, Carlyle and Emerson and show that almost all of the immortal names in literature, art and philosophy either spoke their message to the world or received the intellectual or moral shock that quickened them into activity in the lifetime of these eight men. The lives of eight men can epitomize all human progress. Why is it that great thinkers, poets, artists and musicians do not come singly, but in groups? It is because one human mind is stimulated and inspired by another mind. The example of one mind putting forth creative activity arouses the creative impulse in another. Kant aroused Fichte and Herder aroused Goethe. Then the encouragement such as Baron Bunsen and the Oxford professors gave Max Müller nerves one to explore the untraveled paths of scholarship, to enlarge the bounds of human knowledge and peer into the realms that lie beyond the ken of human vision. I have seen Dr. George A. Gordon, pastor of the South Congregational Church of Boston, grow as a theologian. When I was an undergraduate of Yale, he had not written any of the books that have since made him famous. The first course of lectures which, being afterwards embodied in book form, made him famous, were delivered before the Yale Divinity School. The enthusiasm that their delivery and their publication evoked, and the fact that his own congregation grew with his growth and encouraged and sympathized with his efforts as a theologian, inspired him to deliver three more courses of lectures at Yale, one in Boston and one in Harvard, which, being published, increased his fame. Had he remained in the small country church in Maine, where he began his pastorate, he would not have been the Gordon he is to-day. Boston, Yale and Harvard developed him as a theologian and quickened the spark of genius that slumbered in his soul.

What encouragement does the colored man, who has spent a score of years in school and college, who has delved in philosophy and history and literature, and whose aim and ambition in life is to produce a work in literature, philosophy or history, that shall live after him and cause the youth of his own race to feel that his own race has made some contribution to civilization and wrought something in the world of ideas and the realm of letters, get? The Anglo-Saxon race will regard him as an impractical dreamer, who is wasting his life, while the head of one of the great industrial schools of the South will speak of him as a literary bum and educated tramp and speak in contempt of a rosewood piano in a log cabin or country school-house or a colored youth studying a French grammar in the backwoods. He will be pointed to as an educational failure; even if he has written and had typewritten a work on philosophy, history and literature, he can arouse no interest in the Anglo-Saxon race and no enthusiasm in his own race. If, however, by dint of nerve and grit and pluck he succeeds in getting his book upon the market, and the world recognizes his genius, his own people will then crowd around him for the purpose of basking in the sunshine of his greatness, in order that he may shed lustre upon them. But while he is panting and struggling and striving to rise, to mount the heights of achievement and climb the ladder of fame, he will find few in his own race or the Anglo-Saxon race who will give him an encouraging word or a helping hand.

I remember how three conversations with Hon. William T. Harris, former United States Commissioner of Education, opened a new world to me. Ten and twelve years ago I read Carlyle and Emerson and Goethe and Hegel, and thought I understood them. A few years ago I returned to Washington, after having lived two years in the South in intellectual loneliness and isolation. Just in three conversations, Dr. Harris opened up a new mine of riches in Emerson, Carlyle, Hegel and Goethe, in discussing the philosophy of history and present-day politics. I returned to Emerson's works and Hegel's philosophy of history, and saw in those writers that which I had overlooked or passed by ten years ago. This impulse and inspiration, which contact with a superior mind gives, is not as a rule open to the colored scholar, after he leaves college. This is not a plea for social equality, but a statement of the cause of the dearth of Negro literature and Negro scholarship of a high grade; a statement of the reason why the budding Negro genius is nipped by the chill and frost of unsympathetic criticism and lack of appreciation.

The North desires to develop the Negrosaxon as a man, the South to repress his development. I believe that the North's attitude towards the Negrosaxon is wiser than the South's attitude. Both regard the Negrosaxon as a crude and undeveloped race in comparison with the Anglo-Saxon, which has had the discipline and training of centuries. The South says: "The Negrosaxon is inferior to the white man and we will keep him so. We will Jim-Crow, segregate and disfranchise him. We will eliminate the higher courses from high schools and State colleges. If he indulges in the luxury known as freedom of thought and expression, we will shoot him down, string him up to a tree or run him out of our community. We must teach him to know his place and that he is a Nigger." While the North says: "The Negrosaxon is a child in comparison with the Anglo-Saxon. He is a good-hearted, genial, generous, kindly and religious being and he has produced some exceptional men and women. But he is vain and imitative, caring more for show and display and glitter and glare than for solid intellectual and moral worth. Then he manifests a spiteful and envious spirit towards the more gifted and successful men of his own race. What will we do with him? Why we will give him everything that can exalt him and dignify him as a man." Then the North put the ballot into his hands, gave him equal civil rights and privileges and then admitted him to the public schools in New England, New York, New Jersey, Pennsylvania and the West, and spent millions of dollars in erecting, supporting and endowing Southern schools and colleges to fit the Negrosaxon to become a full-fledged American and to exercise the duties of citizenship. The solution of the so-called race problem will never come until the South learns to respect the Negrosaxon and teaches the Negrosaxon to respect himself. The best way for the South to prevent intermarriage between the races or any longings for such among the colored is to regard and so treat the Negrosaxon with respect and consideration that he will look with honor and reverence upon his own race and women. How can the Negrosaxon be taught self-respect when he is humiliated and snubbed at every turn, when the consciousness of his inferiority is forced upon him in the South every moment of his life? I recall an amusing incident in this regard. A few years ago I visited a Southern school. The State Board of Education was also visiting and inspecting the schools that day. I heard the children read and recite in the various rooms. Then the children convened in the chapel and sang and marched. The brilliancy of their recitations, their gracefulness in calisthenics and marching, the beauty and weirdness of their singing, made a powerful impression upon one member of the Board of Education. And he enthusiastically exclaimed, "Isn't that fine!" "Yes," the other man replied, "but they are Niggers just the same." And that represents the normal Southern attitude.

## THE AMERICAN NEGRO ACADEMY IDEA

And this brings me to the American Negro Academy idea. The American Negro Academy is an organization of Negro scholars, which was founded by the late Rev. Alexander Crummell, its first president, at whose death Dr. W. E. Burghardt DuBois was elected president, and whose present president is the Hon. Archibald Grimke, whose secretary is and has been Professor John Wesley Cromwell. Its membership is limited to forty and it meets every year during the Christmas holidays in Washington to read and discuss papers relating to various phases and aspects of Negrosaxon life. Its last session was held in Howard University, whose noble president, Dr. Wilbur P. Thirkield, offered the university for its annual meeting place. By prefixing the adjective American to the odious word "Negro," the Academy has partly robbed it of its hateful meaning.

Now what is the spiritual meaning and epical significance of the word American Negro Academy, which endeavors to foster scholarship in the Negro race and encourage budding Negro genius? On January 11, January 13, January 14, 1907, I was an interested spectator in the Senate galleries, when, in the discussion regarding the Foraker resolution regarding the dismissal of a whole battalion of the Twenty-fifth Infantry, because a few were charged with shooting up the town of Brownsville, Senator Tillman flayed the Negrosaxon race, and Senators Spooner, Patterson and Nelson made pleas for fair play for the colored brother, and Senator Gallinger stated that one colored man had been appointed Assistant District Attorney in Boston. I was especially interested when, on January 13, Senator Tillman declared, "I do not hate the Negro, but I regard myself as his superior, that is, I mean the white race is superior to the colored race." That pithy sentence of Senator Tillman explains why the South Jim-Crows and disfranchises the Negro and why the North acquiesces in the South's setting at naught the Fourteenth and Fifteenth Amendments to the Federal Constitution. It is because the country regards the Negrosaxon as an inferior race. Now Crummell's idea was that the Negro thinkers, scholars, writers, poets, artists and musicians, must demonstrate to the world the intellectual and spiritual equality of the Negrosaxon race with the Anglo-Saxon race.

One friend said to me, when I said that the Negrosaxon race must acquire prestige and standing to secure respect and recognition, that that was Dr. Washington's doctrine. Hardly. He says: "Get wealth and all other things will come to you." Wealth is a necessary and fundamental factor in the evolution of the Negrosaxon race. For the bread problem is the first problem of life. But wealth alone will not save the Negro. Without a ballot, and justice in the court room, he cannot keep his wealth, but is at the mercy of the whim and caprice of his Anglo-Saxon neighbor. Two thousand years ago the saying was current in Rome, "There is only one thing in the world more despicable than a poor Jew and that is a rich Jew." Through the middle ages the Jews possessed wealth. But they were hounded, persecuted and murdered, driven from post to pillar, forbidden to own land and conduct manufacturing industries. Only towards the close of the nineteenth century have they been able to breathe easy in Europe. A few years ago we read of the anti-Semitic riots in France. Only recently the Kishenev massacre in Russia took place. The Jew's fate in Russia is worse than the Negro's in America. Babylon, Carthage, Rome, Venice and Florence were once powerful and rich kingdoms. But who knows who the rich men of antiquity were. Croesus and Crassus are the only rich men of antiquity whose names have come down to us from the ages and ring in the class room. But every schoolboy has heard of Socrates, Plato, Aristotle, Homer, Demosthenes, Cesar, Cicero and Vergil. The fame of Dante and Raphael and Michel Angelo will outlive that of the famous Medici family. The names of Goethe, Milton, Shakespeare, Spencer, Beethoven, Wagner, Carlyle, Emerson, Browning, Tennyson, Whittier and Wordsworth are household words, while few people know or care who were the rich contemporaries of these gifted souls. Rich men, as a rule, are forgotten as soon as their remains are deposited in the ground. Rich men like Lorenzo the Magnificent, who was a patron of art and letters; or like Robert Morris, the patriot; or like Peabody, the philanthropist, are the only rich men who live in history or literature. So, if we, as a race, would gain recognition, we must not only absorb and assimilate, but must add ideas, must not only be an imitative but a creative race in art, letters, science, statesmanship and finance. In some way or other we must make the world our debtors. If this be true, then we must honor the scholars and thinkers in our race and regard Alexander Crummell as one of those prophetic minds who looked beyond the immediate present and down the vista of the ages.[3]

Dr. Washington has thus expressed the watchword of the modern world, "The world does not care so much what you or I know, as what we can do." And the masses of colored men and women have forsaken soul-hunger for land-hunger and gold-hunger. In a certain sense, it is true that the object and aim of all education is not to make men dreamers and bookworms, but to fit and prepare men to play a man's part in life. We are living in an age when men have harnessed the wind and the rain, the waterfall and brook, fire and electricity to turn our mills, run our errands, transmit us over land and sea, permit us to converse with friends hundreds of miles away and transmit messages to our cousins across the sea. We have compelled the forests, gold, silver, copper, iron, coal and oil and other earthly deposits to yield up their energy for our use. We manufacture ice by machinery and make by machines most of the things that we formerly made by hand. We erect skyscrapers twenty-four stories high. We live in steam-heated, electric-lighted houses, and cross the ocean in floating palaces. We fill in marshes and swamps and build cities upon them. We honor the man who can increase the output of the

3. Reverend Alexander Crummell (1819–1898) founded the American Negro Academy in 1897. He is mentioned by W. E. B. Du Bois as his mentor and friend and called a prophet by Anna Julia Cooper for his essay "The Black Woman of the South." For a comprehensive work on his life and relationship to antebellum Black thinkers, see Wilson Jeremiah Moses, *Alexander Crummell: A Study of Civilization and Discontent* (Oxford: Oxford University Press, 1989).

world's food or clothes supply or cheapen transportation. The watchword of modern life is "bring the comforts and luxuries of life within the reach of the masses." And we exclaim, "great is the man of action, great is the man who can do things."

But wait a minute. Why is it that we moderns have so many more conveniences and inventions, and a more scientific agriculture and a more antiseptic surgery than the ancients? It is only because we know so much more about the laws of nature and human nature; it is because we know so much more about the properties and laws of matter, about the properties and qualities of coal, iron, fire, water, steam and electricity, about the soil and about the human body and have formulated and have systematized such knowledge into science, that we may enjoy the material blessings of our modern civilization. Had it not been for the fact that for nearly ten thousand years men have been questioning nature, unraveling her secrets, discovering her laws and systematizing them in the form of science and leaving the permanent records of discoveries and researches and investigations in books, we would not have our modern inventions, conveniences, agriculture and medicine. We can do things so well because we are the heirs of the past knowledge of the world. The real benefactors of the world are the men who have thought and studied and known and deposited their accumulation of the world's wisdom as the priceless heritage for us moderns.

The question whether the man of thought or the man of action is of most value to society, the question as to whether the man of affairs or the scholar has played the most important role in history, has been a debated question for two thousand years. Two thousand years ago Cicero, in his oration in behalf of the poet Archias, gave a classic defense of the literary man. And the question has never been answered yet. Milton, in middle age, flung himself into the religious and political controversies of his time and became a formidable controversialist; but the Milton who has stamped the impress of his personality upon the ages, the Milton who will go down in English history and literature is not the Milton who wrote iconoclastic pamphlets, but the poet who gave the world "Lycidas," "Comus," "l'Allegro" and "Il Penseroso" and created that epoch of Puritanism, "Paradise Lost." Goethe for many years held some state position in Weimar. But the Goethe whose name lives in history is not the State official, but the author of that epoch of the soul life, "Goethe's Faust." He has been severely criticized because he did not, like the rugged and heroic Fichte, enter into the struggle for German liberty, kindle into activity the slumbering flames of German patriotism, when Napoleon plowed his rugged way and blazed his fiery path through Europe, and stamped the iron heel of oppression upon prostrate Prussia; on the contrary, Goethe remained a calm and impassive spectator, while the most stormy and bloody drama the world has ever witnessed was being enacted upon the stage of human history. One wonders how any man could sit serenely in the grandstand or stand idly along the side lines while the greatest battle in human history was being fought and won for democracy, while blood was flowing like water in the streets of Paris, and while Napoleon was crushing and throttling the spirit of German liberty and was riding roughshod over the kingdoms of Europe, while the old aristocratic order was being shaken to its foundation and the democratic ferment and leaven was felt throughout Germany. Fichte towers in his colossal grandeur above Goethe and is worthy of the eloquent tribute of Carlyle when he calls him "the cold, colossal, adamantine spirit, standing erect and clear, like a Cato Major among degenerate men, fit to have been the teacher of the Stoa, and to have discoursed of beauty and virtue in the groves of the Academe. We state Fichte's character, as it is known and admitted by men of all parties among the Germans, when we say that so robust an intellect, a soul so calm, massive and immovable has not mingled in philosophical discussion since the time of Luther. We figure his motionless look had he heard the charge of mysticism which was made against him in England. For the man rises before us amid contradiction and debate, like a granite mountain amid a cloud and wind."

I will admit that Emerson in his address upon "The America Scholar and Literary Ethics," Curtis in his oration upon "The Duty of the American Scholar," and Wendell Phillips in his "Phi Beta Kappa Address" have sounded the bugle call which aroused the scholars of America out of ignoble ease and cowardly leisure, awoke the Puritan spirit in them and transformed them into champions of liberty and self-sacrificing patriots. All this is true and yet many histories of German literature dispose of Fichte with a few sentences, while they devote as many chapters to Goethe as they do paragraphs to Fichte. Only five or six books have been written upon Fichte, while nearly a hundred have been written about Goethe, whose fame is almost as universal as Luther, the greatest figure of modern times.

Matthew Arnold was for many years examiner in the schools of England and his salary of examiner was greater than the average income from his poems and essays, which was only $1,200 a year. But the Matthew Arnold who lives and will live in English history and literature is not Arnold the examiner, but Arnold the chaste and refined poet, the sane critic of literature, the lofty and serene interpreter of Hellenism, the modern apostle of culture. It is as a moral force, expressing itself through literature, that Arnold powerfully affected and influenced his age.

Carlyle found himself too big for the classroom, he found its walls too narrow to compass his mighty spirit, and embraced literature as his vocation. Had he remained a teacher he might have become as famous and noted an inspirer of youth as Dr. Arnold of Rugby, or Professor Mark Hopkins of Williams, but he would never have enriched the world by his wonderful histories, would never have interpreted German thought to England and America, and been, with the possible exception of Emerson, the strongest moral force of the nineteenth century, and the greatest apostle of idealism since the days of Plato. Emerson and Colonel T. W. Higginson found themselves fettered in the pulpit. They discovered that they could not speak freely and express their individuality in the pulpit. So they uttered their divine messages in literature. Had Emerson remained in the pulpit, he might have become an influence in New England theology like Channing, Theodore Parker and Horace Bushnell, might have become a magnetic preacher like Henry Ward Beecher or Phillips Brooks. But he would never have become the American interpreter of German and Neo-Platonic idealism and Oriental Pantheism, and Harvard's Hall of Philosophy would never have been christened after him. Had Emerson remained in the pulpit he would never have become a world genius like Homer, Shakespeare and Goethe, he would not have been free to range over the world of human thought and could never have spoken those mystic words or sang that mystic song that has enthralled mankind. I well remember Henry McLaughlin, the professor of belles lettres of Yale, who was cut off in his early thirties. He longed to preach but his message would have been embarrassed by traditional orthodoxy. He decided to make literature his pulpit and the world his congregation. And his little books upon "Literary Criticism" and "Studies in Mediaeval Life and Literature" indicate that had he lived he would have developed into a literary critic, who would have blended the sanity of Arnold with the spirituality of Newman.

Max Müller, the famous philologist, in a confession in his "My Autobiography," says: "One confession I have to make and one for which I can hardly hope for absolution, whether from my friends or my enemies,—I have never done anything and I have never been a doer, a canvasser, a wire-puller, a manager in the ordinary sense of these words. I have also shrunk from agitation, from clubs and from cliques, even from the most respectable associations and societies. Many people would call me an idle, useless, indolent man, and though I have not wasted many hours of my life, I cannot deny the charge that I have neither fought battles, nor helped to conquer new countries, nor joined any syndicate to roll up a fortune. I have been a scholar, a Stubengelehrte and voilá tone [tout].[4] . . .

"What we do or what we build up, has always seemed to me of little consequence. Even Nineveh is now a mere desert of sand and Ruskin's new

4. Max Muller, *My Autobiography: A Fragment* (New York: Charles Scribner's Sons, 1901), 308.

road also has long since been worn away. The only thing of consequence to my mind is what we think, what we know, what we believe.[5] . . .

"Did not Emerson write: 'The scholar is the man of the age?' Did not even Mazzini, who certainly was constantly up and trying to do, did not even he confess that men must die, but that the amount of truth they have discovered does not die with them. And Carlyle? Did he ever try to get into Parliament? Did he ever accept directorates? Did he join the choruses or the special constables in Trafalgar Square? . . . Nature has not endowed everybody with the requisite brawn to be a muscular Christian. But it may be said that even if Carlyle and Ruskin were absolved from doing muscular work in Trafalgar Square, what excuse could they plead for not walking in procession to Hyde Park, climbing up one of the platforms and haranguing the men, women and children?[6] . . . Gladstone could harangue multitudes, so could Disraeli; all honor to them for it. But think of Carlyle or Ruskin doing so! Striking the shell of a tortoise, or the cupola of St. Paul's would not have been more attractive to them than addressing the discontented when in their hundreds and their thousands they descended into the streets.[7]

"All I claim is that there must be a division of labor, and as little as Wayland Smith could be spared, when he hardened the iron in the fire for making swords or horseshoes, was Carlyle a man that could be spared while he sat in his study preparing thought that would not bend or break.[8]

"But I cannot even claim to have been a man of action in the sense in which Carlyle was in England or Emerson in America. They were men who in their books were constantly teaching and preaching. 'Do this' they said; 'Do not do that!' The Jewish prophets did much the same, and they are not considered to have been useless men, though they did not make bricks or fight battles like Jehu. But the poor Stubengelehrte has not even that comfort. Only now and then he gets some unexpected recognition, as when Lord Derby, then Secretary of State for India, declared that the scholars who had discovered and proved the close relationship between Sanskrit and English, had rendered more valuable service to the Government of India than many a regiment.[9] . . .

"However, I can only speak for myself, and of my idea of work. I felt satisfied when my work led me to a new discovery, whether it was the smallest desert island in the vast ocean of truth. I would gladly go so far as to try

5. Ibid., 309.
6. Ibid., 310.
7. Ibid., 311.
8. Ibid.
9. Ibid., 311–12.

to convince my friends by a simple statement of facts. Let them follow the same course and see whether I was right or wrong. But to make propaganda, to attempt to persuade by bringing pressure to bear, to canvass and to organize, to found societies, to start new journals, to call meetings and have them reported in the papers, has always been to me very much against the grain.[10] . . .

"As students of classical and other oriental history, we come to admire the great empires with their palaces and pyramids and temples and capitols. What could have seemed more real, more grand, more likely to impress the young mind than Babylon and Nineveh, Thebes and Alexandria, Jerusalem, Athens and Rome? And now where are they? The very names of their great rulers and heroes are known to few people only and have to be learned by heart, without telling us much of those who bore them. Many things for which thousands of human beings were willing to lay down their lives, and actually did lay them down, are to us mere words and dreams, myths, fables and legends. If ever there was a doer, it was Hercules, and now we are told that he was a mere myth![11]

"If one reads the description of Babylonian and Egyptian campaigns as recorded on cuneiform cylinders and on the walls of ancient Egyptian temples, the number of people slaughtered seems immense, the issues overwhelming and yet what has become of it all? The inroads of the Huns, the expeditions of Genghis Khan and Timur, so fully described by histories, shook the whole world to its foundations, and now the sand of the desert, disturbed by their armies, lies as smooth as ever.[12] . . .

"And what applies to military struggles seems to me to apply to all struggles, political, religious, social, commercial, and even literary. Let those who love to fight, fight; but let others who are fond of quiet work go on undisturbed in their special callings.[13]

"That was, as far as we can see, the old Indian idea, or at all events the ideal which the Brahmans wished to see realized. I do not stand up for utter idleness or sloth, not even for drones, though nature does not seem to condemn even that genus altogether. All I plead for as a scholar and a thinker is freedom from canvassing, from letter reading, letter writing, from committees, deputations, meetings, public dinners, and all the rest. That will sound very selfish to the ears of practical men, and I understand why they should look upon men like myself as hardly worth the salt. But what would they say

10. Ibid., 312.
11. Ibid., 316.
12. Ibid.
13. Ibid., 317.

to one of the greatest fighters in the history of the world? What would they say to Julius Caesar, when he declares that the triumphs and the laurel wreaths of Cicero are as far more nobler than those of warriors as it is a great achievement to extend the boundaries of the Roman intellect than the domains of the Roman people?"[14]

I believe that Max Müller never regretted leaving fortune-getting and political agnation and concentrating his life and effort to interpreting to the restless, striving, materialistic world the religion and philosophy of the oriental world. He has put the world under an eternal debt of obligation to him for bringing it in touch with the pantheistic thought of the Hindoo seers and sages and showing the kinship of the spiritual hopes and aspirations of the Eastern and Western mind.

The world has forgotten the millionaires and the political agitators who dominated London in the time of Max Müller; but the name of Max Müller will linger in college walls for many generations.

If, then, Milton, Goethe, Matthew Arnold, Emerson, Colonel Higginson and Max Müller affected their age more powerfully through the written world than they would had they confined their activities to the classroom and pulpit and practical affairs, if McLaughlin had become a Matthew Arnold and John Henry Newman rolled up in one, had he lived, who can tell but what my peripatetic mode of existence, my trying my hand at preaching, teaching, journalism, lecturing and farming instead of settling down to any one occupation and driving a peg in one particular place, has done for me what Dante's exile had done for him, given me that range and breadth of experience, that knowledge of men and insight into human nature which I might otherwise have never received? Had I not traveled so widely and visited so many places and met so many different men and women, had my nature not been exposed to so many different influences and impressions, I might not have written this prose epic of the Negrosaxon race.

But the materialist will say in reply, "This age does not ask how much you know, or how good you are; but it asks what can you do?" This is no doubt true. But we know that with the possible exception of Alexander the Great, the nation maker and Julius Caesar, the empire builder, Napoleon Bonaparte was the greatest man of action the world has yet seen. We are told that he carried a history of several hundred volumes with him on his various campaigns. Before he entered upon his Egyptian, Prussian, Austrian and Russian campaigns, he studied the geography and topography of the country, its political history and mode of warfare. And that is one of the reasons why he moved with such wonderful rapidity.

14. Ibid.

The nineteenth century has seen a greater progress in material invention than all the preceding centuries put together. One hundred years ago we traveled slowly in a stage coach. It took nearly a week to go from Boston to New York. Now we have our speedy locomotives that can cover this distance of two hundred and fifty miles in five hours. And we have automobiles that cover two miles a minute. A hundred years ago to-day we crossed the ocean in wooden steamships. Frequently the journey lasted five or six weeks. Now we cross the ocean in our elegantly furnished iron and steel steamships, which are veritable floating palaces, in five or six days. A hundred years ago to-day we dwelt in wooden houses, heated by wood piled up on a hearth and lighted by candles or oil lamps. To-day we dwell in steel-framed, stone-constructed skyscrapers, heated by steam and lighted by electricity. We stand in Boston and converse with a friend in New York over the telephone. We transmit messages across the ocean by wireless telegraphy. By means of the X-ray, we penetrate through the flesh and locate the bullet that has been lodged in the human body. We reproduce the human voice with the phonograph, cast moving pictures on the canvas, reproducing a prizefight or train robbery with the vitascope. We utilize steam to drive our engines and harness the water and wind to run our mills. How did this come about?

The Bell telephone was invented by a man whose grandfather and father and himself were teachers of elocution. His knowledge of the mechanism of the human voice enabled him to invent the telephone. There is one farmer in New England who grows from $4,000 to $8,000 worth of vegetables annually upon eight acres of land and he raises lettuce in a greenhouse in winter time. There is another man in New England who raises roses and carnations in winter time. There is another man in New England who grows in winter time, in his greenhouse, trees, plants and fruits, whose normal habitat is in Florida and the tropics.

How does this come about? These men or their employees were graduates of the best agricultural colleges in New England. Roentgen's discovery of the X-ray came as the culmination of a series of discoveries and experiments in electricity and electric waves by eminent scientists of the nineteenth century. Then take that most marvelous of all occurrences, Marconi transmitting a message across the Atlantic by wireless telegraphy. Who were the forerunners of Marconi? First, Clerk Maxwell demonstrated that electric waves exist. Then Hertz proved the actual existence of electric waves by his experiments. Then someone invented the ball oscillator, by which one sent electric waves, by passing an electric current through an open circuit. Then someone must invent a coherer to catch that electric wave. Then someone must invent the Morse series of letters. Then someone must invent the decoherer, whereby the electric waves, generated by the ball oscillator and caught by the coherer, can give rise to Morse letters. Then one must conceive of the idea of having the instruments that send and the instruments that catch electric waves, similarly tuned. Then, when the apparatus has been prepared, the theory of wireless telegraphy has been accepted by scientific men, Marconi comes along and sends the message.

So, when we with vaunted pride boast of the wonderful achievements of modern science, and of our numerous inventions, which bring the commodities and luxuries of life within reach of the many, let us remember that we have the locomotive, steamship, microscope, telescope, telephone, telegraph, phonograph, vitascope, electric-light, X-ray and wireless telegraphy, because we know so much about the laws and forces of nature and have formulated such knowledge into sciences. It is only because men have for fifty centuries been studying and interpreting nature, been learning her ways and discovering her secrets, and unraveling her mysteries, that we can utilize the knowledge thus gained for our wonderful inventions. We are under an eternal debt of gratitude to Aristotle, Newton, Copernicus, Galileo, Clerk Maxwell, Lord Kelvin and Hertz and their many contemporaries.

Without the labor and discoveries of these men, we could not have the appliances of Edison, the X-ray and wireless telegraphy.

Freeman has said that history is past politics. But I believe that Hegel, Le Bon, Carlyle and Emerson are nearer the truth when they base human history and its changes upon the ideas and ideals that reign in the mind of man. Aristotle ruled the intellect of Europe for two thousand years. Luther shook Europe from the Baltic Sea to the Mediterranean. Kant has been as potent a factor in nineteenth century history as the French Revolution. So we must admit that the men in the long run who know are the moulders of human history.

If a man can understand nature and man, make a comfortable living and rear and educate a family, he can consider himself fortunate and can look back upon his career as a successful one. The bread problem is a problem of life. So, if the colored man is to succeed in life, he must adjust and adapt himself to this complex civilization. If the Negrosaxon race is to make a name in history it must measure up to and square itself with the Anglo-Saxon ideals. I know that Anglo-Saxon prejudice limits and curtails our opportunities. But it is these hard conditions that make and develop men and women of rugged strength of character and sturdy moral fibre. It does seem a hard thing that the bulk of the time and the energy of the masses of men should be devoted to merely eking out a living. And yet it was the struggle for existence in the German forests, in the British Isles, on the bleak New England coast and on the Western prairies that has developed the splendid fighting qualities of the Anglo-Saxon race and made it what it is to-day. The struggle for existence, to which the Teutonic races have been subjected for centuries, weeded out the weak in body and weak in will who could not survive in the struggle with the forces of nature in the battle with wild beasts and fighting with hostile foes in the German forests. The effort to gain the mastery over nature, animals and man developed thoughtfulness, strength of will and strength of body in those who were strong enough to survive in that strife and conflict. That is why, some eighteen centuries ago, the rude but rugged and sturdy Germans could impress Tacitus that they would be the future conquerors and masters of Rome. Now the Negrosaxon, brought up for centuries in a tropical climate, only three hundred years removed from savagery, and with only half a century of freedom, lacks the steadfastness and tenacity of purpose of the Anglo-Saxon.

The Negrosaxon will get this discipline and training in time. He will be compelled to get it, if he hopes to survive in this strenuous civilization, in this intense competition and strain and at this high pressure and tension of life. In fact, he is slowly but surely mastering the alphabet of bread-winning and becoming a more efficient economic, industrial and agricultural factor in this country. But the great and crying need in this country for the colored youth is moral character. Money, education, political rights, and civil privileges and economic opportunities are necessary factors in the evolution of our race. But underlying all is the substratum of moral character. We must dig beneath the subsoil and sand, until we reach the bedrock of moral character and rest and build the civilization of our race upon that. But it is not popular to preach that doctrine nowadays. A man who would preach character at a public mass meeting would meet with a cool reception. The ministers who are sought after by congregations and lauded by bishops are not the ministers who convert the most souls and inspire the youth of the race; but the men who can raise the most money. Booker T. Washington has wittily shown how the Negrosaxon has absorbed Anglo-Saxon materialism by saying that forty years ago people asked about a deceased man, "What did he say?" But now they ask, "How much did he leave?"

But it seems to me that the greatest need in the Negrosaxon race is for the granite of moral character which distinguishes Dr. Francis J. Grimke and Hon. Archibald H. Grimke, and which distinguished the late Dr. Alexander Crummell. It was the granite of moral character, the iron of manhood and the nerve of integrity that made Rome, England and New England great, and that will make the Negrosaxon race great.

What made Rome, a single city, the conqueror of Italy, then the ruler of the Mediterranean, and finally the mistress of the world? It was sturdiness and ruggedness of character. The Romans were not a brilliant, versatile and gifted race like the Greeks; not skillful traders like the Phoenicians; but they were a sturdy and vigorous race, mentally, morally and physically, with a genius for war and government; and the whole world went down before them. Rome never fell until licentiousness, drunkenness, gluttony and dissipation sapped her moral and physical energy, and then she succumbed before the rough and rude but honest and sturdy barbarians. The greatest war in the ante-Christian era was that waged between Rome and Carthage in the second and third centuries before Christ. It was not only a struggle for supremacy of the sea, for the control of the Mediterranean; but it was a struggle between the old and decrepit civilization of the Carthaginians and the vigorous and sturdy civilization of the Romans. It was a struggle between Hannibal, the greatest military genius of antiquity, if not of the entire history, and Rome, the greatest nation of antiquity. It was Roman character matched against Hannibal's transcendent military genius, and Roman character won in that fierce and bitter struggle. In the Second Punic war, Hannibal crossed the Alps in midwinter; gathering his forces together, he pounced down upon Italy with an eagle's swoop, winning victory after victory, until the olive groves and vine-clad hills of Italy acknowledged him as lord and master. At the battle of Lake Trasimenus, Hannibal and his hosts slew 15,000 Romans and took 15,000 prisoners. At the battle of Cannae, Hannibal practically annihilated the Roman army. The defeated and receding Roman army left 70,000 of their slain comrades upon the battlefield of Cannae. It was a fearful slaughter. It showed that Hannibal was invincible, unconquerable and irresistible, and yet Rome did not despair. Instead of meeting Varro, the conquered general, with reproaches and insult, as Russia did some of her conquered generals and admirals after the Russian-Japanese War, the Roman Senate thanked Varro for not despairing of the Republic. It was, with the possible exception of Leonidas' stand with his three hundred Spartans at the Pass of Thermopylae, the sublimest spectacle of heroism that the ancient world afforded. And although Rome lay at his mercy, Hannibal dared not march upon Rome and capture her. He knew that such was the temper of the Roman people, such the sturdiness of their character, that though he had enough troops to take Rome, he could not hold Rome. So we can readily see that it was character that saved Rome in the Punic Wars.

Great Britain is a small island. It is only about one-fiftieth as large as the continent of Europe, which is occupied by some fifteen different nations. All of these European nations were really formed by the breaking up of the Roman Empire, of Charlemagne's empire. And yet the race that settled in the British Isles sent out adventurers and colonists who have conquered and occupied all of North America, part of the West Indies and South America, all of Australia, part of Southwest Africa and the western coast of Africa, and who now rule and dominate India, a country with nearly five hundred million inhabitants. So that we may safely say that Englishmen and the descendants of Englishmen occupy and control more territory in the two Americas, in the West Indies, in Australia, in Asia and Africa than all the rest of Europe put together. And the colonial possessions of England in North America, South America, the West Indies, Australia, Asia, and Africa are greater than the combined colonial possessions of Russia, Holland, Germany, France, Spain and Italy. Then, as we turn over the pages of history, we read that English yeomen and bowmen, led by the bold Black Prince, although greatly outnumbered, defeated French chivalry at Crécy in 1346 and at Poictiers in 1356. It is said that at the latter battle the English were outnumbered seven to one. Then under Drake and other sailors England defeated the Spanish Armada on the high seas of the sixteenth century. Under the gallant Wolfe, she captured Quebec and drove the French out of North America. Under the brave Nelson, she defeated the French Navy at the battle of Trafalgar. Under the intrepid Wellington, assisted by the Germans, she crushed Napoleon at Waterloo. Only once in her history has she retired from a struggle, in which she put forth all of her power, defeated and vanquished. And that was when she attempted to oppress her own children in America, who were bone of her bone, flesh of her flesh, who had inherited her blood, her traditions and her longings for liberty. But the struggle in which the push and plodding pluck of the Anglo-Saxon, which can forge ahead in spite of difficulty, obstacle and danger, fight a hard up-hill battle and hang on with grim, dogged determination, with bull-dog tenacity of purpose, was seen at its best, was the Napoleonic Wars.

When Prussia, Austria, Holland, Russia, Spain and Italy had bowed before Napoleon's power and recognized him as lord and master, England alone of the European nations refused to recognize Napoleon as the arbitrator and dictator of Europe. She encouraged every coalition against him and backed it with arms and money. When Spain rebelled against Napoleon and England assisted her, Napoleon reconquered every section of Spain, except the narrow strip of land where the indomitable Wellington had planted himself with his intrepid soldiers. Try as hard as he might, Napoleon could not drive the Iron Duke out of Spain. Had not England maintained her defiant and independent attitude, the other European states would not have dared to rise up against Napoleon.

On the morning of the battle of Trafalgar, Lord Nelson signalled: "England expects every man to do his duty." The English sailors responded to that bugle call and defeated the French in one of the greatest naval battles of modern times. It was English pluck and bull-dog grit and courage that won for her the battle of Waterloo. Napoleon, that Sunday afternoon, raked the English squares with grape and canister, but they closed up again. Napoleon sent his giant cuirassiers against those squares. Those mighty horses leaped over the squares and landed right in the midst of the squares, thus breaking them up. But the English soldiers, by standing the hammering and pounding of Napoleon's artillery and the resistless charges of his cavalry for six hours, stood off the French until the Prussians could come to their aid. And the splendid, sturdy fighting qualities exhibited by the English soldiers at the battle of Waterloo has given the Anglo-Saxon race the preeminence and ascendency that it has in the world to-day.

What enabled the Pilgrim fathers in the Mayflower to face the dangers of an ocean voyage, the privations of a New England winter, the terrors and perils of life in an unknown land, surrounded by bloodthirsty savages, to hang on with grim determination, to wrest a living from those barren hills, to transform the Naugatuck valley in a stream of cities that teem with mills and factories, to develop an inland town like New Britain and finally to make New England the center and focus of the intellectual and moral life of the country? It was character, nothing more and nothing less.

And, finally, take the great English and American captains. William the Conqueror, the Charlemagne of the Anglo-Saxon race, the man who with the clear brain, stern heart, stout arm and iron hand of a Julius Caesar, laid the foundation of England's government; Cromwell, the victor in England's greatest civil war; Wellington, the victor in England's greatest foreign war; Washington, who was the hero in America's struggle for independence; Grant, who fought to a successful close the greatest civil war in history,—were all men who blended in their personalities the common sense and iron will that is the predominant characteristic of the Anglo-Saxon race. It required a man with a resourceful brain and iron nerve, with an eye to see, with a heart to dare, and with an arm to strike, to be able to charge his own followers with his own reckless daring and adventuresome spirit, embark upon a hazardous enterprise, cross the English Channel and win out at Hastings. On the memorable Sunday afternoon at Waterloo, the Duke of Wellington, pale, but calm and determined, pulled out his watch and said, "Blücher or night." He realized that unless rescue or night came on soon, he would probably go down to defeat before the impetuous charge of Napoleon. But he did not abate one jot of heart or hope and fought resolutely on. His quiet, calm courage, his resolute and determined personality reflected itself in his soldiers. And the English stood their ground, and just before night wrapped its mantle over the historic battle ground, thirty thousand gleaming and glistening Prussian bayonets, reflecting the golden light of the setting sun, gladdened the eyes of the Iron Duke and he realized that he had not waited in vain. And backed by the fresh and vigorous Prussians, he struck consternation into the French and swept them completely before him, driving them in confusion from the field. Our own George Washington was not a military genius. He had none of Caesar's, Hannibal's, Napoleon's or Marlborough's dash and brilliancy, was not so fertile in resources or prompt in emergency as these great captains. At his best he was only a second-rate general; but it was his transcendent character, his indomitable spirit, his unyielding purpose, his unbending pride, his inflexible resolution and superb control exhibited during the trying winter at Valley Forge and the dark days of the Revolutionary War, that made him a tower of strength to the Colonial Army and ranks him as one of the greatest fighters in human history. William the Conqueror, Cromwell, Wellington and Grant alone of the moderns, Leonidas, Alexander, Caesar and Hannibal alone of the ancients, equal him in coolness of head and sternness of heart. Who can look at his picture and observe his steady eyes, his broad brow, his prominent cheek bones, his firm determined lips, his massive chin and square set jaw, without noticing that the wisdom, the majestic calmness, the strength, the silent and inscrutable mystery of the sphinx is expressed and written in the lineaments of that immobile face?

Our Grant in the Civil War was not a more resourceful strategist than the brilliant but vacillating McClellan; but he possessed an unconquerable will and a bull-dog tenacity of purpose. He had the grit that enabled him to hang on. Thus a clear brain and cool head, a steady nerve and an iron will have made the Anglo-Saxon race victorious in war, politics, business, industry and agriculture. And a race that wastes its strength and energy in riotous living and dissipation never can possess the superb mental, moral and physical qualities that are necessary to the preservation and supremacy of a race. The Negro should heed this teaching of history. This is the most practical age the world has yet seen. Men do not desire to know whether you are a scholar, thinker, sage, saint, or seer, but they ask, "How many acres of land, how many houses do you own, how many railroad companies or steamboat lines or copper or coal mines do you exercise the controlling influence in?" The men who can develop a railroad or cheapen transportation, or work a copper, coal, or gold mine, or probe into an oil well or increase the output of shoes, hats, clothes or food are in the limelight to-day, the only men whose names are upon the lips of every schoolboy. We only value the man who can increase our physical comforts and commodities and develop the material resources of this community. With the population of the world steadily increasing, with the struggle for existence growing fiercer and the competition keener, he is indeed a benefactor who can show us how to feed, shelter and clothe humanity, bring the necessities and comforts and some of the luxuries of life within the reach of the poor man and regulate the relation between labor and capital. And yet the greatest wars that have shook Christendom during the past one thousand years have not been wars waged to increase boundary lines, have not been wars of conquest, but have been wars waged in behalf of civil and political rights, in behalf of moral principles or a religious creed. Men have ever been ready to sacrifice the comforts and luxuries of life, sacrifice fame and fortune, and risk not only material possessions but life itself to defend personal liberty, root out a moral evil or uphold a religion.

The psychology of patriotism shows that we go enthusiastic over the Stars and Stripes, not because the flag waves over thousands of acres of fertile fields, teeming meadows and luxuriant forests and rich mineral deposits and precious ores, but because the Red, White and Blue symbolizes certain moral, political and religious ideals. And when a man is ready to die for his country, when he is ready to sacrifice his all upon the altar of his country, it is not of the field, forest, plain and prairie that he thinks, but of the sacred traditions of his country's history, of her past and glorious achievements and of the ideals that are enshrined in the hearts of his countrymen.

The Crusades, the Thirty Years' War in Germany, the struggles of the Waldenses, the Dutch Netherlands and the French Huguenots and the Puritan Reformation in England, when men rose to a lofty heroism that was unsurpassed by Leonidas and his three hundred Spartans at the Pass of Thermopylae or Napoleon's Old Guard at Waterloo, or the Light Brigade at Balaclava, were religious wars. The Revolutionary War, the struggle for Italian independence, the struggle of the Hungarians under Kossuth, and the brave stand of the Boers against the English, are modern instances where men have valued civil and political liberty as things for which they would sacrifice their lives. Men have ever been ready to risk life and the comforts of life for the sake of those things which alone make life worth living.

Why did the Pilgrim Fathers leave their friends and comfortable homes in England? Why did these men and women in the Mayflower risk the dangers of an ocean voyage and the terrors of a winter in a strange land and dare to plant a civilization and try their fortunes in a wilderness, surrounded by savage Indians? It was an ideal of a religious liberty that lured them on. They desired to follow the dictates of their consciences as to the manner in which they should worship God. The Stamp Act and the other taxes imposed by England upon America were petty and insignificant taxes. They could easily have been paid by the colonists. Why then did they refuse to pay them, plunge this land in war and drench it in blood for eight years, suffering untold hardships and misery, facing death and bitter poverty? It was a principle for which they were contending. The love of liberty, the instinct of free-born men was asserting itself in them. They would have no taxation without representation.

Why did not the North let the South secede and have her own peculiar institutions? It was the ideal of a united country which Webster pictured in his famous peroration that hovered before their imaginations and welded the North and West together. Why do we celebrate Washington's birthday, Decoration Day, the Fourth of July, Thanksgiving day and Christmas as holidays? It is because the first three days commemorate the men who risked their lives for the sake of a political ideal, for the love of country; while the fourth commemorates the men and women who sacrificed physical comforts for their religious faith; and the fifth commemorates the birth of God-Man, who gave a divine meaning and significance to human life on earth. From the time when the Greeks at Marathon and Thermopylae fought as heroes, and defended the liberties of Greece, from the time when the Christian martyrs would rather be thrown to the lions or burned at the stake before they would bow before Diana, forsake their Christ and tell a lie, men have ever been ready and willing to give their lives for the sake of their liberties and the principles and ideals which alone dignify life and make it worth living. From the time when the daughters and wives of the Cimbri committed suicide rather than become the slaves of the Romans, from the time when the Roman Tribune stabbed and killed his daughter before he would see her the mistress of a king, women have ever valued their virtues and chastity and purity as more sacred and precious, as of more worth and value than life itself.

And why is it that the proud, scornful, haughty Anglo-Saxon refuses to intermarry with the Chinaman, Japanese, Indian and Negro? Is it because he fears that this country will become poorer and more poverty stricken? No, he fears lest merging the Anglo-Saxon blood with the colored races would cause their descendants to lose their psychological qualities, moral and spiritual ideals, which have forced the Anglo-Saxon race to the forefront of civilization and given the world the best civilization it has yet seen. And I believe that the Negrosaxon will receive recognition in America not so much by piling up wealth as by developing those psychical qualities and realizing that type of personality that is the dream of the Anglo-Saxon race and the goal of human development.

Many Anglo-Saxon friends and many Anglo-Saxon critics of the Negrosaxon claim that he can acquire culture and refinement, but lacks the rugged character and sturdy moral fibre of the Anglo-Saxon, that he does not possess that simplicity and sturdiness of character that characterized the Duke of Wellington, Wordsworth, Whittier, Emerson, Bryant, Lincoln and Grant. I believe that the answer is at hand. The Anglo-Saxon socially ostracises the cultured and refined colored people and noble colored youths in order to prevent intermarriage of the races. I will not go into the debated question as to whether contact between the races will lead to intermarriage. I honor the

Anglo-Saxon for desiring to keep his race stock pure and preserve those psychical and psychological characteristics which have forced the Anglo-Saxon to the forefront of civilization; but I desire to say a word about the reflex influence of a crushing environment upon a cultured and refined Negrosaxon.

Emerson in his essay upon heroism says: "We have seen or heard of many extraordinary young men who never ripened, or whose performance in actual life was not extraordinary. When we see their air and mien, when we hear them speak of society, of books, of religion, we admire their superiority; they seem to throw contempt on our entire policy and social state. Theirs is the tone of a youthful giant, who is sent to work revolutions. But they enter an active profession and the forming colossus shrinks to the common size of man. The magic they used was the ideal tendencies, which always make the actual ridiculous; but the tough world had its revenge the moment they put their horses of the sun to plough in its furrow. They found no example and no companion and their heart fainted."[15]

Mr. B. Flower in his brilliant book upon "The Century of More" said: "The philosopher who ascends the mountain of the ideal receives truths larger and more potential for good than aught man has before conceived. But when he returns to earth, that is to say, when he is jostled by the positive thought of positive brains, when he is confronted by dominant ideas struggling to maintain supremacy in the empire of thought, he is in peril; that which was a blessing upon the mount becomes a dirge in the valley, for unless he is great enough to hold steadfastly to the high new truth and rise above sensuous feeling, personal ambition and innate prejudices, he is likely to yield to the psychic forces in the atmosphere below. Painful to relate, this was, I think, to a great degree true of Sir Thomas More, as we shall presently see.[16]

"But the point I wish to illustrate just now is the liability on the part of historians and biographers to misjudge persons who are profoundly sensitive and endowed with a wealth of imagination, but who also possess deep-rooted convictions—men who love the good in the old and yet yearn for the new; those who in moments of ecstacy speak for the ages to come, but when oppressed by the fears and prejudices which environ them reflect the dominant impulses of the present. Without a clear understanding of the mental characteristics of such natures, it will be impossible to understand, much less

---

15. Ralph Waldo Emerson, *Character and Heroism* (New York: H. M. Caldwell Company, 1900), 74–75.

16. The book is actually Benjamin Orange Flower, *The Century of Sir Thomas More* (Boston: Arena Publishing, 1895), 184–85.

sympathize with, the noblest and most far-seeing English philosopher of his age."

What Emerson and Flower say with such earnestness and eloquence of the tragedy in the lives of idealists like earnest young men and Sir Thomas More, applies with double force to the colored idealist. The white idealist, if he desires, can come in intimate and personal association and contact with men of like minds with himself, can come in intimate and personal association with men who can inspire and ennoble him; but this sacred privilege is denied ambitious colored youths.

In the summer of 1895 and 1896, just entering my career as a graduate student, I met six colored idealists. They were young men in college or just out of college. They were interested in philosophy, literature and art, and admired Carlyle, Emerson and Browning. The ostracism of the Anglo-Saxon race and the lack of sympathy and appreciation of their own people with whom they were forced to associate, who only cared for eating and drinking and wearing fine clothes and who cared little or nothing for books and culture, drove all six to the verge of despair and to the brink of moral suicide. Two grew dizzy and sank to menial employment. The other four wavered for a while, trembling from stem to stern like a storm-tossed ship and then, regaining their balance, righted and sailed through the storm and mist and foam to the haven of usefulness and noble endeavor. There is one tragedy that has never been written. DuBois sketched it in his chapter upon Alexander Crummell, in his "Souls of Black Folk"; and that tragedy is the loneliness of the colored idealist who sails between the Scylla of the lack of sympathy of the Anglo-Saxon race, and the Charybdis of the lack of appreciation of his own race. Would that some Whittier would come along and touch with his magic lines the hopeless outlook before a dreamy colored youth as he has immortalized the longings and aspirations of a poor country girl!

The tragedy in the life of a colored idealist is that he reads Plato, Wordsworth, Kant, Hegel, Fichte, Carlyle, Emerson and Browning and forthwith goes off into a world that cares nothing for the great idealists and seers and where everything is at variance with the teaching of the classroom and the atmosphere and influence of his favorite authors. To descend from the mountain lands of inspiration to the valley of temptation, hostility and opposition—that is the fate of the colored idealists.

The Negrosaxon has high ideals, but he is born and reared in an environment that makes it very difficult for him to live up to his ideals. I appreciate the Anglo-Saxon's desire to preserve his own racial integrity; but his Jim-Crowing the Negrosaxon, crowding and segregating the good and bad together in large cities, prevents educated colored men from receiving the blessings of an inspiring environment. Unfortunately, the herding of the

Negrosaxons together often compels the cultured and refined to live as hermits or recluses or else to associate with the coarse and ignorant. Many a pure and pretty colored girl has suffered because of the social ostracism that compels her to live in isolation or else associate with the impure of her own race.

There is one thing that I will refer to again that I have briefly touched upon. The saddest spectacle that I witnessed was in a backwoods town of the South. The mother of a beautiful and brilliant group of daughters suddenly died. Some of them were entering, others were leaving their teens. All of them were girls of remarkable beauty, intelligence and refinement. One of them was of an ethereal type of beauty. With her exquisitely molded features she seemed the prototype of Hawthorne's "Hilda." Another, though a mere child in years, was the personification of womanly dignity, queenly grace and maidenly purity of mind and reserve in manners. Now, owing to circumstances over which they have no control, they are unable to associate with people of culture and refinement and are compelled to come in contact with men and women of coarser make than themselves. I regard it as a tragedy that these girls, at a period of life when their natures are plastic, susceptible, impressionable and receptive, at a time when habits are crystallizing into character and ideals are being formed, are prevented by their environment from coming in touch with uplifting and ennobling influences. The problem is, will the memory of a saintly mother be a sufficient charm to ward off evil influences and hold them up against the degrading tendencies of their environment? I remember, too, how a lonely Methodist minister in a country town, living in intellectual and spiritual isolation in a rural community, so hungered and thirsted to converse with and associate with one of similar taste and inclinations with himself that he begged me, passing through the town, to remain as his guest six months, so that we might browse over the field of literature, history, science and philosophy together. There was nothing in that man's immediate environment to inspire him.

I will now add a word. Carping critics pronounce a Negro who does not become wealthy or famous within five years after his graduation from college, a failure. But notice: Hawthorne, the Beethoven of English prose, was not able to buy a house of his own until he was forty-seven years old; Bancroft, a failure as an educator, afterwards wrote the prose epic of America; Motley, a failure as a politician, wrote the immortal work which chronicled Holland's struggle for liberty; Irving was a failure as a hardware merchant, but won a world-wide reputation as a man of letters; Cooper was an indifferent lawyer but a brilliant novelist; Patrick Henry failed as a farmer and merchant, but succeeded as a lawyer and became the fiery, impassioned Revolutionary orator, whose name is indissolubly linked with that of the

American Revolution. Shakespeare, a failure as a wool merchant, a poor actor, became the world's dramatic poet.

Emerson, not a howling success as a teacher or preacher, became the seer and prose poet of America. Verdi's first two plays were failures. The audience hissed the players of one of his comedy dramas off the stage before the completion of the last act. His wife and two babies died of starvation and neglect, and he was on the verge of suicide, while he was winning his matchless fame. Verdi, whose musical harmonies have dazzled the world, labored for ten years in poverty and obscurity, before the world recognized his productions. Henry Grady's first two journalistic ventures in Rome and Atlanta were failures, but he afterwards became the South's most gifted journalist and delivered a speech in Boston, which, while unjust to the Negro, reached the high-water mark of American eloquence. Demosthenes, ridiculed in his first speech, afterwards became Greece's greatest orator. Disraeli, coughed at, hissed and hooted down in his maiden speech in Parliament, defiantly cried out, "The time will come when you will hear me," and afterwards became the Prime Minister of England. Phillips Brooks, a failure as a teacher, became the preacher whose eloquent and fervid sermons stirred the country. U. S. Grant was a failure as a farmer, a cordwood merchant and a clerk; but he afterwards became the greatest soldier America ever produced and ranked as a general with Wellington and Von Moltke. Samuel Johnson, underrated by Lord Chesterfield, was on the verge of starvation; but he was immortalized by Boswell and Carlyle and became one of England's noted writers. Goldsmith would have been jailed for debt had not Addison come to his rescue; but he was the author of "The Vicar of Wakefield" and "The Deserted Village." Millet, jeered at by fellow students and nicknamed "The Wild Man of the Woods;" Millet, who for twelve years barely eked out a living in Paris; Millet, whose first wife died while he was forging his way to the front; Millet, who often couldn't buy fuel for his family—painted "The Angelus," which sold for 800,000 francs, and touched the heart as few paintings have. Wagner, arrested on the charge of being a rioter; Wagner, whose Tannhauser was greeted with hisses, catcalls, jeers and outcries when first performed in 1845, when he was forty-eight years old; Wagner, the composer, whose unpopularity as a musical revolutionist caused him to go into voluntary exile for ten years in Switzerland; Wagner, not rich enough at a period of life when most great men have achieved fame or fortune, to own a piano; Wagner, barely able to earn a living by his music until fifty years of age,—now ranks as a musical genius above Beethoven and Mozart. Sir Isaac Newton, turned down by the Royal Society of London, was too poor to publish his "Principia," but Edmund Halley came to his rescue, printed it at his own private expense and Newton won undying fame. Herbert Spencer, whose fame is world-wide as a philosophical scientist, whose writings have been more widely read than any other philosopher of the nineteenth century, exhausted his small fortune in publishing his first three or four books and was forced to accept a loan of a few hundred pounds from an American friend and a loan also from John Stuart Mill. Elias Howe, the inventor of the first sewing machine, in 1845 was compelled to sell a machine and pawn his American patent for fifty pounds sterling. He was forced to work his passage home from England on an emigrant steamer and on reaching Spencer was forced to borrow a suit of clothes in which to attend his wife's funeral. And yet his royalties afterwards netted him $4,000 a day. Carlyle, who struggled in poverty the first forty years of his life, barely eking a living, afterwards became the most potent and dominant literary force of the nineteenth century. Samuel Adams was so poor that he had to borrow a suit from a friend to attend conventions and speak at meetings, but now every schoolboy knows that he was the Father of the American Revolution.

Do not despair if the Goddess of Fortune does not at first smile upon you and if prosperity does not at the start crown your efforts, but persevere, persevere, plod on, plod on. Remember that the race is not to the swift nor to the strong, but to him who endures unto the end. Go forth to make your contribution to civilization and success will finally perch upon your banners. And the world will at last give you the recognition that she withholds now.

*Part Two*

# AN ETHNOLOGICAL ACCOUNT OF NEGRO THOUGHT AND LIFE

## *Chapter Six*

# Typical Negro Traits

The first fact that strikes us as we study history is the solidarity of the human race. All the great race stocks, all the different races in America, the English, the Irish, the German, the Frenchman, the Italian, the Jew, the Indian and the Negro have certain human traits common alike to all. All have an innate longing for life and liberty, all grope towards the Eternal and reach in their soaring aspirations the thought of some Great Mysterious Power, who is the creator of this universe; all strive to express and give utterance to what is deepest and most fundamental within them; all shudder at the mystery of death. The Negro shares these hopes, strivings, aspirations with other human beings.

The second fact that strikes us is, the psychical differences between the great race stocks. The great race stocks which have made contributions to civilizations have psychical and psychological qualities peculiar to themselves alone. The Hebrews were endowed with peculiar religious gifts; the Greeks with philosophic, artistic and poetic gifts; the Romans with a genius for war and government; the Germans with a remarkable insight into philosophy and theology; the Anglo-Saxon possessed a genius for war and parliamentary government and a desire for simple home life and a settled mode of industrial life. So too in America the native Yankee, the Irish immigrant, the Italian and the Jew have psychical and racial characteristics peculiar to themselves. In this sense and this sense alone the Negro has race traits and tendencies peculiar to himself alone; but I do not believe that he is outside of the pale of humanity.

Nine special race traits are often attributed to the Negro. He is said to be immoral, to have a happy-go-lucky disposition, to be jealous of his fellows, to be deceitful, to be imaginative, oratorical, musical, emotionally religious and imitative. The first four traits or qualities certainly are not peculiar to the Negro. We cannot call those traits or qualities typical which the colored man shares with all undeveloped peoples that have not long been brought under the refining influence of civilization, but those race traits which are not destroyed by civilization, and which persist in a modified form, in cultured individual, these only can be called typical race traits. Thus the Celt is naturally more imaginative, romantic and sentimental than the Teuton. The Irishman has a wit and humor, the Frenchman a faculty for making fine aesthetic and literary distinctions, that the Englishman does not possess. There are then five race traits and characteristics that distinguish the Negro. He is imaginative, possesses the gift of gab, is musical, is religious and imitative.[1]

## 1. NEGRO IMAGINATION

I will admit that the Negro race is not as practical and hard-headed as the Anglo-Saxon, that the black man has not the grim dogged determination and bull dog tenacity of purpose of the white man; but neither had the Greeks of long ago, nor have the Germans, Irish, French, Italians, Russians or Spaniards of to-day the temperament that can calmly and coolly view every subject as the Anglo-Saxon does. The Negro race is by nature as imaginative, versatile and imitative as the Greek was, although he has not, as yet, developed his constructive and creative genius. He has a native poetic imagination.

Those who have studied the Negro closely have observed that his imagination is tropical in its fertility and luxuriant richness. He is gifted with graphic descriptive powers. He is a vivid word painter. He can give a pen picture of an event that interests him. He has an eye that can take in the beauty of nature. He is keen to observe misfit of clothes and quick to catch the changing thoughts and emotions that mirror themselves in the human countenance. He has a native sense of humor. I have, in Washington, D. C., North Carolina, South Carolina, Georgia and Florida, heard uneducated and untutored Negro preachers describe the radiant splendor of the dawn, the beautiful tints of the rainbow, the golden glories of the setting sun, the buoyant freshness of a springtime, when nature bursts into life and weaves a new garment, and pulses into beauty in blade and grass and flower, with natural poetry. I have heard them picture the pensive sadness of the Indian summer and the crimson yellow glory of autumn and the golden glories of the setting sun in a way to thrill me.

1. William H. Ferris, "Typical Negro Traits," *American Missionary* 62, no. 4 (1908): 99–102.

## 2. NEGRO GIFT OF GAB

The Negro preeminently possesses the faculty of language. Not since that fair moment in Grecian history when their philosophers discoursed often on high themes before the "Hoi Polloi" in the market place, nor when the choice disciples of the peripatetics eagerly hung upon their lips in the groves of the Academy; not since the palmy days when the eloquence of the Athenian orators speaking in the open air thrilled their audiences; not since that high hour in Greek civilization when, as DeWitt Clinton declared, "Herb women could criticise the phraseology of Demosthenes, and the meanest artisan pronounce judgment upon the work of Phidias or Apelles" has any race of natural talkers appeared upon the stage of history who could compare in the "gift of gab" with the Negro orators. One has only to attend the revivals, camp meetings, funerals and Emancipation Day celebrations in the South and he will wonder how the illiterate and ignorant preachers and orators can talk with such ease and fluency for one or two hours. He may laugh at some of their uncouth phrases, but he will marvel at the wealth of their illustration and their copious supply of words, and at the tumultuous, torrential flow of their sentences.

Upon the street corners, in the barber shops and political clubs of the North, he will note this gift of fluent speech, this natural ability to talk for the mere sake and love of talking as it is manifested during election times. In the North the beneficent restraint of the Anglo-Saxon civilization has curbed and repressed the effusive, effervescent, enthusiastic oratory of the Negro; but in the Southland, the Negro's imagination riots in barbaric splendor and wild extravagance to his heart's content, unhindered by the standards of the civilization of another race. In the South no wet blanket, in the sense of propriety of another race is so likely to chill and dampen the fire of Negro eloquence.

## 3. NEGRO RELIGIOUS EMOTION

It is said that the Negro is prone to emotional excitement, but the only difference between the Negro camp meeting and the camp meetings of the poor white is that you can hear the whites singing and shouting two miles away, while you can hear the colored people singing and shouting three miles away. The rites at the Delphic Oracle, the Bacchanalian Festivals in Greece and Rome and the miracles at Lourdes exhibit as much excitement and frenzy as do those recent converts who let themselves go crazy when they picture themselves wearing white robes and golden slippers, and treading upon a sea of glass, surrounded by jasper and sapphire walls, as they go up and down the streets of the New Jerusalem. The influence of the kind of education given by the American Missionary Association, the Freedman's Aid and Southern Educational Society, the Presbyterian and Episcopal churches, in furnishing an educated ministry has raised the tone of the Negro's religion. But through his poetic imagination, his eye for color, his native fluency, his ear for melody, his impassioned soul instinctively bursts into expression and utters itself in the soaring flights of untutored Negro preachers often in torrential streams. Witness the jubilee songs and plantation melodies of the old slaves and the ravishing harmonies and rich voluptuous strains of Taylor's "Hiawatha": I believe the Negro will yet make his own contribution to civilization, and will produce songs and poems that will ring in the hearts of men and go singing down the ages.

## 4. NEGRO IMITATIVENESS

The Negro is an imitative being and as yet in this country is largely the reflex image of the white man. Thus the aristocratic colored man of Charleston, S.C., is the reflex image of the white aristocrat, and the sporting Negro of New York City is the reflex image of the sporting white man. The insolent and impudent Negro of Georgia is the reflex image of the arrogant and coarse Georgia cracker. In the Boston, New York, Philadelphia, Washington, Wilmington, Charleston, Savannah and Louisville Negro, I see a reflection of the civilization or lack of civilization of the white man in these places with whom he comes into contact. The white man cannot ascend higher in the scale of civilization than the Negro can follow. Berial Green might say that his blood would dry up in his veins before he would endorse slavery, and Alexander Crummell, his colored pupil, catches the fire of his spirit and likeness.

So the Negro is usually a thermometer registering the ideas and opinions of the white people he works for or associates with. I can tell what sort of people the white people of any community are by association with the colored people.

I have met few colored men who were original thinkers. They could sit in judgment upon the American civilization and critically dissect and analyze the ideas upon which it is based. Three of these completed their education in England, and another in Germany, and two of the three who studied in England lived and traveled in Africa for over a score of years. In order for a man to pass from the imitative to the reflexive stage of self-consciousness, in order for him to set up a higher ideal than his own age and country affords, he must take a deep dive into history and philosophy. He must drink deeply of the Pierian springs. Then only can he compare and contrast the American civilization with the civilization of other times and other countries.[2]

But when I say that the Negro race is largely imitative the fact must not be overlooked that most of the ideas underlying the Anglo-Saxon civilization do not originate in Anglo-Saxon brains. Some were contributed by the Hebrew race; others by the Greeks; others by the Romans. The twentieth century Anglo-Saxon is thus a stream that is fed by currents of thought from other nations. Still it remains true that the Negro race in selecting its leaders needs to put more emphasis upon brain power and the iron of character to improve the type.[3]

---

2. When Du Bois delivered the "Conservation of Races" at the inaugural meeting of the American Negro Academy, Ferris adamantly disagreed with his position. As David Levering Lewis writes of that exchange, Ferris "thought Du Bois had got the picture upside down. Men were great not because of the races they represented; races were great because they reflected the contributions of outstanding individuals" (*W. E. B. Du Bois: Biography of a Race, 1868–1919* [New York: Henry Holt, 1993], 173).

3. Imitativeness was a quality of assimilation. It was the ability of a race to learn from the milieu of its time. At the turn of the twentieth century, this was the basis on which a race was deemed plastic or rigid. Ferris's use of imitation was as subtle reformulation of the term as used in nineteenth-century ethnology. Many ethnologists believed that the Negro race was savage. For example, Frederick W. Farrar suggests that while ethnology cannot tell the world the origin of the different races, it is nonetheless able to describe three distinct strata or stages of humanity. He explains, "Those three classes are the Savage races, the Semi-civilised races; and finally the two Civilised races. The facts on which I shall dwell, tend to show that these races have always been as distinct as they now are, and that it is impossible for their limits to be confused either by degeneracy on the one hand, or progress on the other" ("Aptitudes of Races," *Transaction of the Ethnological Society of London* 5 [1867]: 115–26, 116).

Farrar maintains the view of many nineteenth-century ethnologists. He argues, "Of the seven or eight civilisations which the world has seen, not one, if we except the Egyptian, which has been grossly exaggerated, which was probably due, such as it was, to Semitic and Aryan influences, and which was deeply marked by the Negritian stains of cruelty and Fetichism, not one has been achieved by a black race" ("Aptitudes of Races," 116). Blacks were

> invariable and expressionless, and their minds characterised by a dead and blank uniformity. Among them generation hands on no torch to generation, but each century sees them in the same condition as the last, learning nothing, inventing nothing, improving nothing, living on in the same squalid misery and brutal ignorance; neither wiser nor better than their forefathers of immemorial epochs back, mechanically carrying on only a few rude mechanical operations as the bee continues to build her waxen hexagon, and the spider to spin his concentric web; but in all other respects as little progressive, and apparently as little perfectible, as the dogs which they domesticate, or the monkeys which chatter in their woods. They are without a past and without a future, doomed, as races infinitely nobler have been before them, to a rapid, an entire,

The Negro is not to be blamed, however, because he does not soar into the realms of intellect. Twenty years ago a Negro philosopher or scholar was almost deified and worshiped by members of his race, but now when the current industrial fads so often look upon the Negro scholar as a bookworm and as an impractical dreamer, the imitative Negro has shared in this contempt for pure intellectual attainment.

The Negro should continue to absorb, assimilate and appropriate the highest elements of the Anglo-Saxon civilization as he has done during the past forty years. And he must retain his buoyant, hopeful, optimistic nature, his warm sympathy and rich emotional equipment and endowment. With education he must preserve the type. Then, indeed, the prophecy of Mr. E[dward] H[enry] Clement may be realized when he declares that "The Negroes surpass the Whites in artistic temperament, and with education and refining may become what the Greeks were to the Romans in their later centuries; for the prosaic, energetic and practical peoples of the North have been especially gifted with industry and application and the power to dominate, but have not the sensibility of the Blacks to impressions of nature, nor equal intensity of sentiment and emotion. The culture of the Blacks in art is sure to yield rich results and produce incalculable effects upon the status of the race socially and politically." Mr. Clement further says: "The contempt which the ignorant or prejudiced of 'the general' show for the Blacks cannot hold against signal honors paid by 'the judicious' among the Whites to the gifted artists of the race. This is the side on which the settled antipathy for the Negro will probably first decay and give way to the positive appreciation of acquisitions for civilization." It seems to me that Mr. Clement, who for a quarter of a century as editor of *The Boston Transcript* has encouraged and cheered many ambitious colored youths by his kindly sympathy, has pointed the way in which the black man may overcome race prejudice. It is the way that has also been steadily pointed out by the American Missionary Association during the past forty years.

---

and, perhaps for the highest destinies of mankind, an inevitable extinction. They have not added one iota to the knowledge, the arts, the sciences, the manufactures, the morals of the world, nor out of all their teeming myriads have they produced one single man whose name is of the slightest importance in the history of our race. Were they all to be merged to-morrow in some great deluge, they would leave behind them no other trace of their existence than their actual organic remains. (Farrar, "Aptitudes of Races," 116)

Ferris was able to show, and this claim is extended in *The African Abroad*, that imitativeness was not isolated to the so-called inferior races. It was Ferris's position that so-called civilized races imitate, or assimilate the lessons of, the dominant group to advance throughout history. Imitativeness then becomes a means by which knowledge and civilization are transmitted throughout history, not evidence of originality or creativity in so-called inferior races. In fact, the absorption of the lessons of civilization was necessary for races, specifically the Negro, to enter the reflexive stage of consciousness.

*Chapter Seven*

# A Historical and Psychological Account of the Genesis and Development of the Negro's Religion

The theory of evolution has revolutionized modern thought. By this I do not mean the Darwinian theory of natural selection, but that the religion, politics and art of any era can be best explained by evolution, by growth, by development, by the unfolding of germs that existed before, though in a dormant state.

The genetic method of explaining the present by the past is the only satisfactory way of dealing with any problem. The reason is obvious. The present is the outgrowth of the past and has its roots deeply grounded in the past. Hence the present can only be understood in the light of the past. And we cannot understand things as they are, save as we understand how they came to be. To illustrate, we don't really know the oak tree, save as we understand how the acorn, through the combined action of soil and rain, of light and the air, unfolded its latent powers, reacted upon its environment and grew into the majestic oak. When we see how the oak came to be, then and not until then will we really know what the oak tree is. We cannot understand the adult man, save as we trace his genesis and growth, from infancy through childhood and youth to maturity.

Men apply this same principle to the origin, evolution and development of various religions. The religions of the present day are growths from more primitive conditions. We cannot understand the present religions of the world save as we understand their origin in the distant past. Men find, then, in the history of religion a perspective, which, like a view from a mountain top, enables them to see things in their proper relations.

Formerly church historians and theologians discussed the various systems and views of different theologians and philosophers as if they were isolated phenomena; but now Windelband in his "History of Philosophy," and Harnack in his "History of Christian Dogma," show that the various philosophical and theological conceptions go through an orderly process, an orderly unfolding and development, one from the other.

Then again, when men discussed the various religions, such as Christianity, Judaism, Mohammedanism, Buddhism, Confucianism, Brahmanism, Mazdeism and the various nature religions which culminated in the Graeco-Roman religions, they put the Christian religion in a special category by itself, whereas it is now seen that no religion has its hold upon mankind by virtue of the error that is within it, but by virtue of the truth that it contains. The Christian religion is a mighty stream into which currents from Jewish, Greek, Roman and Persian civilizations flowed. Christianity differs, then, from other religions in that it appeals to all instead of to some of the elements of human nature, and especially to the higher elements.

But this genetic method of explaining things by the principle of growth by and through development, this comparative method of showing how all religions necessarily appeal to some fundamental element in human nature, is entirely forgotten and lost sight of when we study the Negro's religion. Men approach the Negro's religion as if they were about to enter a curiosity shop or hospital or dime museum. They seem to think that they will only find pathological cases of the aberration of the human intellect, religious freaks who foam at the mouth, go into hysterics, prance and shout, and faint away, when in reality the truth is the Negro's religion is not outside of the stream of the general religious development of mankind.

In our account of the genesis and development of the Negro's religion we shall endeavor to show that the colored man is not constructed psychologically different from other men. His religion is not, as commonly supposed, a phenomenon that is separate and apart from the historical development of the human race. In his religion, as in the white man's religion, we see but stages in the evolution of human thought. In the colored man's religion we but see the Anglo-Saxon's religion objectified. The Negro in Africa and America is now passing through the same process of religious development that the Anglo-Saxon and other races have passed through. He is gradually shuffling off his old superstitions and absorbing from his environment materials for a more renewed growth. It is the comparative method in the study of religion that has revolutionized modern theology. And when we approach the colored man's religion from the comparative point of view, we see that it contains the same psychological elements as do other men's religion. And we cannot understand it then save as we make a brief survey of the history of the religious life of mankind and see what are its permanent psychological elements.

Many persons never carefully distinguish between religion and theology, and yet there is wide difference between them. Religion is first in the order of time and is more fundamental and vital. Religion is the soul's inner communion with and relation to God; while theology is the system of religious dogma and faith. Religion is the outgrowth of certain cravings and aspirations of man's innermost heart and nature; while theology is man's thought of the relation of God and man. Religion is a matter of the heart; while theology is an affair of the intellect.

A man may have a wrong intellectual dogma, but yet may feel the presence of God and be perfect in his life. On the other hand, a man may have a correct intellectual dogma, but yet never experience a deep religious feeling; may never really know that God stands in a personal relation to him. Abraham's theology was far from being perfect, yet God was near to him. Many theologians can discourse on the ways of God to man, and yet religion is not a reality to them. Religion brings a man into relation with his fellows; but theology oftentimes never leads a man to acts of benevolence. In a word, religion is the life of God in the soul of man, while theology is man's philosophical interpretation and explanation of that life.

Religion, too, is not to be confused with the church, which is an ecclesiastical organization. Religion is the spiritual life of the individual believer, while the church is the organized body of believing Christians, whose desire for fellowship draws them to worship in common. Religion as a life in the soul of the believer existed before the church as a religious body came into being. Thus those who assembled in the upper chamber were first moved by the Holy Spirit before they came together. Man is a gregarious being. He loves the sympathy of his fellow men, and that is why his courage and his faith is reinforced in a crowd. While public worship and prayer meetings stimulate one's spiritual life, yet the lowly Nazarene chose the quiet of the mountains in the evening and the lonely walk by the seashore for his meditation and communion with the unseen God. During the Middle Ages, when the church was corrupt, many mystics in study and prayer and meditation nourished their piety apart from the church.

In seeking a definition for religion we must have a broad conception of religion and find a definition that will apply to all the varied forms of religion, from the religions of savages up to that of the enlightened Christian. It must take in the most primitive as well as the most developed form of religion. The Hottentots and Bushmen have moral ideas which are crude and distorted. The Vikings, the Spartans, the Zulus, the Kaffirs, the wild Indians, the Mohammedan warriors, the Goths and the Huns have many notions of right and wrong that are at variance with the Sermon on the Mount. We see at times an unscrupulous treatment of foes, a fiendish cruelty towards their enemies, a demoniac fierceness of spirit and many revolting practices, and yet these savage and relentless barbarians are guided by what to them seems their ideal of a brave and faithful man. They follow what to them appears to be the highest conception of life. Their reverence for courage, their fidelity to their chieftain, their loyalty to their tribe, may manifest itself in grotesque and unnatural forms, yet it is this that dominates their actions. Their rude notions of what is right and wrong, their instinctive ideas of justice, prompt these men to action.

Our conception of religion must be broad enough to take these in. It must include the fetish worship of native Africans; the worship of gods many and lords many who were half men and half beasts, which we find in the old Dravidian, and the religion of the Tetaonian, the Egyptian religion and the religion of the American Indian. It most also include the superhuman and semi-ethical deities of the Vedic, Zoroastrian, various Semitic, Celtic, Germanic, Hellenic and Graeco-Roman religions; the legislative or nomistic religions of the Brahmans and Hebrews and the universal and ethical religions such as Confucianism, Buddhism, Islamism and Christianity.

I think the late Dean Everett of the Harvard Divinity School hit the nail on the head when he said, "Religion is a feeling towards a supernatural presence," and that in the higher religions this "Supernatural Presence is manifested in Truth, Goodness and Beauty."

Without feeling there may be a philosophical conception of the universe; without feeling there may be a moral life; but without feeling there can be no religion. But what distinguishes religious feeling from other forms of feeling is this: In the religious feeling there is always a reference to unseen and invisible powers, with whom the worshipper desires to get into right relations and whose favor he seeks. The higher and lower forms of religion differ in two respects; in the lower forms of religion we find superstitious and slavish fear, while in the higher forms of religion we find a worshipful reverence. In the lower forms of religion the deities are endowed with the lower attributes of the human spirit, while in the higher forms of religion the deities are endowed with the higher attributes of the human mind. Thus when we say that "religion is a feeling towards a supernatural presence" we have a definition that is comprehensive enough to take in all.

Each race is modified and influenced by its religion. This fact is so well known that it does not need elaboration. We have all seen the wonderful transforming power of Christianity in the case of individual men and women. To see what it has done with a race we have only to reflect that it has tempered, mildly though it may be, the original barbarity of the Teuton and

Anglo-Saxon. Buddhism has made the Hindoo more passive and less aggressive. Confucianism has made the Chinese more practical, while Mohammedanism has sent its converts out with that unconquering faith and infectious enthusiasm that have ever moved the world.

Each race, too, prefers the religion that is suited to its temperament. Thus we see the preference of the Anglo-Saxon for Christianity, of the Hindoo for Buddhism, of the Chinese for Confucianism, and of the African for Mohammedanism. Some wonder why fierce and aggressive peoples, like the Teutons and Saxons and Normans, could so readily assimilate a religion that emphasizes self-renunciation, self-sacrifice and self-denial. It is because Christianity laid stress upon the worth and sacredness of the human personality and hence touched what was deepest in the Teuton's nature, namely, his nascent sense of personality. Again the Chinese are a practical and non-poetic and non-heroic people and hence like a religion that does not call for heroic self-sacrifice, but looks to the temporal comfort of a people, while Buddhism with its dream of a Nirvana appeals to the languid Hindoo nature.

Before Mohammed's time the Saracens were men of a narrow iconoclastic spirit and were scattered into a few Bedouin tribes. But what did Mohammed do? In the brilliant words of Professor George Burton Adams, of Yale, "Putting into definite and striking form the unconscious ideas and aspirations of his people and adding a central and unifying teaching and inspiring and elevating notions from various sources, he had transformed a few scattered tribes into a great nation and sent them forth under a blazing enthusiasm upon a career of conquest entirely unparalleled in motive force and extent." Mohammed starts out with a few Bedouin tribes and yet a territory 6,000 miles in diameter was occupied and conquered within a hundred years. The native African tribes, both then and now, took to Mohammedanism as a duck takes to water.

Christians may point with pride to the Christian martyrs and heroes going singing and crying "Hosannahs to the Lord of Hosts," to be torn into pieces by the lions in the Roman amphitheater or burned alive at the stake. But Islam can also point with pride to the fanatical enthusiasm and death-defying courage of the followers of the Mahdi, who repeatedly rush to be mowed down by thousands by British musketry and British cannon.

The African Negro takes so readily to Mohammedanism because it fits in so well with his previous modes of thought and feeling and appeals so powerfully to all that is deep and fundamental in him. The fatalism and sensuousness of Mohammedanism, its picture of a heaven with its fair gardens and luxuriant vegetation that has ever delighted the eye of man, its soothing music and beautiful women touch a responsive chord in the heart of the native of

Africa. In the Mohammedan Paradise the African beholds his dream of earthly happiness visualized and realized. Again while Mohammedanism does not particularly encourage, it does not distinctly forbid polygamy and slavery. Thus we can see why Islam can sway the native African in the way that it does.

The truth which is illustrated and brought out in this survey is this: The religion of a race or nation cannot be arbitrarily imposed upon it from without, but springs up and grows from within. It is the resultant of the longings and desires, the hopes and aspirations of the race. It wells up spontaneously and unconsciously from the soul depths of the race, issuing forth just as the spring, rising in the hills and expanding on its downward career into the river, on whose noble bosom the ships of the nations float, gushes forth from the mountain side, because impelled by unseen, elemental forces from below.

Israel, Greece, Rome, the Germanic and Saxon races are the five great races that have thus far made important contributions to civilization. Each race developed a peculiar genius along one line and perfected it in an organized and national life.

Now each race has followed the dialectics of its own nature in developing in the way that it did. It developed in ways peculiar to itself, because it was true to the trend of its own genius, because it followed the tendencies and bent of its own peculiar temperament. It passed its environment through the crucible of its own race psychology. We cannot understand how these races developed in the way that they did, unless we understand the peculiar and inexplicable soul life of the race. Now each of these five great race stocks not only was influenced and modified by Christianity, but each left its own impress upon Christianity and contributed its own distinct genius to it. It made its distinct and permanent contribution by following the dialectics of its own nature.

The Greeks, like Justin and Clement and Origen, who had studied Greek philosophy, embraced Christianity and they had to interpret Christianity in terms of the Greek philosophy. And Christianity in adapting itself to the Greeks had to recognize the truth in the philosophical systems. Now the Platonic philosophy with its conception of an unknowable God who was apart from the world, and the Stoical philosophy with its conception of the Logos or Divine manifestation of God in the universe, these two systems of philosophy influenced the Christological conceptions of the day. Also Persian and Oriental notions of sin and Neo-Platonism influence Christian thinkers. The Alexandrian thinkers represented by Clement, Origen and Athanasius were largely given to recognizing Christ as the incarnation of God. It recognized and emphasized the divine element in Christ, while the influence from Antioch emphasized the human element in Christ.

Those who were steeped in Platonic and Neo-Platonic philosophy found difficulty in the conception of the union of the human and divine. Thus one Christological problem was the incarnation, "How could the human and divine be united in one person?" Clement solved it by showing that Christ was the Logos which was the Word of the Father, was the manifestation of the Father, who had always been in the world inspiring heathen moralists and philosophers and the good in all ages, and in so far as Socrates and Plato knew the Logos, they knew Christ. And the divine Logos or the indwelling Christ or Father was manifested in the reason, conscience and hearts of all men. He was the divine light of the reason of all men. The Christians must believe in the divinity and humanity of Christ at the same time.

The problem in the first three centuries was, "How could the unity of God be harmonized with the Trinity? How could the Absoluteness of God be harmonized with the Divinity and Deity of Christ? How could the Divinity and Humanity of Christ be harmonized?" Clement solved the last by showing that Christ as the Logos of God was present in the world and in man from the beginning, hence it was easy to see how Logos, who was imperfectly manifested in men heretofore, could be perfectly manifested in one man. Thus we see how the Greek philosophy and the philosophical trend of the Greek mind profoundly influenced and modified the theology of Christendom.

The Hebrew gave us the monotheistic conception of an ethical deity. It was from the Hebrew mind and spirit that Christianity derived its conception of the ethical perfection of God and of the reality of sin as an alienation from God. The gifted Greek mind, more versatile and poetic, gave to civilization, philosophy, poetry and sculpture, to which men still repair, as to perennial founts of inspiration and perennial well-springs of wisdom. And it was from the Greek mind that Christianity obtained its conception of the immanence of the Divine Mind in nature, obtained its Logos doctrine that every visible thing was but the symbol and manifestation of an invisible thought. The practical Roman mind gave us a system of law and a policy of assimilating rather than subjugating a conquered people, that has revolutionized political history. Rome thus became the purveyor of the Hebrew and Greek civilization, and so unified the world that it was possible for Christianity to be disseminated over the entire civilized world. And when the hosts of the barbarians swarmed over the Roman frontiers and poured down upon Rome, sweeping everything before them, there was one thing that challenged the admiration of these rude Titanic tribes and that was the Roman civilization as embodied and crystallized in the Christian religion. It was this that really conquered the youthful and victorious barbarians. The Roman mind had expressed its monotheistic genius in the Roman Catholic Church and it was this that held the vigorous and untutored races together during those ten silent centuries that are fitly termed the Dark Ages.

The profound and mystical Teuton mind gave the theology, pietism and mysticism to modern Christianity. We find the German spirit free and independent. It emphasized the worth and sacredness of human personality. During the process which began with the mediaeval mystics and culminated in the heroic pleas of Luther for the sanctity of inward piety, of the soul's communion with God, and for individual freedom in studying and interpreting the Bible, up until the present time, inward piety, philosophical and theological freedom have been the distinctive contribution of the Germanic race to Christianity. And it was from the mediaeval mystic that the Lutheran Reformation in Germany received its theological impulse.

Fifteen hundred years ago the hardy Norseman and fierce Vikings made their presence known and felt in Europe. They laughed at the perils of the deep, courted danger, burned villages and pillaged houses. The Anglo-Saxon race ever since has stood forth as the perfect embodiment of daring courage and adventurous aggressiveness. By its bold, daring, adventurous and aggressive spirit the Anglo-Saxon race has conquered every race that it has ever come into contact with. It has preeminently originated and developed the idea of representative government, and has emphasized personal liberty in religion and politics.

What Rome did for the Hebrew and Greek mind the Anglo-Saxon race has done for the German mind. The Anglo-Saxon has assimilated the results of the Hebrew, Greek and German genius and it is aggressively carrying forward to all parts of the world the indestructible elements contributed by the Hebrew, Greek and Roman mind. The Anglo-Saxon is, then, the advance guard of civilization and it is the source from which the great missionary movements have sprung. It is the embodiment of a progressively aggressive missionary spirit and is actively interested in social reform. It must not be understood by this that the Anglo-Saxon is the only race that embodies the missionary spirit. Thus we see that religion is transformed and modified in passing through the crucible of race psychology.

Some say that the intellectual, moral and spiritual differences of the various races are due to the geographical location of the race. But we cannot explain the psychological genius of the Greeks, the monotheistic and ethical genius of the Israelites, the political genius of the Indo-Germanic races on geographical grounds. Neither can you explain the great racial characteristics or psychological peculiarities of the different races on biological and anthropological grounds. The race reacting in a different way on its environment, determines the course of development the race will take. The inexplicable soul life of the Germanic nations is the thing of main account that will explain what the Germanic nations have done and will do in history. How account for the psychical and psychological differences between races so that one has a genius for religion, another for art, and another for politics? It cannot be done upon merely geographical grounds.

## A HISTORICAL AND PSYCHOLOGICAL ACCOUNT OF THE GENESIS AND DEVELOPMENT OF THE NEGRO'S RELIGION.

*Is there anything that psychologically differentiates the Negro from other races?* Every time the Negro minister is referred to before a white congregation, immediately a broad grin spreads over the countenance and they call to mind the darkey preacher often referred to, who looked apprehensively at the sun and said, "De grass am gittin' weedy, de sun am gittin' hot, dis man's gittin' old and feeble; guess dis darkey am called to preach." When you speak of the Negro's religion, this audience will immediately call to mind another Negro, also often referred to, who pays his respects to the chicken coop on his way home from the prayer meeting. The Negro's religion is not taken seriously, and yet despite the superstitions, the incongruities and inconsistencies manifested in the Negro's religion, there is a deep vein of serious religion in the Negro's nature.

I will admit that the Negro race is not as practical and hardheaded as the Anglo-Saxon race, but neither had the Greeks and Romans of long ago, nor have the Germans, French, Italians, Russians or Spaniards of to-day that phlegmatic temperament that can coolly and calmly view every subject. But the Negro is as imaginative, versatile, plastic and imitative a race as the Greeks. He has a poetic imagination. Even the illiterate Negro has fastidious notions as to dress. The Negro has remarkable ability in adjusting himself to a varied and changing environment. That is why he thrives under changed surroundings, where other races perish.

The Negro race is the greatest race of natural talkers that ever appeared upon the stage of history. It is preeminently endowed with the gift of gab. It has its oratory on tap. All you have to do is to turn the faucet and a copious stream of oratory will gush forth. On election days, in the large cities of the North and East, every street comer is a rostrum, every barber shop a forum and every bar-room a free lecture platform. We think then of that brilliant epoch in Greek history, the days of Pericles, when the Athenian orators made the market place ring with their eloquence, when the peripatetic philosophers discoursed of high things in the grove of the academy and Socrates held his divine conversations in the streets of Athens. The Greeks were a race of talkers. But they could not compare with the Negro race. I know you will think of that fair moment in Grecian history when, as DeWitt Clinton declared, "the herb women could criticise the phraseology of Demosthenes and pronounce judgment upon the works of Phidias and Apelles." I know you will recall how Pericles, Aeschines and Demosthenes held the Athenian multitude spell-bound under the magic wand of their matchless eloquence. But reflect that in the cotton and corn fields of the South, our sugar and rice plantations and in the turpentine camps, there are untutored Negro preachers from whose lips issue forth eloquence that, though rude, is noble.

I know you will say that the Negro is prone to emotional excitement. But the only difference between the Negro camp meetings and the camp meetings of the poor whites is that you can hear the whites singing and shouting two miles away, while you can hear the colored singing and shouting three miles away. The rites at the Delphic Oracle, the Bacchanalian festivals in Greece and Rome and the miracles at Lourdes exhibit as much excitement and intoxication and frenzy as do those recent converts who go crazy and let themselves go when they picture themselves wearing white robes and golden slippers, and treading upon a sea of glass, surrounded by jasper and sapphire walls.

Then, again, the Negro race has an innate ear for harmony, an instinctive love of music. The aspiration and longing and sorrow and cravings of the Negro burst into expression through the jubilee songs and plantation melodies. Besides the soothing and plaintive melodies of these songs the gospel hymns of Moody and Sankey sound like sounding brass and a tinkling cymbal. These songs touch and move everyone because they come up out of the elemental depths of the Negro's nature. The Negro race is richer, then, in emotional endowment than any other race in the world.

It has an inspiring nature, for immediately after his emancipation the Negro began to aspire after the highest things in the American civilization. He tried to absorb the most complex political psychology ever evolved from the brain of man. The Reconstruction politicians even aspired to using Dresden china cuspidors.

Nature worship is the first form of religion, and the most primitive form of religion. Herbert Spencer seems to think that ancestor worship was the first form of religion, basing his argument upon the fact that the phenomena of dreams, where persons saw their parents and grandparents, was what caused savages to ascribe the good or ill luck that attended them to their dead ancestors. But it is the almost universal verdict of scholars that Spencer is wrong. So far as we can learn by the observation of present peoples and by the study of the past, ancestor worship is found among more highly developed people than nature worship. The worship of crude and unsophisticated savages is almost always nature worship. By nature worship, or animism, we mean that form of human thought which ascribes spiritual life to the objects of nature and animals, or, as it is scientifically defined, "the doctrine that the phenomenon of life in animals is caused by the presence of a soul or spirit."

Professor C. H. Teile, the eminent scholar in the history of religions, in an article upon religion in the ninth edition of the Encyclopaedia Britannica, divides nature worship into three varied forms of nature religions: "The Polydaemonistic magical religions, under the control of Animism; the purified or organized magical religions, namely, Therianthropic polytheism; and the worship of man-like, but superhuman and semi-ethical, being in 'Anthropomorphic polytheism.'"[1] He divides the ethical religions into two great groups, the national nomistic or nomothetic, and the universal religions.

We see the first form of nature religions in the religion of savages. We see the second form in the old Dravidian faith, in the religion of the Finns, in the Egyptian religions and the more organized American Indian faiths. We see the third form of nature religions in the Vedic religions, in Zoroastrianism and various Semitic faiths, in the Celtic, Germanic, Hellenic and Graeco-Roman religions.

I think that Teile is right in making nature religion in the form of Animism, or the religion of savages, the most primitive form of religion. Human nature is everywhere the same. It is the same yesterday as it is to-day. It is the principle of causation and the impulse to interpret nature in terms of the mind's life that leads the speculative philosopher of the twentieth century to his belief in a universal world spirit, immanent in the universe.[2] And it was the same universal desire to seek a cause adequate for every effect and to ascribe to nature a spirit akin to his own that led the untutored savage to worship his Fetich and led the poetic Greeks to people the springs and streams with nymphs, the woods and groves with deities and to represent the thunder and lightning as but the frowning Zeus, hurling his dreaded thunderbolts from

1. Ferris is getting sloppy at this point in the text. He is quoting from the reference entry "Religion" in *The Encyclopedia Britannica Latest Edition: A Dictionary of Arts, Sciences, and General Literature*, ed. Spencer Baynes and W. Robertson Smith (New York: Werner Company, 1902), 20: 368. Ferris actually means to reference the work of Professor C. P. Tiele, *Outlines of the History of Religion* (London: Kegan Paul, Trench, Trubner, & Company, 1896).

2. This moment in the text is interesting, as Tiele suggests that "Animism is not itself a religion, but a sort of primitive philosophy, which not only controls religion but rules the whole life of man" (*Outlines of the History of Religion*, 9). Tiele suggests that we can only seek to answer the question of origin by psychology, and a philosophy which seeks to organize religious experience. His text, however, does not seem to indicate this is the direction of his inquiry (6). We can read Ferris as taking up Tiele's challenge to use psychology and philosophy to inquire into these origins specifically applied to the Negro.

Mount Olympus' rugged heights. The Greek, in letting his imagination go out and paint one of the sublimest pictures that can enter the mind of man, when he conceives of guardian spirits presiding over forest, streams, hills and dales, and controlling the beneficent activities of nature, was but obeying the same universal instinct of the human reason that dominated the thinking of the Apostle Paul when he says, "In him we live and move and have our being," or the poet Wordsworth when he says,

> There was a time when meadow, grove and stream,
> The earth and every common sight
> To me did seem appareled in celestial light,
> The glory and the freshness of a dream,

or the astronomer Kepler, when in reading aright the meaning of those grand elemental laws that control the movements of the stars in the Milky Way, he said he was thinking the thoughts of God after Him.

The poet-philosopher Plato calls God the great Geometer. The philosopher Kant says that there are two things which fill him with awe, the starry heavens above him and the moral law within him. The old prophets in the calm of the midnight sky saw God face to face. Who of you that has beheld the stars shining so calmly in the immensity of space has not felt that he was in the presence of forces and powers that were above and beyond him. The savage, the Apostle Paul, the poet Wordsworth, the astronomer Kepler, the poet-philosopher Plato, the philosopher Kant and you and I obey the same innate laws of human thought, the same constitutional principles of human reason, when we strive to get back of the phenomena to that which produced them.

Some have made the distinct characteristic of man that differentiates him from the lower animals, to lie in the fact that man is a tool-using being. Others have laid stress upon the fact that man is a being who has the gift of speech. But the peculiar characteristic of man that differentiates him from the lower animals is that he is a metaphysical and reasoning being. Behind the ability to handle tools lies the ability to think, back of the power to use speech lies the power to frame a concept and carry on a consecutive chain of thought.

You throw a stone at an animal and conceal yourself—it will give a start, look around and go about its business; but you throw a stone at a savage and hide yourself and he will immediately begin to reflect, and that is what the primitive men of all races and nations have done. That is what primitive man has always done in unconsciously obeying that constitutional tendency of the human mind which leads it to seek a cause for every effect.

The savage saw the sun rise and then set. He saw the stars shine in the firmament. He saw the trees and grain and grasses and fruit and flowers grow.

He saw the frost and rain spoil his crops. He saw the cyclone sweep everything before it. He saw the rivers rise and surge and rage. He trembled at the thunder and lightning. He saw sickness and disease and death take away his fellows. He felt the rheumatism steal in upon him and was driven by the necessity of human thought to account for it. What more natural than that he, in seeking causes for the beneficent and baleful operations of nature, should ascribe them to good and evil spirits with a conscious, sentient and volitional life that was akin to his own. From the time when primeval man looked up to the stars and at the world around him and peopled nature with spirits akin to his own, up to the present time this has ever remained the process by which religion has germinated and unfolded in the mind of man. The wild African, the ancestors of the Aryan race on the hills of Northern Asia, and the poetical Greeks, all saw nature throbbing and pulsating with animate life.

Now if nature was believed to be peopled with good and evil spirits, where will these spirits exist. Primitive man had not reached that stage of advanced thought where he could conceive of disembodied spirits, neither could he believe that the objects of nature that he saw moving and growing were inanimate. He believed that all the physical objects and all the animals were impelled by some spirit. What more natural, then, than that he should believe that the unseen and invisible spirits that lived and moved in things and animals should be the spirits who benefited or harmed them?

It is significant in this respect that animus is the Greek or Latin for spirit, and this is the step from nature worship to Fetichism. "A Fetich," in the words of one scholar, "is not an idol and is not properly a symbol, but is looked upon as the actual and visible dwelling place of a preternatural power."[3] In Fetichism, then, the object is not worshipped or prized highly because it itself has power to benefit or harm a man, but because it is the abode and habitat of some invisible spirit or unseen power.

"Every object," says Peschel, "that attracts the glance of the savage, who espies a ghost in every corner, may become in his eyes the abode of a deity."[4] Sticks, stones, household utensils, ornaments, plants, trees, snakes and animals were thus looked upon and regarded as fetiches.

---

3. Ferris gets this definition from Marcus Benjamin, ed., *Appleton's New Practical Cyclopedia* (New York: D. Appleton, 1913), 376. The rest of the quote says, "It may be thus some fixed object in nature, as a mountain or tree; it may be an animal, as a snake or a crocodile, and often is a sheep or goat; or it may be any object on which the fancy has fixed, as the beak of a bird, the hoof of quadruped, a stone, a feather, a nail or almost anything else" (ibid.).

4. Oscar Peschel, *The Races of Man, and Their Geographical Distribution* (New York: D. Appleton, 1906), 247.

Oscar Peschel, on page 77 of his "Races of Man," says, "All true Negroes adhere either to a rude animal and fetich worship or to Islam."[5]

Now these seem to be rather sweeping statements, but if the reader will but turn over the pages of Ratzel's "History of Mankind," by far the most exhaustive and comprehensive account of the darker races, their customs, institutions and religions, he will observe numerous instances which verify these statements of Peschel.[6]

Fetichism is now common in Central Africa, among the Kaffirs, in Dahomey and among the degraded tribes of Senegal and Congo. At one time or another Fetichism has been common among the Red Indians, the Mexicans, the Germans, the Saxons, the Brahmins, the Hindoos and other tribes. When the fetich was a household utensil, it was punished or beaten or broken if misfortune befell its owners, or it did not grant his wish. Says Peschel again, "Before every great enterprise, the Negro of Guinea, if no old and tried fetich is at hand, selects a new one; whatever his eye falls upon as he leaves his house, be it a dog, a cat, or any other creature, he takes as his deity and offers sacrifices to it on the spot. If the enterprise succeeds the credit of the fetich is increased; if it fails, the fetich returns to its former position." African fetichism is not different then from the Fetichism that is found among other peoples and has been found in other ages.

It is but a step, then, from African Fetichism to African Shamanism. If nature was looked upon and regarded as peopled with invisible spirits, who bring not only beneficent results, but also misfortune, calamities, sickness, disease and death upon men; if in the religion of ancestor worship, the departed spirits of ancestors must be propitiated when angry, what more natural than that the primitive savage should seek for some means of counteracting the baleful operations of these evil spirits. In this way, priests or magicians, such as the African Shaman or Indian medicine man, grew up.

The Shaman, by his magic and peculiar medicines, is supposed to be able to cure sickness and disease, prolong life, ward off death, counteract the effect of witchcraft and come into direct communication with evil powers and the spirits of departed ancestors, thus receiving supernatural knowledge.

Says Peschel, "Of all nations the South African Bantus suffer most from this mental malady of Shamanism. Whenever a death occurs, inquiries are made of the Mzango or local Shaman as to its author. . . . When the seer indicates a suspected person, a trial by ordeal takes place, etc."[7] Thus in

5. This quote from Peschel is actually on p. 477 of *The Races of Man*.

6. Friedrich Ratzel, *The History of Mankind*, vol. 3 (London: MacMillan and Company Limited, 1898).

7. Peschel, *The Races of Man*, 266.

African Shamanism, no man is regarded as dying from a natural cause; but from the malice of some wizard or some person who sought its evil powers.

African Shamanism is not only the religion of the South African and Bantu Negro, the Australians, Papuans and the Kaffirs, but is the religion of some Siberian tribes, of primitive North Asiatic and Central Asiatic tribes, of the Brazilian peon and of the North American Indian. It is something that is not peculiar to the Negro per se.

Now this native African, with tropical and luxuriant imagination, a passionate, sensuous, voluptuous and emotional temperament and nature religion, taking the form of a crude and superstitious Fetichism, was suddenly imported to an alien country as a slave. His condition here has been graphically portrayed by Dr. W. E. B. DuBois. He says, "Endowed with a rich tropical imagination and a keen delicate appreciation of nature, the transplanted African lived in a world animate with gods, devils, elves and witches, full of strange influences of good to be implored, of evil to be propitiated. Slavery then was to him the dark triumph of evil over him. All the hateful powers of the underworld were striving against him and a spirit of revolt and revenge filled his heart. He called up all the resources of heathen sin to aid,—exorcism and witchcraft, the mysterious Obi worship, with its barbarous rites, spells and blood sacrifice even, now and then, of human victims. Weird midnight orgies and mystic conjurations were invoked, the witch woman and the voodoo priest became the centers of Negro group life and that vein of vague superstition which characterizes the unlettered Negro even to-day was deepened and strengthened."[8]

But this is where I differ from Professor DuBois: the woman conjurer and voodoo priest were not creations of the American Negroes in their slave life; they were rather modifications of the African Shaman or Medicine Man, who was at the same time judge, physician, priest, magician and wizard. What more natural than that the Negro in his new environment and new sorrows and trials should turn for comfort and solace to his old healer, the African Shaman.

To-day, even, in some sections of the Bahama Islands and the South, no man or woman is supposed to die of a natural disease, if consumption or typhoid fever takes him off. If rheumatism or paralysis afflicts him some

8. Ferris could have gotten this quote from two places in W. E. B. Du Bois's extensive corpus. The most obvious articulation of this quote is in *The Souls of Black Folk* (New York: Penguin Books, 1995), 217–18. Ferris could also have found this quote in Du Bois's essay in *The New World: A Quarterly Review of Religion, Ethics, and Theology* 9 (1900): 614–25. For a discussion of the revisions Du Bois made between the two pieces, see David Murray, *Matter, Magic, and Spirit: Representing Indian and African American Belief* (Philadelphia: University of Pennsylvania, 2007), 59–61.

enemy is supposed to work a charm and the man or woman conjurer is consulted and sought after.

*What was there in the environment of the American Negro which caused his religious development to take the form it did?* We have seen how the native African, following that primal instinct which is common to every primitive race, was led in seeking a cause for every effect to believe in the existence of unseen forces and invisible powers who could help or injure him. We have seen how he worshipped the various objects in nature, or animals in which these supernatural spirits were supposed to reside. We have seen how next he had recourse to the Shamans who were magicians or priests supposed to have the power to ward off the witchcraft of evil-minded persons and the mischievous designs of wizards and departed spirits. We have seen, too, how Negro Voodism, Gopherism and Conjurism is a direct evolution from African Shamanism. And the medicine men and women conjurers who were familiar figures on Southern plantations were lineal descendants of the African Shamans.

Professor W. E. Burghardt DuBois, the eminent sociologist, in his article upon the religion of the American Negro in the New World for March or June, 1901, gives a graphic and eloquent picture of the transformation of the family and clan life of the newly imported slaves. He there says, "He (the slave) was brought from a definite social environment, the polygamous clan life under the leadership of the chief and the potent influence of the priest. The first rude change in this life was the slave ship and the West Indian sugarfields. The plantation organization replaced the clan, and the tribe and the white master replaced the chief, with his thirst for greater and more despotic powers. Forced and long-continued toil became the rule of life, the old ties of blood relationship and kinship disappeared, and instead of the family appeared a new polygamy and polyandry, which, in some cases, almost reached promiscuity. It was a terrific social revolution, and yet some traces were retained of the former group life, and the chief remaining institution was the priest or medicine man. He early appeared on the plantation and found his function as the healer of the sick, the interpreter of the unknown, the comforter of the sorrowing, the supernatural avenger of wrong and the one who rudely, but picturesquely, expressed the longing, disappointment and resentment of a stolen and oppressed people."

Before we proceed, it will be well for us to make a résumé of the ground already covered. We have shown that the genetic method of explaining things by the principle of growth by and through development, the comparative method of showing how all religions necessarily appeal to some fundamental element in human nature, is entirely forgotten and lost sight of when we study the Negro's religion, when in reality the Negro's religion is not outside of the stream of the general religious development of mankind. His religion is not, as commonly supposed, a phenomenon that is separate and apart from the historical development of the human race. In his religion, as in the white man's religion, we see but stages in the evolution of human thought. The colored man is gradually shuffling off his old superstitions and absorbing from his environment materials for further growth.

The presentation of a religion whose heaven and hell gave his imagination room to play, the presentation of a God and Saviour who awakened his religious aspiration and satisfied the cravings of his spirit, the songs of Christendom that appealed to his sense of music, was what caused the transported African to embrace Christianity.

The depression of slavery caused him to rest his hopes of happiness in heaven. His utter helplessness caused him to lean upon an unseen friend for comfort. And the aspiration and longing and sorrow and cravings of the Negro burst into expression through the jubilee songs and plantation melodies. The emancipation hope may be likened to the Jewish hope of the coming of a Messiah. And the relation between sexual and religious excitement is illustrated in the emotional excitement of the Negro in the ecstacies of the religious fervor.

The consequent effect of the change in the Negro's soul life that was produced by his emancipation upon his religion must be noted. The influence of the American Missionary Association, the Freedman's Aid and Southern Educational Society, Wilberforce University, the Presbyterian and Episcopalian churches in giving the Negro an educated ministry, raised the ethical standard of his religion. The general diffusion of intelligence among the masses broadened their faith. But the irreligious tendencies of the new Negro must be noted. The sportive and epicurean tendencies of the young Negro is the reflex manifestation of the irreligion of the present day. The rise of the Gospel of industrialism, of the "Get Cash Gospel," has caused men to forget that man has higher aspiration than feeding his belly; that eating and drinking and sleeping do not circumscribe and limit man's activity. What is needed is a higher gospel than get bread and nothing but bread.

There was often a divorce between religion and ethics in the ante-bellum days, and even now the Negro has not sufficiently shaken off the influences of slavery, which disrupted family ties, and has not completely assimilated the civilization and religion of a race that differs in history and tradition from his own. But the day is breaking; the Negro will never completely lose his rich emotional endowment, but his rich emotional life will be a life directed by intelligence and controlled by the will.

*Chapter Eight*

# Is the Negro an Imitative or a Reflective Being? To What Extent Is the Present Anglo-Saxon Civilization Original and Underived?

It will be observed that I speak with what the philosopher Kant would term epideictic certainty. Perhaps it may be well for me to quote authorities: G. F. Riching's "Evidences of Progress among Colored People," DuBois's "Suppression of Slave Trade in America," Williams's "History of the Negro Race in America," William T. Alexander's "History of the Colored Race in America," Johnson's "School History of the Negro Race," Professor Daniel L. Williams's "Freedom and Progress," and H. F. Kletzing and Crogman's "The Progress of a Race" have furnished me with several facts. I read Simmons's "Men of Mark" and Wilson's "The Black Phalanx" when I was a schoolboy. But it might interest the reader to know what first inspired me to so patiently study the lives of prominent colored men. In the fall of 1896 I met two men who changed and directed the course of my life. In September, 1896, Rev. A. Clayton Powell of New Haven, Conn., was advertised to lecture in a Baptist Church in Newport, R. I., upon "The Stumbling Blocks of the Race." In company with Rev. Dr. Mahlon Van Horne, formerly consul at St. Thomas, West Indies, I attended the lecture. At the close, a tall, slender, dark-complexioned man, of stern and grave countenance, arose in the audience to express his appreciation of the address. His sentences were short, crisp and nervy; he spoke rather rapidly, but every word was clearly enunciated and he threw his whole soul, his entire personality, into what he said. Soon everyone was feverishly leaning forward listening to what he said. I eagerly hung upon his every word. I asked Dr. Van Horne who the gentleman was. Dr. Van Horne said, "That is Dr. Crummell." When Dr. Crummell sat down, a large man, with a prominent brow and a face upon which determination and a resolute will were stamped and written arose, and spoke in calm and measured words. Dignity and pride were expressed in his attitude and manner of speaking. That was George T. Downing. A recent graduate from college, I hurried forward, at the close of the meeting, to meet two men whom I had long regarded as heroes. The next day I called and spent the day with Crummell and Downing. Then every pleasant morning for two weeks Crummell and I would go down to the beach together; and such delightful conversations we had, as we looked out of Downing's window upon Bellevue Avenue, watching the gay equipages rolling by.

Crummell and Downing were then nearly eighty years old. They had been personally acquainted with all the prominent white and colored abolitionists and had been eye-witnesses of and actors in some of the most stirring anti-slavery scenes. They told me of Remond and DeGrasse of Boston, of Reason and Dr. McCune Smith of New York, of Purvis and Forten of Philadelphia, of Ward and Nell, Still, Wells, Brown, Garnett, Varshon and Frederick G. Barbadoes, the prominent colored abolitionists. In the summer of 1898, I met Mr. William Burr of Norwich, Conn., then a colored barber over seventy years old. He, too, had participated in some of the events of those days. He confirmed what Crummell and Downing had told me and added several new facts. In some respects he was one of the most remarkable self-made colored men I have ever met. His judgment was so sane and unerring, his estimates of men and women were so critical, his ideals were so high, the language that flowed from his lips was so beautiful, his literary tastes were so fine and true, there was such an air of refinement about the man that even his shabby clothes could not conceal, that I spent hours at his house, talking with him. At one time he and Jefferies of Meriden wielded considerable influence in their respective communities. The infirmities of age, with his failing eyesight, prevented his making much money at his calling; but he had seen better days.

Then, the last year that I attended Harvard, I boarded with Mr. Emery T. Morris of Parker Street, Cambridge. Colonel Higginson said that he had never met a man colored or white who had more books dealing with the anti-slavery movement and Negro question. Morris had gathered together books and pamphlets that are now out of print and that were written by colored people and about colored people thirty, forty, fifty, sixty and seventy years ago. What is the significance of all this? Why, prior to my meeting Crummell and Downing, I didn't rate colored men so highly. I had been a student with and under white men so long that I, a colored man, had absorbed and assimilated the Anglo-Saxon's attitude towards the Negro intellect. And I am afraid that many colored men are now as I was then. Every time a colored man distinguishes himself at Yale or Harvard or rises to eminence, as a writer, educator, inventor, fortune accumulator, lawyer or physician, the whole country is surprised and astonished. Imagine my surprise when Downing and Crummell informed me that fifty, sixty and seventy-five years ago there were colored men living in Boston, New York and Philadelphia who were looked upon in those days as intellectual prodigies and literary curiosities. Imagine my surprise when I learned that John V. DeGrasse was admitted to the Massachusetts Medical Society in August, 1854, and that Charles Remand was seriously considered as a prospective member of an exclusive Boston literary society in the early fifties. Imagine my surprise when Downing one day read me what a white man had written in the early fifties about Rev. Samuel Ringgold Ward, rating him as a scholar and logician far above Douglass. Imagine my surprise when I heard that George B. Vashon received an A.B. degree from Oberlin College in 1843. I told Downing then that someday I would write a book or booklet about the colored heroes of the anti-slavery days, and behold the hour is at hand when the desire and wish is to be gratified.

When I think what high-minded and high-spirited colored men and women lived in the stirring times that preceded the Civil War, I wonder why the spirit of those heroic men does not live in the colored editors, educators, preachers, politicians and business men of to-day. I wonder why so many of them will, like Esau of old, sell their spiritual birthright for a mess of pottage, bartering away their own manhood and the rights of the race they represent for a petty political job or for a position in, or subscription for, a petty school. At last, I have discovered the answer. The Negro is largely an imitative being and is largely the reflex image of the white man.[1] Thus, the aristocratic colored man of Charleston is the reflex image of the white aristocrat, and the sporting Negro of New York City is the reflex image of the sporting white man. The insolent and impudent Negro of Georgia is the reflex image of the arrogant and coarse "Georgia cracker."

1. Some readers may find Ferris's language off-putting here, given our contemporary racial sensibilities. I remind the reader that this was an actual ethnological debate at the turn of the twentieth century and builds off the questions Ferris puts forth in his piece titled "Typical Negro Traits," *American Missionary* 62, no. 4 (1908): 99–102. Ferris is in fact making a revolutionary intervention into the inclination behind much of the work and literature produced at the turn of the century. Much as Frantz Fanon calls for an actional man in *Black Skin, White Masks*, trans. Richard Philcox (New York: Grove Press, 1967), Ferris asks for a reflective capacity to be demonstrated by the American Negro, whom he will soon term the "Negrosaxon." This work cuts against the current Hegelian framing of Du Bois's description of the Negro's spiritual strivings. Ferris suggests an evolutionary model and a critical mode that originates from, or rather differentiates itself from, the Anglo-Saxon spiritually—being of a different type and kind altogether. This situates the debates of the day much differently than do previous texts encountered.

Whatever the white man approves of or admires, that the Negro will admire, too. If the white man admires most the bold lion, like Douglass, every Negro will try to be a little Fred Douglass. If the white man approves of a cautious, conservative educator and industrialist of the Booker T. Washington type, then you will observe a change of front among the Negroes. Little, petty, industrial schools will suddenly spring up all over the country. Colored ministers will have a little industrial attachment to their churches. Nearly every Negro will become a little Booker T. Washington, and then the Negroes will regard it as an unspeakable crime for a colored man to attempt to assert his rights as a man and an American citizen. The Negro is usually a thermometer which registers the ideas and opinions of the white persons he works for or associates with. Why, once I met two colored men, one in Georgia and another in South Carolina, who were unusually proud, haughty and self-assertive. And, behold, I found that one had been raised with, and another had worked for, Benjamin Tillman, and he was their ideal. In Booker T. Washington we see the faint reflection of General Armstrong and New York plutocrats. Why, I can tell what sort of people the white people of any community are by associating with the Negro.

In the Boston, New York, Philadelphia, Washington, Wilmington, Charleston, Savannah and Louisville Negroes, I see a reflection of the civilization, or lack of civilization, of the Boston, New York, Philadelphia, Washington, Wilmington, Charleston, Savannah and Louisville white man. The white man cannot ascend higher in the scale of civilization than the Negro can follow. Charles Sumner might be heroic and aristocratic but a George T. Downing can grow into his likeness. Beriah Green might say that his blood would dry up in his veins before he would endorse slavery and Alexander Crummell, his pupil, catches the fire of his spirit.

Now, the Negro, to me, is an interesting being. He not only imitates the dress and manners of his white brother, but absorbs and assimilates his civilization and the ideas upon which that civilization is based. In Charleston, S. C., I met an uneducated colored man who was the prince of gentlemen, he was a Lord Chesterfield in his manner, and his ideals were high and fine and true. In him, I saw a reflection of the finest type of the Caucasian aristocracy of Charleston. He spoke of the white people of Charleston, what they say and think, as though he were one of them. The Negro is a perceptive, imaginative and emotional being. He has a creative and constructive imagination. He is original as a thinker and productive as an inventor. Why, then, is he an imitative being? Why, simply because the American white man, whom he imitates, who is his god, is an imitative being, too.

In my travels I believe that I have met three colored men who were original thinkers, three men who could sit in judgment upon the American civilization and critically dissect and analyze the ideas upon which it is based. They were Alexander Crummell, Edward Blyden and Hon. Archibald H. Grimke. All three were profound students of history. Crummell completed his education in Cambridge University, England, and lived for several years in Africa; Blyden lived most of his life in Africa and visited England frequently; Grimke completed his education at Harvard. They could compare and contrast the American civilization with the civilization of other times and other countries. In order for a man to pass from the imitative to the reflective stage of self-consciousness, in order for him to set up a higher ideal than that his own age and country affords, he must take a deep dive into history and philosophy.

I have said that the American white man is an imitative being. Of the epoch-making discoveries in science, biology and medicine very few originated in America. Newton, Laplace, Copernicus, Clerk Maxwell, Hertz, Marconi, Helmholtz, Lord Kelvin, Roentgen, Darwin, Huxley, Spencer, Pasteur, Koch, Metchnikoff and Professor Willard Gibbs of Yale, these are the men around whom modem science has revolved. And only one of these is an American. Some critic may point to Edison, the inventor, but Edison has not discovered any new principles in electricity as Tesla has. Edison and the other American inventors have merely applied the principles. And Granville Woods, the Negro electrician of Cincinnati, has done the same thing. Then, going to the realm of speculative philosophy, going back to the time of Jonathan Edwards and coming down to the present day, I find only two American philosophers—Professor Ladd of Yale and Professor Royce of Harvard. I find only two American psychologists—Professor Ladd of Yale and Professor James of Harvard, who have made a positive contribution to philosophy and psychology. Professor Ladd derived his starting point from Kant, Lotze and Wundt, three German philosophers, and Professor Royce derived his starting point from Kant and Hegel, two German philosophers. Hon. William T. Harris, United States Commissioner of Education, the world's greatest interpreter of Hegel, built upon Hegel.

Professor John Watson of Kingston, Canada; Professor Edward Caird of England, and the late Thomas Hill Green and John Caird, probably the most potent English philosophers of the nineteenth century, received their cue from Hegel. The gifted Seth brothers went back to Hegel for their point of view. Professor Howison of California is a Neo-Kantian; so we can safely say that all of the profoundest English and American philosophers of the nineteenth century are Neo-Kantians, Neo-Hegelians or Neo-Lotzians or they represent a fusing and blending and developing of ideas of these three philosophers.

I will go a step further. What have we in Thomas Carlyle, the greatest prose writer the Anglo-Saxon race has yet produced, but German idealism grafted onto Carlyle's rugged dyspeptic nature? What have we in Carlyle's "Sartor Resartus," his masterpiece, but German idealism breaking into expression in poetry and eloquence, and somehow or other mingled with Scotch wit, humor, pathos and cynicism. As Professor Beers of Yale would put it, in Carlyle we see "the hot heart of the Scotch married to the transcendental dream of Germany." What have we in Coleridge but a reflection of German idealism? Then, take Emerson, the most original mind America has produced, and what have we but Yankee keeness and shrewdness and Puritanic moral fibre, touched and transfigured by Oriental mysticism and Platonic and German idealism?

I will go a step further. The Anglo-Saxon race has contributed no new ideas to civilization. Some of the ideas which underlie its civilization were contributed by the Hebrew race, others by the Greek race, others by the Roman race, and others by the German theologians and philosophers. If the Anglo-Saxon race has any genius, it is the genius of common sense. In Grant we see the genius of common sense applied to war, in Hon. James Bryce and Elihu Root we see the genius of common sense applied to law and statesmanship. In Professor Ladd, Professor Sneath and Professor Duncan of Yale and Professor Royce of Harvard, we see the genius of common sense applied to philosophy. In Professors Sumner, Adams and Wheeler of Yale and Professor Hart of Harvard we see the genius of common sense applied to history. In Professor Seymour of Yale we see the genius of common sense applied to the Greek language and literature. In the late Dean Everett and Professor Toy of Harvard we see the genius of common sense applied to theology. In Charles Eliot Norton of Harvard we see the genius of common sense applied to art and literature. In Professor Palmer of Harvard we see the genius of common sense applied to ethics, and in Deans Wright and Phillips of Yale we see the genius of common sense applied to the administration of practical affairs. In Professor H. A. Beers, Professor William Lyon Phelps and Professor A. S. Cook of Yale we see this genius applied to literature. What do I mean by the genius of common sense? The Anglo-Saxon intellect does not, like Plato, the Greek idealist, or Luther, Schleiermacher, Kant, Fichte, Schelling and Hegel, the German philosophers and theologians, spin and weave a system of theology and philosophy out of its own mind. It does not, like Rousseau, evolve a theory of natural rights out of its own brain. Kant for twenty-five years brooded over and meditated upon the problem of sense perception, upon the problem of how the mind can know anything at all, and then he revolutionized modern philosophy, so that he is justly called the Copernicus of modern philosophy, the man that was the pivot around which modern philosophy revolved. What do I mean by this?

This is how the Anglo-Saxon mind acts. I was a student of Professor Ladd for three years. Successively the philosophers Kant, Lotze, Wundt, Schopenhauer, Riehl and Bradley were laid upon the dissecting table and critically analyzed by Professor Ladd's searching and penetrating intellect. As a result of such critical analysis, certain fundamental physical, psychological, moral, aesthetical and religious facts were disclosed and revealed as facts that must be accepted as the fundamental truths of our human experience. Then came the problem, how can such facts be harmonized in a theory of the universe that shall be self-explanatory and self-consistent? And then Professor Ladd proceeded to construct his system of philosophy. He built it out of the facts that emerged as the result of his critical analysis. Professor Royce constructed his system of philosophy by analyzing the four fundamental conceptions of being and then constructively synthesizing the results of such analysis. And I might go on still further. The philosophy of the Declaration of Independence is not the product of Thomas Jefferson's brain. That philosophy originated in the minds of Rousseau, Voltaire, Diderot and the French encyclopaediacs of the eighteenth century.

What has the great Anglo-Saxon race contributed to civilization? It has contributed its spirit. The love of liberty, the desire for personal independence and insistence that reverence and respect be paid to its personality is an inborn quality of the Anglo-Saxon mind. And that is the issue in the South. The Southerner does not dread physical contact or nearness to the Negro as much as the Northerner does. The presence of thousands of mulattoes, quadroons and octoroons in America is a living witness. Whence the ground of the race friction in the South? The Southerner demands that the Negro look up to him as a superior being, as a sort of demigod. If the Negro will but acknowledge his inferiority, mentally, morally and physically, to the Southerner, will but recognize him as lord and master, and will but say to him, with upraised hands, on bended knee, "My lord and my god, what will thou have me to do?" why the Negro will have a friend who will "stand by him until hell freezes over," as one Southern aristocrat put it; he will have a master who will be lenient with his shortcomings and deficiencies. But if, on the other hand, the Negro says, "I am a man the same as you are. You are dealing with a man and not a slave," then there will be war to the knife and the knife buried up to the hilt. The recognition of the importance of his own selfhood and the demand that others recognize it, that is the fundamental fact in the Anglo-Saxon's history.

The Anglo-Saxon is the greatest fighting race that has yet appeared upon the stage of history, combining aggressive force with dogged determination and a bulldog grit and tenacity of purpose, combining a daring, adventurous spirit with the ability to fight a hard, uphill battle. I believe the English-speaking people could stand off the combined armies of the entire world. Then in the leaders of New England transcendentalism and the anti-slavery movement we see this rugged strength blossoming into the fruit and flower of Christian kindness. But I do not believe the Anglo-Saxon intellect has the versatility of the Greek mind, and except occasionally in a Professor William James, the scintillating brilliancy of the French mind, or the speculative depth of the German mind.

On the other hand, is there such a thing as real originality? No one thinker, by solitary meditation, ever spun the philosophy and theology prevailing to-day out of his own unaided intellect. The world's system of thought is a stream that was fed from a thousand channels. Ideas from Hebrew, Greek, Roman and German sources have all contributed to make Christianity what it is to-day. Aristotle, the greatest intellect the Greek race has yet produced, sat at the feet of Plato, the prince of idealists, and Plato was a pupil of Socrates, who had derived his inspiration from Anaxagoras. Even the philosopher Kant, the father of modern philosophy, said that it was Hume who roused him out of his dogmatic slumber. Thus it has ever been in the world of thought. One thinker has added somewhat to the stock of thought and knowledge that was furnished him by his predecessors.

Rarely, in the world of science, has a great discovery or invention suddenly sprung from the brain of one thinker alone, like Archimedes' discovery of the law and principle governing the buoyancy of water, Newton's discovery of the law of gravitation, Harvey's discovery of the circulation of the blood, Isaac Watts' invention of the steam engine or Roentgen's discovery of the X-ray. Usually there has been a series of steps preparing the way for the epoch-making discovery. Darwin had his forerunners, who blazed the way for him. Few discoveries and inventions are suddenly shot out of the mind of one thinker, who had none to prepare the way for him. Not at a single bound was the palatial and commodious ocean liner evolved from the dugout of the savage, or the locomotive that pulls the Empire State express evolved from the old-fashioned stage coach, or the record-breaking automobile evolved out of the wagon; but many stages were passed through before the modern steamship, the modern locomotive and the modern automobile were evolved.

Some may point to Marconi's sending a message across the sea as a refutation of what I say. Clerk Maxwell had to prove theoretically the existence of electric waves, Hertz had to actually discover the electric wave, someone had to invent the ball oscillator, then the coherer and decoherer, someone had to conceive the idea of similarly tuned instruments, someone had to formulate the system of Morse letters before Marconi could send or receive a message by wireless telegraphy across the seas.

It is a law of the human mind and it applies to the Negro, Anglo-Saxon, French, German, Roman, Greek and Hebrew intellect, that the mind must first be roused to action by stimuli from the outside world before it unfolds its latent capacity and develops as a reasoning, moral and religious being. Material facts, physical, mental, moral, aesthetic and religious, must first be presented to the mind before it can construct its physical world, its world of thought, its moral world and its religious world out of them. The prophet Moses differs from the worshipper of Baal because he reacts in a different manner to his moral and religious environment. The poets Tennyson and Wordsworth differ from ordinary men because they see in the "flower in the crannied wall" and in "the clouds that gather round the setting sun" that which the ordinary man does not see; Carlyle differs from the ordinary man because the French Revolution starts in motion and sets in operation trains of thought and reflection that they do not to the ordinary man. The man of genius differs from the ordinary man because he constructs a more magnificent edifice out of the material presented to him by his experience.

Civilization moves forward by one race appropriating the achievements of another race and adding to it. Greece absorbed and assimilated the civilization of Egypt. Rome absorbed and assimilated the civilization of Greece. The barbarians, who swept over the Roman frontier and captured Rome, were awed by the Roman civilization, as expressed in the Christian religion, and it took them over one thousand years to absorb and assimilate the civilization of Rome. The so-called Dark Ages mean that the English, French, German and Spanish people were, for ten silent centuries, slowly taking in and mentally digesting the ideas underlying the Roman civilization. And then the revival of learning, the rediscovery of the Greek world means that at the close of the Middle Ages, the mediaeval mind bathed and steeped and saturated itself in the Greek civilization. The Protestant Reformation, however, was a distinctly forward move. It resulted from the brooding and meditation of a lonely monk in his cell. Some say that the Reformation would have come anyway without Martin Luther. But it would not have come so soon and would not have taken the form that it did.

So, then, when the American Negro builds the ideas underlying the American civilization into the structure and texture of his mental and moral life, he is only doing what mankind has ever done. The question remains, Is the Negro a reflective as well as an imitative being? Kelly Miller is not the only Negro scholar or writer who is endowed with an analytical mind. Mr. L. M. Hershaw of Washington, a graduate of whom Atlanta University may well be proud, is a logician and dialectician. And he is not the only Negro, unknown to fame, who is gifted with a keen and penetrating mind. The fact that the Cuffes, in the eighteenth century, petitioned for their rights as Negroes; the fact that colored men formed an anti-slavery society in 1831, seven years before the big anti-slavery society; the fact that Downing, Crummell and Garnett, as boys in New York City, formed an anti-slavery society, shows that the Negro has done some thinking for himself in the past.

But in the last ten or twelve years he seems to have taken his ideas ready-made from his Caucasian friends, and to have let his Caucasian friends do his thinking for him. In a blind, naive, unquestioning and unreflective manner, he has accepted whatever Mars' John has told him. If Mars' John tells Aunt Dinah that it is dangerous for her boy to go to college, if Mars' John tells Ephraim Jim Crow cars are good for him, medicine for the weary soul, if Mars' John tells Sambo that God didn't intend the Negro to be a voter and office-holder, why Aunt Dinah, Ephraim and Sambo will forego their right to think for themselves. Why is it there seems to be a fatalistic tendency in the Negro's nature? He submits gracefully to fate and bows to the inevitable. He submissively submitted to slavery. He accepted Booker T. Washington as a leader without hardly an audible murmur or dissenting voice, when Washington asked the Negro to forego those rights and privileges which the Anglo-Saxon race has ever held dear. The Negro can easily adjust and adapt himself to a changed condition and a different environment.

I have seen colored men and women suddenly step from prosperity to adversity, from wealth and affluence to poverty and pauperism. I have seen one United States Congressman, who was once wealthy, eking out a living by doing menial jobs. I have seen a prominent business man become a janitor. I have seen cultured and refined preachers who once were pastors of large, wealthy and aristocratic churches, take small and poor churches. I have seen colored persons who once lived in palatial mansions living in huts. And they bore this change of fortune with good grace. They accepted it philosophically. The reason why the Negro surrenders his individuality to the Anglo-Saxon is not because he is conquered by the Anglo-Saxon's intellect but by his will. The Negro has the plastic nature and temperament which conforms to its present environment instead of moulding its environment to the likeness of its ideal.

But the day is breaking. The Negro is going back to the temper that prevailed in the days of Crummell, Downing and Garnett. The Boston Guardian, DuBois's "Souls of Black Folk," DuBois's "Moon," "The Voice of the Negro," the Boston riot in the summer of 1903, the recent Niagara movement and the recent Macon conference to me are very significant facts. Some people see in them only jealousy of Mr. Washington on the part of overeducated Negroes. But I see deeper. It has been repeatedly said that the Negro is a child race. Well, these seven happenings and the successful attempt of the colored people of Darien, Ga., to avert a threatened lynching, the refusal of the Thomasville, Ga., colored people to have anything to do with a fair and show that barred them on Washington's birthday, the attempt of the Jacksonville, Fla., colored people to challenge the legality of the Jim Crow law in the city of Jacksonville, and their subsequent boycotting of the Jim Crow cars, the fact that the colored people of Nashville ran busses of their own rather than ride in the Jim Crow street cars, Professor W. H. H. Hart's winning his case against the Maryland Jim Crow law in January, 1905, Professor Kelly Miller's reply to Dixon's Leopard Spots, the articles of Archibald Grimke and J. Wilson in the Atlantic Monthly, all these indicate that the Negro mind has roused itself from the former lethargy and that the Negro is beginning to think for himself.

Some people do not take the Niagara movement or the recent Macon conference seriously. They have been so accustomed to think of the Negro as a happy-go-lucky fellow, with simian traits well developed, that they pass lightly by with a toss of the head or a wave of the hand anything that he says or writes. It has been repeatedly said that the Negro race is a child race. But the movements and events referred to above indicate that the Negro has emerged from childhood to manhood. He is no longer a child but a man who has put away his childish clothes and toys, his childish way of looking at the world and viewing life. He has passed from the imitative to the reflective stage and DuBois is the leader of those who are in the reflective stage.

What do I mean? A Negro is in the imitative stage of self-consciousness when he swallows whole and gulps down everything his Caucasian friends tell him. Those colored men who look cross-eyed at the higher education of the Negroes, who regard the ballot box as a dangerous quicksand or a mirage in the desert, who regard Jim Crow cars as a boon and blessing in disguise, because Uncle Jonathan and Mars' John tell him the two former things are poison to him and the latter thing something God intended him to have, are imitative beings.

But when old Uncle Eff, Uncle Mingo, or young Caesar, Scipio, Pompey, and Rastus begin to scratch their heads and thus soliloquize, "Is what is meat for the white man, poison for the Negro? If voting and office-holding are good for the white man, why are they not good for me? My Caucasian friends make light of my rights. And yet the pages of English and American history, which tell how English and American statesmen, orators, soldiers and patriots struck out for their liberties and their rights are the pages which are lighted up with a divine lustre and glow. In order to have liberty to worship God, as their consciences directed, the Pilgrim fathers left their happy homes in England, faced the terrors of an ocean voyage and braved the rigors of a New England winter on a bleak and barren coast. For the sake of a principle the American colonists refused to pay a petty tax that would not affect their pocketbooks to any appreciable extent, and thus forced a terrible war upon themselves. And now, my Anglo-Saxon friend, asks me to hold lightly the principles that he has treasured so highly and regarded so sacredly. On George Washington's birthday, Decoration Day and Fourth of July orators will tell of the courage of the Revolutionary soldiers at Valley Forge, they will tell of the brave Netherlanders who said, 'We will cut down the dykes and give Holland back to the sea' before we will yield to Spain. And yet they ask me to be Jim-Crowed. Now does my Caucasian friend think I haven't any intelligence or any feelings? Does he think that I do not recognize an insult and resent a snub?"

When I say the colored brother asks these questions, he has passed from the imitative to the reflective stage.

The Anglo-Saxon gods and goddesses, throned high upon the rugged heights of Mount Olympus, and basking in the sunshine of prosperity, hear the grumblings, complainings and mutterings rising from the vale below. They lean over the edge of the mount, look down into the valley and ask, "What is this noise that I hear? What is the matter with the colored people? Do they want to be invited to the feasts of the gods? Do they want to drink of our ambrosial nectar at our banquets? Do they want to listen to this seraphic music and view the intoxicating splendors of this dreamland?[")]

No. Old Uncle Eff and young Rastus are not languishing and pining away, or dying of grief and sorrow because they are not invited to the banquet of the Olympian dieties. They don't care a picayune or one scintilla about being invited to the private dinners, private parties, private receptions and private dances of their Caucasian neighbors. They do not desire to marry any of the Olympian goddesses, because they have handsome women, dazzling beauties in their own race, whose souls are as pure and fresh as the morning dew, whose honor is as stainless and unsullied as the snow when it first falls from the ethereal dome.

Then Father Zeus, who used to feast with the blameless Ethiopians, will ask, "Well, then, what is the matter with DuBois and Trotter and the men who are interested in the Niagara movement and Macon conference?" I will tell you,—the colored brother wants his humanity recognized. He wants to be treated as a human being and not as an animal. He, whose brawn and muscle, whose toil and sweat has developed the resources of the Southland, and for two hundred years has sustained and made possible the aristocracy of the South, desires to receive citizenship on the same terms that are offered to the ignorant and illiterate foreigner who seeks an asylum in this country. He asks the labor unions and employers in the North and West to give him a man's chance to earn an honest living. In a word, he asks for civil, political and industrial equality, in a country that is the haven for the persecuted and oppressed of every land and clime.

In my travels in the Southland, I have met Southern aristocrats from whose hearts the very milk of human kindness flows towards the Negro. In Mr. Smith, the city editor of the Charleston News and Courier, I have met a gentleman who is as noble-hearted as Editor E. H. Clement of the Boston Transcript. I realize, too, that there are some bad and vicious Negroes in the Southland and that they need to be handled with kid gloves off. But the Southerner does not discriminate and distinguish between the first class and the low down Negroes.

I will take Savannah for instance. Tom Dixon speaks of the Negroes of Savannah being impudent. I have met more insolent and ill-mannered Negroes in Savannah than in any other town I have ever been in. On the other hand, the colored brother may be seen at his best in Savannah. Along literary, political and financial lines, he has reached a high state of civilization.

There is the Men's Sunday Club of which Professor M. N. Work of the Georgia State Industrial College was the president, and of which Mr. G. S. Williams and E. W. Houston, both brilliant men, were active workers. Every Sunday, cultured and handsomely dressed men and women meet there and listen to a splendid literary and musical programme. Then, once a month, they invite some distinguished man to lecture for them in the Beach Institute Lecture Course. Professor George B. Hurd, a New England white man, is principal of the popular Beach Institute. Then there is the Colored Republican Poll Tax Club of Chatham County, of which J. C. Williams is president, James T. Burton, secretary, and the brilliant lawyer, H. A. Macbeth, chairman of the executive committee. This impresses upon the youth the duties of citizenship and inculcates civic pride to virtue.

Then there is the Metropolitan Mercantile and Realty Company, of which J. W. Armstrong was general manager and F. M. Cohen, teller and cashier; the Wage Earners' Loan and Investment Company, of which L. E. Williams was president and W. S. Scott is secretary and treasurer; and the Union Savings and Loan Company, of which L. S. Reed is president, D. C. Suggs, vice president, J. T. Burton, secretary, T. M. Bell, treasurer; H. A. Macbeth, attorney; and W. A. Newsome and Wylly A. Thrash, two of the directors. I believe that it would be difficult to find three more wide-awake, aggressive and up-to-date business men than J. W. Armstrong, L. S. Reed and H. A. Macbeth. In Dr. T. B. Belcher we see a physician of the finest type, and Sol. C. Johnson is the progressive editor of the Savannah Tribune. So, after all, if Tom Dixon says there are some impudent Negroes in Savannah, there are also some very intelligent and refined colored people. And my bone of contention with the

Southern white man is that he does not recognize the presence of the higher and better class of colored people.

To return to the point from which we have digressed. Is the Negro an imitative or reflective being? The Negro who believes in the Niagara movement, in the Macon conference, in the "Souls of Black Folk," and in the principles enunciated in this book is a reflective being. The Negro who does not, is an imitative being. Ask any Negro if he thinks DuBois has the key to the solution of the Negro problem. If he says "No," he is an imitative being. If he says "Yes," he is a reflective being.

I have long been thinking of writing a book of some thousand pages along the lines laid down in this chapter. DuBois's "Suppression of the Slave Trade in America," Williams's "History of the Negro Race in America," are masterpieces. But no discriminating accounts of colored history-makers have been written yet. All of the books eulogizing the great Negroes lack the historian's perspective. Giants, pygmies and ordinary men are thrown together, and you can't tell the heavy-weights from the light-weights. None of them combine the philosophic grasp of a Thucydides with Plutarch's insight into men and motives, and Carlyle's dramatic instinct, which seizes the spectacular events in a man's or nation's life and paints the heroes in flesh and blood colors, so that you can see them living, moving, struggling and striving, yea points them in a way to stir the blood and thrill the nerves. Sometimes I think the story of the great men and women of the race could be written so that it would read like a romance. That is the way DuBois has treated Alexander Crummell in his "Souls of Black Folk."

It is said that Aesop, the creator of those famous fables; Terence, the Latin poet; Alexander Hamilton, the constructive statesman; Robert Browning, the English poet; Henry Timrod, the poet of South Carolina, and General Lew Wallace, the novelist of Indiana, were of Negro descent and had a slight strain of Negro blood in their veins. Whether or no[t] this is true, I do not know. But this has been asserted by both white and colored scholars. I believe that such sane thinkers as E. H. Clement, of the Boston *Transcript*, and Professor W. E. Burghardt DuBois believe it possible that these gifted writers may have been one-fourth or one-eighth or one-sixteenth Negro. It is claimed that one of the great-grandmothers of Hamilton, Browning and Timrod were Africans or mulattoes. That would make them octoroons or one-sixteenth Negro. You may lay it down as an axiom that in nineteen cases out of twenty DuBois is right when he makes an assertion about the Negro. He is cautious and conservative as well as heroic and poetic. Whether these assertions about these men are true or not, I trust that this book will be a storehouse of information, a mine teeming with rich and pregnant factors. Whether I have found any nuggets amongst the dross, or discovered any ore in the rocks, the perusal of this book will disclose.

## *Chapter Nine*

# Reason Why the Term "Negrosaxon," or Colored, Better Characterizes the Colored People of Mixed Descent in America than the term "Negro"

### I. INTRODUCTORY REMARKS. MY POINT OF VIEW

Scholars and scientists are in despair as to what term will best classify the hybrid and ostracized group of individuals who are known in America as "Negroes," "colored people," and "Afro-Americans." "Negro" will not do, because that ethnologically refers to the full-blooded Negro in Africa, or of African descent living elsewhere, whereas more than fifty per cent of the colored population in America has more or less of Anglo-Saxon blood in its veins and ten per cent has Indian blood or the blood of the Indian, Jewish, Spanish, Italian, French and German races in their veins; "colored" may not do because the Indians, Mexicans, Chinese, Japanese and Philippinos are colored people as well as the American Negro. While not a scientific, it is a good colloquial term.

"Afro-American" will not do, because it is a geographical rather than an ethnological term.[1] The Canadians, Indians, Mexicans and Brazilians are just as much Americans as the citizens of the United States. And the Egyptians, Berbers, Arabs, Phoenicians and Carthaginians are just as much natives of Africa as the Negroes. What word will do then? Why, Negrosaxon, or colored.

---

1. This is a key moment in the text. Notice his distinction between the geographic and the ethnological, which aims to tell us the purpose, the development/evolution, of a racial stock.

We must remember that the colored race is a heterogeneous group of individuals in whose veins Negro, Indian, Jewish, Celtic, Teutonic and Latin blood is mingled, rather than a homogeneous race.[2] The colored race has no ethnological integrity. It does not spring from the same stock, has not similar physical and psychological traits and characteristics, nor common ideals. The force that welds it together does not come from within, but from without. The colored race is held together by adhesion rather than by cohesion. It is the oppression of a more powerful and more dominant race, rather than similar physical characteristics, similar race ideals that bind the colored people in America into a unity. When the external pressure and oppression is removed, it will fly apart. Why, because there is nothing to hold it together, no inward or compelling impulse which unites and binds together the different molecules and particles.

The machine is constructed by an external artificer. He puts it together or pulls it apart, piece by piece. He gives it an artificial unity by a mechanical arrangement of parts. When that mechanical arrangement of parts is changed, the machine collapses. But the organism has its principle of growth residing within it. That life principle in its growth development, unfolds itself in that inner structure and constitution that gives its unity to organism. Only when the life principle is affected, the vital process interfered with, does the organism die. Break the hour hand, minute hand and second hand of a watch and it is no longer a watch. Remove the wheels, the cow catcher, etc., and leave only the boiler and furnace and burning fuel and you no longer have a locomotive. But you can lop off all the limbs and branches of a tree, and it is still a tree, as long as there is the inward vitality. For it will put forth, from its resident and unimpaired forces, new limbs and branches, shoot forth new buds and blossoms and come to fruitage in new leaves and flowers. You may cut off a man's limbs; but as long as his brain centers, his lungs, heart, liver and kidneys, the vital organs are unimpaired, he will live on,—he is still a man. Now, the Negrosaxon or colored race in America has a mechanical and artificial rather than an inner and organic unity like the Anglo-Saxon or Jewish races. The integrity of the Negrosaxon or colored race in America will be destroyed the moment Anglo-Saxon caste prejudice is destroyed or removed. But the integrity of the Anglo-Saxon and Jewish races will not be destroyed until they amalgamate with other races and lose their predominating physical and psychological race traits and tendencies, and their peculiar and inexplicable psychical, moral and religious ideals.[3]

2. So much for the idea that Black thinkers uncritically accepted racial determinism. Ferris acknowledges the plurality of racial constitution in the American Negro.

3. Ferris rejects the idea that racial solidarity can simply be environmental or historical. He is arguing for a spiritual/ethnological integrity.

Then, again, the Negrosaxon or colored race in America has no spiritual integrity, no common religious hopes and beliefs and aspirations like the Jewish race. In the Babylonian, Assyrian, Greek and Roman dispersion of the Jews, caused by the Babylonians, Assyrians, Greeks and Romans conquering the Jews and carrying some away into captivity, the Jews were scattered all over the world two thousand and nearly three thousand years ago. To-day there are American Jews, English Jews, French Jews, German Jews, Russian Jews, Palestinian Jews and Armenian Jews. Yet the world over the Jew is the same dogged, determined, resourceful individual with a genius for finance. They have no home, no nationality, they are not a farming or manufacturing people, they live by buying and selling the products of other men's toil and labor, by lending money and banking. Two thousand years ago there was a saying current in Rome, "There is only one thing in the world more despicable than a poor Jew and that is a rich Jew." But to-day, some of America's most noted philanthropists and most brilliant preachers belong to the Hebrew race, which has produced some noble men and women. The school teacher who inspired me, a schoolboy nine years old, with the desire and ambition to rise in the world was a Jewess, Miss Fannie Ullman, one of the noblest women that gifted race has ever produced. But what causes the Jewish race, scattered all over the world, to hang together and to preserve the same psychical and psychological race traits and tendencies. It is their race pride and peculiar religious beliefs which prevents their intermarrying with other races and losing their race identity and individuality. Now, this Negrosaxon has not this Hebrew pride of race, or Hebrew religious pride that its race was the chosen people of God. His only God is the God that he borrowed from the Anglo-Saxon.

Again, the Negrosaxon has no territorial, geographical integrity or community of political ideas. The Englishman in Australia, China or India has a country he can call his own, a government that can protect him, a political history and political traditions that he is proud of, and certain political ideals of justice and liberty that he believes in. That is why the Englishman is an Englishman the world over. Now, the colored man is a pariah in American society. There is no country he can call his own. He is a social and political outcast. His only political faith is the political faith of a country that rejects him as a citizen and does not regard him as a full-fledged man. Now, how shall we name and classify a heterogeneous and discrete group of individuals, who have no racial, territorial, geographical and political integrity, who are not unified by a peculiar religious faith as are the Jews, or the scattered Bedouin tribes under the Mohammedan religion, and who are only held together by the iron hand of American caste prejudice. Name them by the predominant bloods that enter into their composition? Negro and Anglo-Saxon blood predominates in the colored population of the United States. For in the Southland the bulk of slave holders and overseers who had children by the slave women were pure Anglo-Saxons. And while the colored people of America cannot boast of the manner in which they came by their white blood, they at least have this consolation,—most of the Caucasian blood that flows in Negrosaxon veins is the blood of Southern aristocrats. If, then, Negro blood is in every colored person in America and Anglo-Saxon in over fifty per cent, why not call the colored American a Negrosaxon? I am justified in my observations, for I know two noted colored educators who are black or very dark in complexion and yet their grandfathers were white men, and they are Anglo-Saxons. And there are many others such. The same ethnological considerations that apply to the term Anglo-Saxon applies to the term Negro-Saxon or Negrosaxon. Some may ask, why not be correct and call the colored people of America the Negro-Anglo-Saxon race? My reply will be, "for the same reason we do not call the English-speaking people, the Jute-Anglo-Saxon, Norman-French race. This is how the term Anglo-Saxon came to ethnologically characterize the English-speaking people.

When Julius Caesar began the conquest of Britain in 55 B. C., he found a Celtic race there who were known as Britons. In the fourth and fifth century, A. D., Rome was hard pressed because of the tide of barbarian invasion which was sweeping over her frontiers. Then in 407 A. D., the Roman legions were withdrawn from Britain for the purpose of helping Rome to stem the advancing tide of sturdy and rugged Goths. After the Roman soldiers were withdrawn, the peaceful and semi-civilized Britons were unable to defend themselves against the fierce Scots and Picts, who came surging like a mighty wave from Scotland and Ireland.

But meanwhile a mighty race of tall, fair-haired and blue-eyed Teutons, who were known as Saxons by the Britons, was arising in the north of Europe. They were the forerunners of those daring navigators, reckless pirates and formidable warriors who were afterwards known as the terrible Vikings, or Northmen, whose name brought terror to whatever shore in Southern Europe upon which they landed, and who afterward sailed up the Seine and sacked Paris. Three of these Saxon tribes, the Angles, Jutes and Saxons, occasionally attacked the east coast of Britain. So, imitating her mistress, Rome, who pressed into service one Gothic tribe to fight another Gothic tribe, the Britons, unable to cope with the Saxons, the wild Picts and Scots, promised the greatest fighting race known to history, land in return for services rendered in driving back the Picts and Scots. As the first tribe of Teutonic invaders who came from Northern Europe and attacked East Britons were Saxons, the Britons afterwards called the various tribes of Germanic invaders by that name. So that is how "Saxon" in the course of centuries came to ethnologically characterize the Teutonic branch of the Aryan race that conquered Britain. That is why Wendell Phillips in his oration upon Toussaint L'Ouverture could say, "Now, blue-eyed Saxon, proud of your birth," etc.

But to return to our story. In 449, the Jutes, who were the first Teutonic settlers in England, came from Jutland, landed on the Isle of Thanet in the southeastern corner of England, near the present Canterbury, and vanquished the Picts. They spread and established the kingdom of Kent. Then the Saxons and Angles came over in greater numbers. Not receiving enough land and rations to satisfy them, they turned against the race that had invited them over and swept it off the face of history. They conquered the Britons in battle after battle and absorbed the remnant that they did not exterminate and annihilate.

Thus, three Teutonic tribes, the Jutes, Saxons and Angles, invaded and conquered Britain. But only the Angles and Saxons gave their name to the race. As the first tribe of Teutonic invaders who landed in Britain were Saxons, the Britons called all Jutes, Saxons and Angles, by that name. So that is why the term Saxon has clung to the Teutonic settlers. The Jutes were few in number and formed a small and insignificant settlement. So their name was last. The Angles, who settled on the eastern coast, on the other hand, occupied the bulk of the land, a much greater portion than the Saxons, who settled on the southern shores. Hence, when the Teutonic settlers called themselves by a common name, it was Angles or English, and the island was called England. Thus Saxon is the name the conquered Britons gave to the Teutonic invaders and Angles is the name the Teutonic settlers gave to themselves, and that is how, in the course of time, they were called the Anglo-Saxon race and the language they spoke was called the Anglo-Saxon language.

But in the ninth century, four centuries after the Saxon tribes invaded Britain, Danish pirates began to make raids upon the east coast of England, and conquered the Anglo-Saxons in 1016, but their kings only ruled England for a quarter of a century. So, from 449, when the Jutes conquered the Picts, until 1066, when the Norman-French, under William the Conqueror, Duke of Normandy, crossed the English Channel and defeated Harold at the battle of Hastings, the Anglo-Saxon race was supreme in England. But the conquering Danes or Northmen, who came over from Normandy, on the northeast coast of France, and subjugated the Saxons, did not exterminate them or drive them out. They lived side by side, the Norman-French as the aristocratic and ruling, the Saxons as the serf and peasant class. Finally they mingled their blood. But why did not the conquerors, the Norman-French, give their name to the mingled language and blended race? For the first time in history, the conquered or subjugated people gave their name to the mingled language and race. How explain this ethnological and philological miracle? The answer is near at hand. Immediately there began a struggle for the supremacy of the Anglo-Saxon and the Norman-French language. It lasted for four centuries; and when, in 1475, Caxton gave the printing press to England, the Anglo-Saxon language had won the battle, two-thirds of the words in the English language being Anglo-Saxon words and only one-third being Norman-French words; and over three-fourths of the words in daily use being Anglo-Saxon words and less than one-fourth of the words being Latin-French words. So that is the race stock, at the beginning of the sixteenth century, which represented the blending of the Jutes, Angles, Saxons and Normans, who were called the Anglo-Saxon race. So we can see that by ethnological and philological laws of the survival of the fittest the race of Teutonic or Germanic settlers of Britain was called the Anglo-Saxon race. And the word Saxon, which was the name of the first Teutonic invaders of Britain, has in the course of centuries come by natural psychological and ethnological laws to be a synonym to represent the entire race of Germanic settlers in Britain. So that is why I call the race in which is mingled the blood of the Negro and Anglo-Saxon race, the Negro-Saxon or Negrosaxon race.

## II. ETHNOLOGICAL CONSIDERATIONS

Colored Americans do not belong to the Negro, but to the Negrosaxon race.

What do we mean by Negro? Most of the encyclopaedias, geographies and dictionaries define him as a black person, of African descent, low, receding forehead, knotty, kinky, woolly hair, broad, flat nose, enormous lips, a monkey grin that stretches from ear to ear, thick, coarse, heavy, brutal features, guttural utterance, flat-footed and either bow-legged or knock-kneed and usually reeking with the malodor of perspiration. He is described as an emotional and excitable creature, devoid of reason and conscience, and with the passions and instincts of a brute or beast. This is the picture that is conjured up by the words big burly Negro, and this is the picture of the Negro brute, who only represents one-tenth of one per cent of Negro society. Does this represent the Negrosaxon in America? No, the Negrosaxon varies in complexion, from deep black to blond white, in hair from woolly knots to flowing, flaxen locks; in features from heavy African to refined Caucasian. I know families in whose veins course Negro, Indian, English and Spanish blood. Does Negro ethnologically describe that group? No, the only ethnological term to describe the mixed colored population in America is Negrosaxon.

## III. PSYCHOLOGICAL CONSIDERATIONS

The colored man is not psychologically different from other individuals. One eminent Negro divine said that the colored man who points with pride to the Anglo-Saxon blood in his veins is boasting of his bastardy, and that the colored man is the only being who boasts of his bastardy. There is a large measure of truth in this. But in coining a new name to describe the colored people of mixed descent in America there is only one that is ethnologically true and that is Negrosaxon. Just as there are differences in color and hair and features in the Negrosaxons, so there are intellectual and moral differences. There are all grades of intelligence and character in the Negrosaxon race. The Negrosaxons, even those of pure Negro descent, have forsaken their African heritage and absorbed and assimilated the political, social, moral and religious ideals and conceptions, the language and religion and the social manners and customs and usages of the Anglo-Saxon race. In fact, Alexander Crummell, who became metamorphosed into a cultured and polished Englishman, was a pure-blooded Negro. And Kelly Miller, the mathematician, and Judge Joseph E. Lee, the astute politician, who possess the phlegmatic temperament and analytical mind of the Anglo-Saxon, are almost pure blacks. These three, one of whom was a pure black, the other two almost pure blacks, possess as many of the psychical and psychological characteristics of the Anglo-Saxon as any colored men I have ever met. Crummell was a born aristocrat and a born autocrat. He was an intrepid, dauntless soul and was steeped and bathed and saturated and dyed with English ideals, traditions and prejudices. And yet he had not an ounce of Caucasian blood in his veins. Kelly Miller has not the aggressiveness of the Anglo-Saxon, but, like Francis Bacon, he is the incarnation of pure intellect, and has the calm, judicial mind and cool and calculating intellect of the Anglo-Saxon. Judge Lee is as gracious and polished in his manners as a Lord Chesterfield and as shrewd, as far-seeing and as discreet and self-controlled as a Tom Platt. And yet he and Kelly Miller have very little Anglo-Saxon blood in their veins.

## IV. SOCIOLOGICAL CONSIDERATIONS

Our destiny is not to build up peculiar racial ideals, but to become American citizens. Calling ourselves Negrosaxons defines our race ideals. The American Indian was exterminated because he would not adopt the Anglo-Saxon civilization. If the Negrosaxon expects to share in the political inheritance of the Anglo-Saxon, he must be made over in the likeness of the Anglo-Saxon. He cannot bleach out his complexion, or straighten his hair, or sharpen his nose, or thin his lips. But in mind and character and disposition he must become a black white man. After the Negrosaxon has been made over into the likeness of the white man he can hope to be made over into the image of God.

I have just spoken of three Negrosaxons of pure or almost pure African descent. Take now three who have more Caucasian than Negro blood in their veins. I refer to the gifted Grimke brothers and the peerless writer and brave champion of the black folk, DuBois. Not only by blood and descent are the Grimkes from the best Huguenot stock, but in intelligence, refinement, aristocratic bearing and puritanic fibre, they are Huguenots through and through. They have not the slightest trace of Negro characteristics, although I suppose that they are one-fourth Negro. There is DuBois,—what is there Negro about him, except that he is one fourth Negro by blood and descent? While he has the poetical nature and tropical imagination and gift of language of a Negro, in intelligence, pride and sensitiveness, he is an Anglo-Saxon of the bluest blood.

I desire to say that I regard the term Negro, to characterize the mixed race, in whose veins flow Negro, Caucasian and Indian bloods, as a misnomer. It is an opprobrious, disingenuous epithet, into which has been packed all conceivable and imaginable hatred venom, disdain, contempt and odium. What causes more of a shudder or revulsion to run through the frame than the phrase, "A big, burly Negro." The term Negro is so loaded down and freighted with ignominy and contempt that the colored man who brands himself as a Negro thereby catalogues and labels himself as a being who is outside of the pale of humanity, as a being who is separate and distinct from other men. So much that is low and degrading is suggested by the name that the colored race can never hope to dignify and exalt the term.

When a colored man calls himself a Negro he puts himself upon the defensive. He then has a case to prove. He calls himself by a term that suggests a low type of man. Then he has to prove and demonstrate that he possesses the higher qualities and finer characteristics of the Anglo-Saxon. The odor of that word Negro will cling to him like mud upon trailing skirts. It will be as easy to eradicate a birth mark as to purge out the objectionable and offensive features of that word.

We must forget the word Negro and all that is connected or associated with it. We don't want any Negro philosophy, Negro theology, Negro religion, Negro art, Negro music and Negro literature. Our destiny is not to build up a separate nationality in America but to become American citizens. Let us call ourselves the "Negrosaxon race" or the "Colored race" instead of "Negro race"—"Negrosaxons" or "Colored Americans" instead of "Negroes."

Thoughtful Negrosaxon leaders have observed that there has been a change of sentiment on the part of the white man towards the colored brother during the past twelve years. A wave of anti-Negro sentiment has swept over the country. Some have attributed the change to the fact that the old abolitionists and Grand Army heroes have died and that their sons have become engrossed and absorbed in money-making and have hardened and deadened their consciences to moral appeals and sentimental considerations. Others have shouldered Booker T. Washington's industrial-and-surrender-civil-and-political-rights fads with the responsibility for the changed attitude of the country regarding the colored brother. Some have thought that the Associated Press, siding with the South and branding the Negrosaxon as a criminal, has turned the North against him. But we colored people ourselves are partly responsible for the changed attitude of the country. When we called ourselves Negroes, when Negrosaxon teachers, editors, orators and preachers made the term popular, we tagged ourselves with a name that suggested that we were a peculiar class of beings, different from other men, that we were a little higher than the ape, and a little lower than the rest of mankind. Then, when we dubbed and labeled and catalogued ourselves as inferior beings, we laid the burden of proof upon ourselves. Then we had to establish the fact that we were equal to other men.

And that reminds me of a story. Once upon a time a dog bit a man; the man was a Quaker, averse to the shedding of blood. So he said to the dog, "I will not kill thee, but I will give thee a bad name." So he yelled out, pointing his finger at the dog, "Mad dog, mad dog, mad dog." Soon others took up the cry, "Mad dog, mad dog," chasing the dog meanwhile. And finally someone shot him. Now, that is what we did. When we called ourselves "Negroes" we gave ourselves a bad name. What was the result? In October, 1898, the Red Shirts in North Carolina yelled out, "Negro, Negro, Negro, Negro this and Negro that," and the Wilmington riot resulted. In September, 1906, Hoke Smith's and John Temple Graves's newspaper repeated, "Negro, Negro, Negro, Negro this and Negro that," and the world was horrified by the spectacle of the Atlanta massacre. In October, 1906, the citizens of Brownsville, Texas, proclaimed, "Negro soldiers, Negro soldiers, Negro soldiers this and Negro soldiers that, and Negro soldiers the other." The result was that President Roosevelt in November, 1906, discharged without honor a whole battalion of 167 colored soldiers, simply because he could not detect or discover the thirteen who were supposed to be guilty of murder or attempted murder. In December, 1906, the white people of Scoobo, Miss., set up the howl of "Negro, Negro, Negro, Negro this, Negro that, and Negro the other." The result was that Nicholson, a prosperous Negrosaxon farmer, and other innocent Negrosaxons were murdered in Scoobo, Miss. And unless the Negrosaxons or colored people stop blackguarding and libeling themselves and besmirching their reputations by calling themselves Negroes, the lynching, shooting down and stringing up of often innocent Negrosaxons by crazed mobs will continue to go on in the South.

To mention or use the word "Negro" to a white man of the South or a white mob is like waving a red flag before an angry bull. Why? Words have a history. In the course of time certain associations and traditions become attached to the word. Immediately the Negro is mentioned, certain suggestions are called up by the word. Now the word "Negro" originally referred to a native African black, who was a barbarian and a savage. When this native African black was imported and transported to America, a genuine infusion of aristocratic Anglo-Saxon blood into his veins took place, due to white slaveholders and overseers having children by black, mulatto and quadroon women. Then, too, this transported slave absorbed and assimilated the civilization, language and religion of the Anglo-Saxon race. He forgot his own native language and spoke the English language; he forgot fetichism and idol worship and accepted Christianity; he forsook polygamy and accepted monogamy. Ethnologically and psychologically he is a different being from the being to whom the word Negro originally applied. So the being to whom the word Negro originally applied is different entirely from the being who is now called by the word Negro. For there are five million Negrosaxons with Anglo-Saxon blood coursing in their veins. Even the five million American Negrosaxons who are pure blacks are psychologically different from the native African blacks. As long as the Negrosaxons call themselves Negroes they will be disfranchised, Jim-Crowed, segregated and lynched. The loophole out of our political and civil ostracism is to call ourselves Negrosaxons or Colored people.

But you can't make the colored leaders see this. The Negrosaxon has shown a remarkable faculty for appropriating the Anglo-Saxon ideals and absorbing and assimilating the Anglo-Saxon political sagacity and foresight. He can master Greek, Latin, French, German, science, mathematics, mechanics, agriculture, philosophy and literature. But when it comes to his own salvation, you have to take a sledge-hammer to drive anything into his head or hammer any ideas into him. He possesses more hindsight than foresight. He is as slow of comprehension of what concerns his own future welfare as the Englishman is of a joke. The Negrosaxon, Irishman or American catches on to the joke immediately. But the Englishman is slow of comprehension. He goes home, thinks it over and the next day it dawns upon him, and then he will collapse and explode with laughter.

I have said that the race problem will be solved by the colored people calling themselves Negrosaxons, or Colored people, instead of Negroes, because the word Negro misrepresents us and conveys a false impression in the minds of our Anglo-Saxon friends and critics, and suggests that we are a peculiar people. Three things will result from our calling ourselves Negrosaxons. In the first place we will see that our mission and destiny as a race is not to build up a Negroocracy or little Africa in America, but to appropriate Anglo-Saxon ideals and absorb and assimilate the Anglo-Saxon civilization. Some say this is a servile imitation. No, I do not think so. The Anglo-Saxon civilization is the highest and best yet evolved in the history of the human race. The twentieth century Anglo-Saxon civilization is a stream that is fed by currents from Hebrew, Greek, Roman and German thought. It is a thread into which are woven strands of Hebrew monotheism, Greek art and philosophy, Roman law, German mysticism and philosophy and Anglo-Saxon aggressiveness and reverence for women. Fibres of Hebrew, Greek, Roman and German civilization grafted onto the Anglo-Saxon's power of initiative and love of personal freedom and independence of character, is what we find in the Anglo-Saxon civilization. And what higher purpose could the Negro have than to enter into the spiritual inheritance of such civilization and regard Milton, Hampton, Chatham, Clarkson, Wilberforce, Chinese Gordon, Samuel Adams, Emerson, Sumner, Garrison and Phillips, and Mrs. Harriet Beecher Stowe as his spiritual heroes and heroines and grow into their likeness. I know that reading Tom Brown's School Days and Tom Brown at Oxford when I was about fourteen years of age fired me with the ambition to get an education and be a man.

In the second place, if we call ourselves Negrosaxons or Colored people the white people will ultimately call us Negrosaxons or Colored people, and, in the third place, as a consequence of this, they will recognize that their blood is in our veins, and that even those Negrosaxons or Colored men who have not a drop of Anglo-Saxon blood in their veins, have partaken and shared in the Anglo-Saxon civilization and built Anglo-Saxon ideals in the roots of their being and fibres of their nature. And while the Anglo-Saxon will not permit our children to marry his sons and daughters, he will still permit us to share in his civil and political life.

The carbon, oxygen, hydrogen, sulphur, potash, iron and magnesium and silicon in the blood of the pure black comes from the same American soil as do the chemical elements in the blood of the American white man. He, with the other social units in America, comes from the same American earth and draws his sustenance and nurture from the same natural bosom. And, if this is true of the physical elements that go to make up the physical structure of the pure black or Negrosaxon, how much more real and identical is that kinship which comes from moral ideals and aspirations and intellectual faculties and their development, with all of its binding threads of language, love, labors of hope and of righteousness, the only rational end of life—to say nothing of those enduring bonds which bind the creature to the Creator, and the religious work and worship of this great Christian American nation, which has exalted in its secular and sacred life the brotherhood of man equally with the fatherhood of God; to say nothing of all the devout hearts and souls of all this nation, black and white, believing in the immortality of the soul and the eternal responsibility of man to his Maker for the observance of the divine law. This divine leaven of Christianity will yet impress itself fully and freely upon all of our government institutions and over social intercourse. To hasten that day of the new world and new social order, when the Lord's Prayer shall become the world's heritage, when His Will will be done on earth as it is in Heaven, is the duty of every American citizen, black or white, and this book is the fruit of my abiding conviction on this point—of this fact.

The term "Negro" suggests physical and spiritual kinship to the ape, the monkey, the baboon, the chimpanzee, the ourangoutang and gorilla. The term "Negrosaxon" denotes the physical kinship of half of the colored people of America and the spiritual kinship of ninety per cent of the colored people of America to the noble Anglo-Saxon race. It is up to the Negrosaxon or Colored man to say which badge he shall wear, the badge of monkeyhood or of manhood, the badge of brutehood and bestiality or the badge of humanity. Calling ourselves "Negrosaxons" or Colored people will not let down the social barriers to us and give us entrance to Anglo-Saxon society; but it will give us the only kind of equality and opportunity that we need and desire—civil and political equality and industrial and economic opportunity. This is my commonsense inquiry, What is the use of our taking a name that misrepresents us, ethnologically and psychologically, and then hope by our deeds and achievements to purge the name of its odium? Why not take a name that ethnologically and psychologically represents us?

The term Negro passed into general circulation about three centuries ago, early in the seventeenth century, to characterize tribes of African savages and barbarians. Its original meaning has clung to it during the past three hundred years. By the term "Negro" a being who possesses the instincts of a brute, who is uncouth in his manners and hideous to look upon, is conjured up by the imagination. This colored race is no longer a pure Negro but a mixed Caucasian and Negro race, no longer a savage but a civilized race that is fast becoming cultured. In a word, it is an entirely different race of being from the African savages to whom the term "Negro" was originally applied. We colored people in America create the race problem by calling ourselves by a name that ethnologically and psychologically suggests what one side of our ancestors were three hundred years ago. Negrosaxon, both ethnologically and psychologically, suggests what we actually are to-day, and why not call ourselves by our proper name?

Judge Samuel Hoyt of Atlanta, Ga., believing that a rose by any other name would smell as sweet, said, "That which we call Negro would smell as bad by any other name." But the Judge, while eminent in legal lore, is not a philologist or psychologist. If he had understood the history of language he would have known that words have a history, certain meanings become packed up in them and they come, in the course of time, to suggest certain ideas. Now the word Negro suggests what over fifty per cent of the colored people are not, ethnologically and psychologically, and what seventy-five per cent will not be ethnologically and psychologically twenty years from now. It may be that the colored American is an offensive and an objectionable being to the Anglo-Saxons and always will be. But he is a little higher in the scale of being than the word "Negro" represents him to be.

Now the word Negrosaxon sounds rather queer and strange. It suggests incompatible ideas. "Negro" calls up a black, kinky-haired and heavy-featured being; "Saxon" calls up a very white, flowing-haired and thin-featured being. But the term "Negrosaxon" is a linguistic symbol for a physical fact. It represents a race that is the blending of the blackest and the whitest race known to history. The sons of Japheth, seeking the black but comely daughters of Ham, gave rise to the mixed race that I call Negrosaxon or Colored. Some say that is a base origin for a race. But the duke of Normandy by his deeds and achievements changed his title name from "William the Bastard" to "William the Conqueror." Abraham Lincoln made the world forget the dishonor that shrouded his birth and he goes down in history as the "savior of his country." Some of the ancestors of the present aristocrats and millionaires of America came over to this country two and three hundred years ago as redemptionaries, paupers, adventurers and social outcasts. So the obscurity and shame, for which black women were not responsible, of the origin of the Negrosaxon race need not deter its members from ascending the highest pinnacles of fame. Colored, then, is the colloquial and Negrosaxon the scientific term to designate the individuals now called Negroes.[4]

NOTE.—While the author does not think the term "Negro" properly characterizes the colored American or Negrosaxons, he uses it because of common custom and because he realizes that Andrew Carnegie and Col. Theodore Roosevelt, far more powerful than he ever dreams of becoming, were unable to reform American spelling.

4. Ferris is suggesting that there is not a tension between the Negro and Saxon parts of his term. He is not suggesting, as is usually done in reading Du Bois's *The Souls of Black Folk* through Hegelian dialectics, that Americanness and Negroness are antithetical. We can see the influence of Josiah Royce's themes of assimilation.

*Part Three*

# RACIAL IDEALISM AND THE COLOR QUESTION

## *Chapter Ten*

# The Key to the Solution of the Race Question

### I. THE PHILOSOPHY OF THE COLOR QUESTION.

I believe that in a few paragraphs I can state the philosophy underlying this book. I do not believe that the Negro is outside of the pale of humanity and that he is such a peculiar being that he needs a different kind of training, a different kind of treatment from other men. I do not believe that any one formula, recipe or prescription will solve the race question. I do not believe that industrial education alone is the universal panacea for all of the colored man's ills and ailments. It took the farm, the workshop, the mill, the factory, the bank, the store, the public school, the college, the church and civil and political liberty to make this country what it is. And I believe that it will take all of these, nothing less and nothing more, to make anything of the Negro. If I am asked, "What does the Negro need most, industrial or higher education?" I reply, "He needs both!" If I am asked, "What does the Negro need most, wealth or the ballot?" I reply, "He needs both." Why? Because he is a man and not a monkey, because he is a full-fledged man in all that the name implies, and not half a man as some of the colored brother's friends would endeavor to make him believe.[1]

Then, someone may ask, "What do you think of the Jim Crow car and of social equality?" I don't care the snap of the finger for social recognition. I

---

1. This is a strong point of William Ferris's text. He demands a sociological, historical, and complicated view of the Negro and the "Negro problem." His work resists mirroring existing debates over race thinking/theory at the turn of the century that reduces all debates to concerns over separatism versus intergrationism or industrial education versus liberal arts education. Ferris is suggesting that the social development of the Negro is a concern that requires attention to the spiritual uplift of a people as well as their economic and political sustenance.

don't hunger and thirst and hanker and crave for the society of men and women. As to whether I am invited to dine by any man, white or colored; as to whether I am invited to any social function, are minor concerns of my life. When I was at Yale, my happiest moments were when I would take my Emerson and Carlyle and my Irish terrier, named "Birdie," go out to the Slaughter woods and West Rock on some spring or fall day, look down upon the dreaming, sleepy quiet village of Westville, which was nestled so cosily among the trees, watch the play of sunlight and of shade, see the stream lazily dreaming its way through the meadows and, with the blue sky above me for a canopy, drink in the beauty of nature, as I brooded over the mystic words of two lofty thinkers. What is the hollow and artificial life of man, with its vainglories and petty rivalries and prejudices, compared to the memory of such golden moments as these, when I saw all nature radiant with the glory of a present God?

Then, too, there were some memorable experiences and memorable days at Harvard, when inspiration came to me in the presence of memorials of the past. I well remember the Sunday in May when I first visited Concord, Mass. It was a beautiful afternoon, with just enough haze in the atmosphere to relieve the glaring brilliancy of the noonday sun and to soften the outlines of the trees. I remember coming to a lonely lane. It was in a quiet, secluded spot, running off from the main road and far away from the business center of the town. It seemed that the Almighty intended to hallow and consecrate this spot, by placing it at a distance from the center of trade and the wranglings, quarrelings, and contentions of men. It was a beautiful lane, shaded by four rows of trees, with the statue of the Minute Man of '76 at the end of the lane. Unless I confuse it with the statue of a minute man I have seen elsewhere, it is a bold, defiant youth, who, with flashing eye, and set lips, and bared chest, holds a gun. The fire of battle is in his eye. He seems eager for the fray. And there is the bridge just beyond and from the bridge rises the hill that is crowned by the house from which Emerson's grandfather witnessed the fight.

It was down this hill that the New England patriots marched and here it was that the "embattled farmers stood and fired the shot heard round the world." I would call this place the meeting of the waters. Three or four quiet, peaceful lakes and lazy, lingering streams seem to meet and mingle their waters under this bridge. Heaven seems to have shed its benediction upon this scene, and then I asked, Will I ever in reality be able to share in the glorious memories of those heroic days?

And then I reflected. The colored boy pursues the same and yet different ideals from the white boy. Ambitions which appeal powerfully to the white boy touch him not at all. Hopes and fears and longings and sorrows, too deep for tears, that the white boy knows nothing of, visit him constantly and stir him deeply. On Washington's Birthday, Decoration Day, the Fourth of July and Thanksgiving Day, he hears of the bravery of the Pilgrim Fathers, of the heroism and patriotism of Samuel Adams and Patrick Henry, of Otis and Hancock and Warren, of Israel Putnam and General Stark at the battle of Bennington, and straightway goes into a world where the rattle of musketry in the streets of Boston and the thunders of Bunker Hill, the story of Paul Revere's ride and the ringing of Independence Bell, sends no thrills of patriotism. The white boy who sweeps out an office may someday become president of the bank. The white boys who sells newspapers in the railroad cars may someday become the president of the railroad corporation, and the white boy who blacks your boots or splits rails may someday become the President of the United States. But no such vista stretches out before the colored boy. His horizon is limited, his sphere circumscribed. His activities are confined to a narrow circle. The trades unions discriminate against him in the North and East. Certain callings are closed to him. He is barred from them. In others he can go to a certain point but there must stop, regardless of his ability, aspiration and ambition. And I regard it as a healthy sign that the caste prejudice is teaching the Negro self-reliance and that colored men are going into business for themselves.

No, I do not care for the attractions of society, but I will speak the truth: I do hate, when I am in the South, to be constantly reminded of the fact that the color of my skin is different from that of most of the other American citizens. I do hate to be constantly annoyed, insulted, humiliated, treated with open contempt, taunted with my inferiority and forced to feel that I belong to a despised race, as when a white clerk in a manufacturer's office told me when I introduced myself as Mr. Ferris, "We don't call you people by the title of Mr." (Mr. is a title of respect in the South and denotes a gentleman, which is of course too high a title for a Negro), or, when I heard the sign over one door at the Atlanta Exhibition read, "Negroes and dogs not allowed." I do not enjoy or relish the inferior and uncomfortable accommodations that are given colored people on the Jim Crow car. I think it a shame that a colored lady of culture and refinement is unable to secure a berth in a sleeping car. I do hate to be constantly reminded of the fact in the South that I am a Negro, not a man. I don't like to always feel I am of a darker complexion, my hair is not as straight and my features not as aquiline as those of most of the other American citizens. It is refreshing for me to visit a little town like Beaufort, S. C., where the thought of color, color, color, color, is not always brought to the front and emphasized and where the two races dwell together in peace and harmony.

I like to feel rather that I am a human being, that I belong to the human family. I like to feel that I belong to the genus *vir* as well as to the genus *homo*.[2] I like to feel that the same flag waves over me that waves over the white man. I like to feel that the Stars and Stripes is the emblem and symbol of the government to which I belong as an integral part and not as an alien. I like to feel that it protects me as well as the white man. I like to feel that there is a divine spark within my soul. I like to feel that a divinity stirs within me no less than in my white brother. I like to feel that I am an immortal soul, dwelling for the space of a few short years in this tabernacle of flesh, in this temple of clay. I like to feel that the same God who speaks in thunder tones in the conscience of the white man lives and moves and has his being and manifests his inmost nature in my reason, and higher impulses and higher instincts, too.

Some people say that the Negro must not expect too much, after only forty years of freedom. But in the year 1800, A. D., everyone of my ancestors, with two exceptions, were living, moving, breathing as free men and women. And the love of liberty was such an inborn quality and characteristic of their souls, that these two would not, and could not, be kept as slaves. They secured their freedom immediately after the War of 1812.

Sixty years ago to-day, both of my grandfathers were property owners. The blood of the warlike Delaware Indians flows in my veins. My father, my uncles and grand uncles, fought in the late Civil War. Some of my relatives baptized with their blood the soil of this country in order that "this nation, under God, might have a new birth of freedom." Haven't I some rights in this country? Does not this country owe me as much as it does the foreigner who came over yesterday?

## II. WILL WEALTH ALONE SAVE THE NEGRO?

Then some say, "The Negro must do something, must have a material foundation for his prosperity." This is all very true, but I believe that the foundation upon which the race needs to build is the bed rock of manhood and womanhood, and not the shifting sands of cowardice and sycophancy.

2. "Vir" and "Homo" are used interchangeably to mean "man" or "mankind," but Ferris seems to be making a subtler but important distinction. He wishes not simply to be an individual or part of mankind; rather, he insists on manhood, or being a political man/citizen. Today our liberal feminist leanings have us overlook such distinctions, but at the turn of the twentieth century, manhood was a racial telos that everyone, man and woman, aspired toward. For texts explaining the complexity and nuance of the ethnological conceptualization of "manhood" and "Black manhood" in the nineteenth century, see

It is as true to-day as it was in the days of Paul, that the things which are seen are temporal, while the things which are unseen are eternal. The works of the hand perish before the wind, the rain, the corroding forces of the atmosphere, and the wear and tear of time, but the products of the mind endure forever. The Parthenon, the marbles of Phidias, the buildings on the Acropolis and all the memorable works of the age of Pericles are crumbling away. Soon not a vestige of them will remain. But the writings of Plato and Aristotle, the orations of Demosthenes, the poems of Homer and Pindar, and the dramas of Aeschylus, Sophocles and Euripides still live; and when every last one of the material landmarks of the age of Pericles shall have succumbed before the corroding forces of nature and the abuse of man, and shall have passed into oblivion, the literary products of that brilliant moment in Grecian civilization will still remain as the imperishable treasures of the human mind.

Go to mighty Rome, that city of one million souls, which once ruled the entire world. What has become of the Coliseum, of the temples of the Gods, and the palaces of the Roman emperors? They are a mass of ruins, but school-boys still read the orations of Cicero, still admire his exposure of Catiline's conspiracy and his eloquent defense of the poet Archias, still delight to scan the lines of Vergil beginning:

> Arma virumque cano. Troiae qui primus ab oris. Italiam, fato profugus, Lavinia venit
> Littora; multum ille et terris jactatus et alto,
> Vi superum, saevae memo rem Junonis ob iram;
> Multo quoque et bello passus, dum conderet urbem, Inferretque deos Latis! genus unde Latinum
> Albanique patres, atque altae meonia Romae,
> Musa, mihi causas memora, quo numine laeso.[3]

The Gothic cathedrals and rugged castles of the middle ages are crumbling into decay. Some of the old mediaeval abbeys are in ruins; but Dante's divine poem, which Carlyle called, "the voice of ten silent centuries," will ever remain as the literary monument, the literary expression of the genius, and the religious hopes and aspirations and cravings and longings of the benighted souls of the Middle Ages.

---

Melissa Stein, *Measuring Manhood: Race and the Science of Masculinity, 1830–1934* (Minneapolis: University of Minnesota Press, 2015).

3. The English translation of Virgil's poem is "I sing of arms and a man. Troy was the first from the mouth. Italy, exiled by fate, came Lavinia coasts; was hunted to much on both land and sea, By virtue of the gods, on the memo Juno anger; Suffered much even in war, until he could found the city, and bring the gods to Latium! whence the Latin race and the Alban fathers and the high Meonia in Rome. Who offended the Muse, tell me the reasons, with what deity having been offended."

Gone is the temple of Solomon, once the pride of the Hebrew world. The glories of the old Jerusalem have passed away, but the reflections of Job, the poetry of the Psalms, the splendid visions of Isaiah, the profound words of John and the burning eloquence of Paul still stir our hearts and minds. Yes, it is true that the works of man shall perish, but the word of our "God" will abide forever.

Despite the *at tuba terribili, sonitu taratantara dixit* of Booker T. Washington, and the other prophets of Baal and worshippers of the brazen calf, I still believe that Jesus Christ is the greatest builder the world has yet seen. You could take all of the kings of finance from the time of Croesus to the present day; all of the statesmen from Khufu to Gladstone; all of the conquerors from Pepi of Egypt to Napoleon, and estimate the permanent value of their works, and you would probably find that their combined influence would hardly surpass that of the lowly Nazarene. He sowed a few germinal thoughts like seed corn in the minds of a few chosen disciples. They grew and developed and were reproduced in ten thousand times ten thousand men. The soul of one man, the Apostle Paul, was touched by these thoughts. He stood against the Roman Empire, which reached from Germany on the north to the wilds of Africa on the south, which stretched from Great Britain on the west to the Parthian empire in the eastern part of Asia. The whole world was shaking beneath the triumphant tread of Roman soldiers. Her eagles were flying at the head of her victorious legions.

Human slavery was embedded in the very fibre and woven in the very web and woof of the Roman civilization. What could one man do against the great, the vast Roman Empire?

But Paul said, "I preach Christ and him crucified." He was stoned by a mob, beaten with rods, and beaten with stripes. He was shipwrecked three or four times. He floated for a day and a night on the great deep. He languished in prison. Bound with fetters upon his wrists, a chained and manacled prisoner, he still wrote letters that thrilled and inspired Christendom. He faced centurions and Roman governors. He addressed the cultured Greeks from the historic Mars Hill. The flaming enthusiasm and burning zeal of those Christian martyrs, who went singing to be torn in pieces by lions in the Roman Amphitheater, and whose burning bodies lighted up the gardens of the infamous Nero, penetrated the inmost core and kernel of his being. What was the result? Christ, through Paul, conquered the Roman Empire.

And when Rome, weakened by licentious ease, was unable to stem the advancing tide of the sturdy, hardy barbarians, and yielded to the rugged Goths, who poured over the Roman frontiers; Christ, through the Christian religion, which was embodied in the Roman civilization, overawed and impressed and conquered and tamed the barbaric Teutons.

I know that this is the age of practical atheism. Men scan the heavens with the telescope, they examine plants and microbes with the microscope, and they say they see no God. But His image is engraved upon the human conscience, and written in the ideals of the human heart, and His nature is expressed in those moral imperatives which, springing up in the human mind, we know not whence, we know not how, are the impulses to all human progress. And unless the iron of manhood enters the blood of the Negro youth, unless the nerve of manliness is incorporated into the sinews and fibres of his moral nature, the Negro will never amount to anything. We must have for our foundation faith in God, and faith in manliness and womanhood. Then we can get all the wealth and buy all the land that we can.

When Christ said to Peter, "Upon this rock I will build my church, and the gates of hell shall not prevail against it," on which Peter was he to build thechurch? On the timid, hesitating, doubting and denying Peter? No, but the Peter, whose God was a man of war, the Peter who was so rooted and grounded in his faith in God that he had the boldness and lionlike courage to defy and face a frowning world; this was the Peter on which Christ was to build his church.

Let us then lay first the foundation, deep and strong, in the manhood and womanhood of the race. And then we can add wealth and culture, and the comforts and luxuries of life.

When was it that the civilizations of Babylon, Persia, Greece, Rome, Constantinople and Spain crumbled away, and when did those nations fall before the attacks of other more vigorous people? Was it not when they had become enervated by luxury and ease and licentiousness? When was it that the Persian, Greek, Roman and Spanish soldiers swept opposing armies before them as with the onward sweep of a mighty torrent? Was it not when those nations were rugged and sturdy and strong, were in the youthful period of life and were characterized by simplicity and simple tastes?

I realize that in an age which has witnessed the invention of the telephone, telegraph, phonograph, and vitascope, etc.; I realize that in an age which has witnessed the marvelous development of the material resources of this country and the miraculous accumulation of great wealth in the hands of a few individuals, the doctrine that the race problem will be solved by the colored man's getting wealth, seems very plausible. But moneymaking alone will not solve the race question.

The Phoenicians were once the traders and merchants of the ancient world. Egypt, Persia, Greece and Spain were once mighty empires, but wealth did not save them. Babylon once reveled and rioted in wealth and luxury. Athens, the home of philosophers, orators, statesmen, scholars, artists and poets, was once basking in the sunshine of material prosperity. Carthage was once the queen of commerce and the mistress of the sea. Rome was once blessed by seeing the wealth of the entire world pouring at her feet, and the nations of the world prostrating themselves before her. Constantinople was once the metropolis of the Eastern world. Florence was once a flourishing and art-loving city. And yet all of these magnificent cities fell in power, and saw their ancient glory fade away. All of them, with one exception, heard the tramp of conquering armies within their city gates. Go to Babylon, Athens, Carthage, Rome, Constantinople and Florence and you will everywhere see the relics and remains of a glory that has departed, of a grandeur that has passed away.

There can be no doubt that wealth gives a man great power and influence. A rich man can surround himself with all of the comforts and luxuries of life. He can go abroad or to the Adirondacks, to California, Colorado and Florida, whenever a whim seizes him, or the necessities of his health require it. He can buy up orators and writers, lawyers and judges, mayors and governors and congressmen and senators. He can control the judiciary and corrupt the fountain sources of legislation. And David Graham Phillips, in his brilliant articles in the Cosmopolitan upon "Treason in the Senate," says that a few multi-millionaires, through Senators Depew, Aldrich and Gorman and others, have their hands upon the throttle valve of the United States Senate. But great as is the power and influence of the immensely rich, unless like the Stokes, Thornes, Harrisons, Schiffs and Sloanes of New York, the Hazards and the Wetmores of Rhode Island, the Masons and Cranes of Massachusetts, and the Hearsts of California, their hearts have been touched by the humanitarian waves of thought and feeling that have swept over the country, their riches avail nothing.

Then, again, the doctrine that a Negro must acquire property before he secures his manhood rights, means that the Negro, whose sweat and toil has made possible the Southern aristocracy, must acquire wealth to secure the rights that the ragged immigrant secures from the mere fact that he is a man. It furthermore means that we must take Jesus Christ, the Apostle Paul, Martin Luther, the Pilgrim Fathers, the Revolutionary Fathers, the Abolitionists, Phillips Brooks, Richard Salter Storrs, Colonel Robert Gould Shaw, George William Curtis, Dante, Milton, Carlyle and Emerson down from the lofty pedestals upon which the gratitude and common sense of manhood have placed them, and admit that they were pursuers of chimeras and mirages. It means that a man must be a millionaire before he is a man. It means that it is no longer the fashion to estimate and rate a man for what he himself is, for his intrinsic worth as a man.

## III. OUGHT THE COLORED BROTHER TO ASPIRE TO BE A MAN?

Some people are confused about the race problem. But I believe that it only requires the exercise of a little common sense to understand and solve the problem. It seems to me that even a child ought to be able to grasp the color question as easily as he learns his alphabet. Let us remove the colored glasses of our preconceived notions and prejudices and look at the problem in the clear light of reason. The Negro is not a dog nor a slave, not a monkey nor an ape, not a jackass nor a mule—but a man. And hence he deserves not the treatment of a dog, slave, monkey, ape, jackass, or mule—but a man's treatment. Let us no longer lump all of the Negroes in a mass and treat all alike. But let us recognize individual differences and treat colored men and women as individuals. Let us give each colored person the education, training, treatment and opportunities that his talents, ability and character, his natural tastes and aptitudes and inclinations require that he should have. If we banish to the limbo of exploded ideas the theory, regnant in the days of slavery, that the Negro is a soulless brute, no longer will the ghost of Negro domination or the nightmare of social equality disturb our peaceful slumbers. The members of New York's Four Hundred do not invite the Irish immigrants to their social functions. The descendants of the old Puritans, who came over in the Mayflower, do not entertain the Jewish banana vender in their parlors, and yet they treat them as human beings and not as beasts of the field.

This is all that the brother in black asks. It is not an abstract question of theoretical rights; but the simple, practical question as to whether the Negro is or is not a man. Our Anglo-Saxon friends are shocked and surprised when they see a colored man manifesting manliness and spirit and sensitiveness. It seems now to be political heresy for a colored man to emulate the spirit of the heroes of the Anglo-Saxon race. And a colored man who is interested in literature, art and philosophy is dreaded as if he were an anarchist or fire-eater.

All my life, I have in the grammar and high schools, in the college and graduate schools, been taught by white men, and sat by the side of white students. Now the Anglo-Saxon ideals of manliness have become part of my mental and moral constitution. No man can study in Yale or Harvard without being affected by the atmosphere and catching the spirit of these two institutions of learning. Besides, my ancestors on both my mother's and father's side were high-minded and high-spirited people. My parents, grandparents and six of my great-grandparents never groaned under the yoke of slavery, never trembled with fear at a master's frown, never heard the crack or felt the sting of a slave-driver's whip, never bled under the lash, nor shuddered at the far-off bay of the dreaded bloodhound. And old Enoch Jefferson, my great-grandfather, resolved one day to be his own master. He rose in the dignity, strength and majesty of his manhood, threw off the yoke of slavery, and stepped forth a free man. It is reported that he spent one Sunday in the woods and by the creek planning his escape. He returned home Sunday night. His master asked him where he had been. He said to church. His master asked him what the text was. Enoch replied, "You shall look for me in the morning and shall not find me." Sure enough, next morning, Enoch was missing. He had taken the wings of the morning and departed for parts unknown. This story has been repeated in different parts of the country. But I understand that my ancestor actually uttered these words. He was the father of about a dozen boys and six daughters. Most of his sons and many of his grandsons became farmers. His son David, who lives in Middletown, Del., and my grandfather Enoch became very successful farmers. The Jeffersons in Delaware excelled as brickmakers, farmers, wrestlers and athletes. My grandfather Enoch and his wife were raised and trained by Philadelphia Quakers, and I suppose that is why their ideals were so high. His wife was one half Indian, one quarter Negro, and one quarter Caucasian. My grandfather, David Ferris, was a hard worker, and a fiery preacher. His ancestors were emancipated at the time of the Revolutionary War. Coming from such a splendid stock, and being bred and born in New England, being saturated with New England traditions, admiring Samuel Adams and Israel Putnam, even as a schoolboy, is it strange that I have absorbed and assimilated the white man's aggressive spirit and ideals, while I still retain the Negro's buoyant, optimistic and hopeful nature?

Professor Ladd, Professor Duncan, Professor Sneath, Professor Sumner, Dean Wright and Dean Phillips of Yale, and the other Yale professors, gave me a sound philosophy. But Thomas Carlyle, Frederick Douglass, Alexander Crummell, and George T. Downing developed the combative instinct which was born in me. But I believe that Professor DuBois has had as much influence over my ideals as any other man. When I heard him read his paper upon "The Conservatism of Race Traits, and Tendencies of the Negro," at a meeting of the American Negro Academy in Washington, in March, 1897, I trained my guns upon DuBois and severely criticised him. But the more I reflected the more truth I saw in his views. Dean Everett, Professor Royce, and Professor James of Harvard broadened my conception of life. But the strenuous spirit of my great-grandfather, Enoch Jefferson, who burst asunder the bonds of slavery, lives in me, and that is why, while I admire Booker T. Washington for the consummate ability with which he organized and marshalled his forces at Tuskeegee, I cannot accept his view that the Negro should remain at the foot of the ladder, should extol as blessings in disguise, Jim Crow cars, and should give up the ballot and office holding.

I look at the situation philosophically. The white man in the South dominates the Negro psychologically and the Negro must adapt and adjust himself to him, because he has the wealth, the government and press on his side. But sooner or later the day must come—it will come, when the civil and political status of the Negro will be determined, not by the color of his skin, but by his intrinsic worth as a man. What the Negro has to do is to make the most of his present opportunities, and never lose sight of the fact that the ultimate solution of the color question will never be found until he has all of the rights guaranteed him by the fourteenth and fifteenth amendments, and is clothed with the full paraphernalia of manhood.

I believe that the race question will be brought to a focus and a crucial test in Georgia, and that Georgia will be the battleground and storm-center where the problems centering around the civil and political rights will be fought out. The situation is more acute and the friction between the races greater in Georgia than in any other State. In the first place, there are more wealthy and educated Negroes in Georgia than in any other State. Then the white men in Georgia taunt and goad and wave the red flag before the Negro more than they do in Beaufort, Charleston, Summerville, Orangeburg, Denmark, or Georgetown, South Carolina, or some towns in North Carolina, Florida, and Kentucky. I don't say that there is any more prejudice in Georgia than in the other States. But the Georgian does not sugarcoat his pills, or administer his medicine in homoeopathic doses.

He is not as courteous and as polite as the South Carolina aristocrat. And one will see the haughty, arrogant spirit, the contempt of the Caucasian for the Negro, in its plain, unvarnished simplicity in Georgia. Thus the Negro, except in Savannah, Brunswick and Darien, is irritated more in Georgia than in the two Carolinas, Kentucky and Florida; and the Georgia Negro is intelligent and wealthy enough to be manly and self-assertive. Hence there is likely to be an interesting development in Georgia. Then again, there are in Georgia men like Rev. H. S. Bradley, D.D., of Atlanta, Judge E. H. Callaway of Augusta, Ga., Attorney D. L. Clarke and Colonel J. H. Estill of Savannah, Ga., who believe in giving the Negro a man's chance in life, and that is all that a sensible man wants.

Editor B. J. Davis, of the *Atlanta Independent*, in the issue of April 19th, in an able editorial under the headlines, "The Case is Made, and Burden of Proof is upon the Negro," says: "The celebration (referring to the twenty-fifth jubilee celebration at Tuskeegee) demonstrates beyond cavil this moral certainty, the white man North and South has agreed upon the solution of the Negro problem. Both sections have agreed to put it up to the black man and leave it to him to fix his status in the social order upon his neighbors and compel the estimate that they shall place upon his worth as a man and citizen. Instead of depending on self, the Negro, to his hurt, depended too much upon the Republican party, and for something to happen out of the ordinary in Yankeedom." Now, Editor Davis in a very able manner unravels his text. It applies to any man, black or white, that he must acquire the wealth, the education, the character and manliness that the community requires and demands in those it would respect and honor. But it seems to me this editorial really begs the question and dodges the main issue. The Negro confronts the bars of race prejudice. Suppose his Caucasian neighbors tell the Negro, "thus high shalt thou rise, and no higher"; suppose the decree goes out, that not even the wealthy and educated Negroes can hold office in the South; suppose the Negro is disfranchised, under terms that are contrary to the spirit and the letter of the fourteenth and fifteenth amendments to the Federal Constitution; suppose Jim Crow car laws are passed that fly in the face of interstate commerce laws,—what then?

There are two classes of men and women in the world. There are those who believe in submitting and succumbing to the existing moral, religious, social and political evils, and there are those who believe in a finish fight with injustice and unrighteousness. They believe in going into the battle determined to conquer or die. They believe in winning out, or going down with their colors flying and banners floating to the breeze. I will admit that there are times when a man must stoop to conquer. But generally the soldiers who go into battle determined, in the words of the Spartan mother, to return with their shields or upon them, are the winners in life's battles as well as in war.

The man who impresses his convictions, his ideas, and ideals, and hopes and aspirations upon his fellows, and dominates his associates by the sheer force of his own transcendent personality, is the real maker of history.

William Pitt the elder, called the Great Commoner, afterwards made the Earl of Chatham, is my ideal leader. He swayed men by appealing to their imagination, by charging them with his own faith and enthusiasm, his own passion and patriotism. If a man is to bring a message to men and implant in them his own fundamental and basal ideas regarding life and its meaning, he must be something more than a tactful diplomat or clever compromiser. To be an intellectual and moral force in the world a man must be free to assert his individuality. A man whose individuality has lost its color and flavor is like a faded rose which has parted with its fragrance and sweetness.

Now the problem is, can this ideal of manhood be realized by a colored man in the South and in a colored college? Can a colored man be a man here? An independent thinker, who, like the Hebrew prophets of old, speaks with a "Thus-saith-the-Lord" authority and blazes a path through the unknown is always a potent factor in civilization, always a force to be reckoned with. Julius Caesar, Oliver Cromwell, John Calvin, and Napoleon Bonaparte, at certain crises of history, saw that to be masters of the situation and control the discordant elements, they must lay aside their democratic and republican ideals and inaugurate an imperialistic form of government, with the seat of authority residing in one man. They burned their bridges behind them, carried the war into Africa, bearded the lion in his den, took the bull by the horns, and came off victors.[4]

The prophets like Paul, Mohammed, Calvin, and Wesley, the soldiers like Caesar, Napoleon and William the Conqueror, the religious heroes like Luther and Cromwell, the statesmen like William Pitt the elder, who possess an irrepressible individuality, who do not get discouraged and disheartened when obstacles and opposition loom up before them in gigantic proportions, but in whom all the lion in their natures rises at the sight of difficulties, who gather all of their forces together, and hurl themselves against the obstacles and drive through the opposition with the force of a moving catapult or flying wedge, these are the great captains of history and the epoch-makers.

It is no doubt true that it is the height of absurdity and foolhardiness for a man to lower his head and run at full tilt against a mountain; it is suicidal for a man to stand in the middle of the track and crash into a locomotive coming at full speed, as an angry bull and an English bull dog once did. But history teaches us that the men who, when they have a fighting chance to win, go into the fray and risk their lives, their all,—go in determined to come out conquerors or meet their Waterloo, usually turn seeming defeat into victory, as Caesar and Napoleon more than once did, as William the Conqueror did at Hastings and Phil Sheridan did at Winchester. It is related that at the Battle of Hastings the report spread amongst the Norman invaders that William the

4. Ferris offers a very interesting point about manhood here. In his time, manhood commonly represented the ability of the race to participate in the political, just as the womanhood of the race was about the character and moral uplift of the people. Klan violence was particularly centered on Black manhood and, as such, Black political and economic participation. See Martha Hodes, "The Sexualization of Reconstruction Politics: White Women and Black Men in the South after the Civil War," *Journal of the History of Sexuality* 3, no. 3 (1993): 402–17. "Manhood Rights" was an inclusive term for race progress that sought to place the aspirations of the race within the scope of civilization. This was a complex debate that supersedes the categorical impositions of gender that we hold in our contemporary moment. For some historical context for Ferris's worry and what he was actually striving for, see Earnestine Jenkins and Darlene Clark Hine, eds., *A Question of Manhood: A Reader in U.S. Black Men's History and Masculinity*, vol. 2 (Indiana: Indiana University Press, 2001).

Conqueror was slain. This scattered and disorganized them. But, in a voice of thunder, William cried out, "I live and by God's grace will conquer yet!" He rallied his disheartened forces and won out on that memorable day at Hastings. Why is it?

There is no one quality of the human mind that is so contagious as courage. The preacher, the statesman, the reformer, the soldier, who possesses an unconquerable and indomitable spirit, who never gives up, who never knows defeat, who never says die, can charge a thousand, yea a million men with his own faith and passion, his own zeal and enthusiasm. Thousands will flock to his banners and rally around his standards. That is why the mighty minds and great souls of history dominate their fellows and followers in the way that they do. The weaker natures gravitate towards the stronger by as irresistible a law of gravitation as that which draws the needle to the magnet or compels the tidal waves of the sea to obey the resistless pull of the moon. What is the secret of eloquence? It is not the voice, the elocution, the gesture, the thoughts, the words and rhetoric that explain the secret of the orator's spell or the preacher's power. The magic wand by which the orator sways listening thousands is a psychic influence. He communicates his mind, his soul, his spirit to his hearers, and by the force of his individuality and personality impresses his ideas and convictions upon those who come within the radius of his influence. His soul illumines his features and transfigures his voice. That is why his countenance is radiant and his voice magnetic.

Milton's Satan is the real hero of his "Paradise Lost," in fact the most powerful character, the most heroic figure in poetry and fiction. The unconquerable, indomitable, invincible, dauntless and defiant spirit that he exhibited when he had been hurled over the battlements of Heaven into Hell, has challenged the admiration of the world. How eloquently does Milton describe his fall and dauntless resolution!

Him the Almighty power
Hurled headlong flaming from the ethereal sky,
With hideous ruin and combustion, down
To bottomless perdition, there to dwell
In adamantine chains and penal fire,
Who durst defy the Omnipotent to arms.
Nine times the space that measures day and night
To mortal men, he, with his horrid crew,
Lay vanquished, rolling in the fiery gulf,
Confounded, though immortal. But his doom
Reserved him to more wrath; for now the thought
Both of lost happiness and lasting pain
Torments him: round he throws his baleful eyes

That witnessed huge affliction and dismay,
Mixed with obdurate pride and steadfast hate.
. . .
At once, as far as Angels ken, he views
The dismal situation waste and wild.
A dungeon horrible, on all sides round,
As one great furnace flamed; yet from those flames
No light; but rather darkness visible
Served only to discover sights of woe,
Regions, of sorrow, doleful shades, where peace
And rest can never dwell, hope never comes
That comes to all, but torture without end
Still urges, and a fiery deluge, fed
With ever-burning sulphur unconsumed.
. . .
There the companions of his fall, o'erwhelmed
With floods and whirlwinds of tempestuous fire,
He soon discerns, and, weltering by his side,
One next himself in power, and next in crime,
Long after known in Palestine and named Beelzebub
Is Satan discouraged? Mark how he holds discourse with the arch fiend Beelzebub:
Since, through experience of this great event,
In arms not worse, in foresight much advanced,
We may with more successful hope resolve
To wage by force or guile eternal war, Irreconcilable to our grand Foe,
Who now triumphs, and in the excess of joy
Sole reigning holds the tyranny of Heaven.
. . .
Consult how we may henceforth most offend
Our Enemy, our own loss how repair,
How overcome this dire calamity,
What reinforcement we may gain from hope.

Though Milton wrote "Paradise Lost" and "Paradise Regained" to justify the ways of God to man, nevertheless the Puritan poet who, when fallen upon evil days, when some of his friends had been imprisoned and others executed, when his enemies were upon the throne and in the saddle, did not abate one jot of heart or hope; thus Milton, I say, unconsciously breathed his own heroic nature, his own intrepid spirit into the being that he intended to represent as the Prince of Devils, the defier of the Powers of the Universe. Milton intended to represent him as the Prince of Demons, instead he made him the King of Fighters. The whole world loves and admires a fighter. I don't know whom to pity the most, the Indian or the Negro. The Indian played the lion, was exterminated, and now is admired and honored by the entire world. The Negro played the lamb, survived and is now despised and proscribed in

America as is no other race or class of people in the world. I believe the Negro assumed the wiser but less heroic role. Too often, though, the Negro leaders have been sickening in their servile sycophancy, sickening in their cowardly cringing.

Why, my grandfather, David Ferris, although only a stevedore and local Methodist preacher, had a spirit within him that might well put to shame these latter-day saints. It was no doubt true that he regarded the whipping of his boys as a religious duty, and consecrated and made too much of a religious ceremony over a mere whipping, for he would first read the scripture, preach a short sermon to them, whip them, and then pray over them. But he was the type of the soldiers who formed the backbone of Oliver Cromwell's "Ironsides." Men had to respect the "House of the Lord" when he preached. One night some brothers began to quarrel in the church. He said, "Go slow, brethren, go slow." They began to fight: he said again and again, in ever louder tones, as he approached nearer and nearer to the combatants, "Go slow, brethren, go slow." He was a tall, powerful man, and as graceful and as supple as a dancing master. They wouldn't heed him, and finally he pitched and plunged into the fray. He picked up first one and then the other, and threw them out of the door. There were no more fights when he conducted the services in the Methodist Church. Now, I believe that the younger breed of Negroes need some of his sterling qualities.

Some think that the race problem will be solved by the Negroes becoming a race of spineless and flexible-kneed sycophants. I notice that if a dog can't fight, nearly every dog in the neighborhood will jump on him, and send him home howling. If a boy is cowardly, nearly every boy in the school will kick and cuff him about. If a man is soft and mushy and short in the vertebrate column, he will be used as a football and a doormat. It requires a man, and not a weakling, to stand the stress and storm, the rivalry and competition of modern life. The men to stand the struggle for existence must be made of stern stuff and cast in a heroic mould.[5]

The moulding of an enlightened public sentiment will solve the race question. Now, no one will be so potent in affecting public opinion in his own behalf as the colored man himself. It is not enough that he be a producer in

5. This was a key debate over the Black man's burden at the turn of the century. Black men and women debated the need for Black men to be fighting men capable of taking up the charge to spread civilization (English and Christianity) to the world, specifically Africa and the Philippines. Many Black men were against such an idea and created Black Men's Burden societies specifically arguing against the link between (white) manhood and imperialism. See Michelle Mitchell, "The Black Man's Burden," in *Righteous Propagation: African Americans and the Politics of Racial Destiny after Reconstruction* (Chapel Hill: University of North Carolina Press, 2004), 51–75.

the agricultural, industrial, commercial, manufacturing world, not enough that he be a creator in the world of letters, art, music and science, but he must manifest and exhibit manliness. The main reason why the Negro is despised and looked down upon by his Anglo-Saxon neighbors is not because of his color and hair, his illiteracy and poverty, but because he and his ancestors so tamely and cowardly submitted to chattel slavery. As many degrees as the Negro race rises in manliness and courage, just so many degrees will the thermometer of the Anglo-Saxon's respect, admiration and appreciation for the Negro rise.

I do not mean that colored leaders should wave the bloody shirt and stir up race riots in the South. On the other hand, I disapprove of Negro educators who are running around the country soliciting funds, painting the South as an earthly paradise, a New Jerusalem, for the colored brother, where the lamb and the lion lie down together and where Leibnitz's preestablished harmony prevails. It is advisable for the Southern Negro, who is in the lion's den, to move with caution, circumspection and discretion for the present and acquiesce in existing conditions. But it seems to me to be injudicious for colored leaders to extol as "blessings in disguise," and laud to the skies, the despotism that crushes them down.

## *Chapter Eleven*

# The Educated Leader the Hope of the Race and the Hero in the Struggle for Negro Liberty

And there is still another reason why there is no room and no place in the South, at present, for educated colored men of advanced and independent thought, of broad and liberal ideas and dynamic force of character, and that is the jealousy, opposition, distrust and suspicion of half-educated leaders, who, like the ass in the lion's skin in Aesop's fables, pose as thinkers and scholars. The thinker in the Negro race will be appreciated by the scholars of the race. Most of the ministers will respect him. The ignorant masses will revere and worship him, but his efforts are constantly thwarted by half-educated, shallow, selfish and superficial demagogues, who are jealous of his superior ability and scholarship. The curse of the Negro race is its false prophets, its political and educational leaders who will compromise the manhood rights of the brother in black and sell him out for a government job or a contribution to a school.

The sudden emancipation and enfranchisement of the Negro brought to the front as leaders men whose only equipment for leadership was a vigorous pair of lungs, the gift of gab, and nerve and brass and assurance that exemplified the motto, "Fools rush in where angels fear to tread." Ignoramuses and illiterates masqueraded as Solons and Solomons, and became national figures. Men who couldn't utter a dozen sentences without butchering the English language became political and religious leaders and educators. Men who couldn't write a short letter without making ten or twenty grammatical errors became secretaries of the deacons' board and chairmen of the trustee board of so-called Congregational churches.

A white man, who can barely read and write and cipher and spell, would never look upon himself as a great man. Why, then, do the untutored Negroes not manifest the humility of ignorant white men in the presence of scholars? I will tell you. I once heard of a famous colored divine, a D.D., who had built up a church of nearly 2,000 members out of nothing. I expected to meet a cultured and finished scholar. Instead, I met a fine-looking, well dressed, suave, unctuous man, who was woefully ignorant and illiterate. He used words of three, four and five syllables, and placed them in the wrong places in his sentences. What sort of a leader is he? I asked. I visited his church and found out the reason. He who knew but a little was a sort of leader to those who knew nothing. He who was tactful and diplomatic was a sort of leader to those who were rough and uncouth in manners. He who was dignified in his bearing and carefully groomed, was a sort of a leader to those who were slouches in appearance and slovenly in dress. He who was moral was a sort of a leader to those who were immoral. No wonder his illiterate and superstitious congregation looked up to him as if he were a demigod. Similarly, the Negro politicians of limited education who forged to the front during the Reconstruction days, men of native ability and force of character, loomed up as intellectual giants in comparison with the colored voter who didn't even know his alphabet. When I consider that these men made such splendid use of their meagre training and slender opportunities, I am constrained to admire them. They performed well the task assigned to them. But the vital questions of the hour demand colored leaders of trained minds and broad scholarship. If the old leaders whose sun has set and whose day is passed will but give the right hand of fellowship to the scholars and seers of the race, they will put the race under an eternal debt of gratitude.

While I differ with Booker T. Washington regarding his attitude towards the educated Negro and the civil and political rights of the Negro, there is one position that he has wisely taken. He has opened his batteries and trained his guns upon the institutions for the higher education of the Negro in the South that spoiled good farmers in turning out poor preachers, lawyers, doctors, editors and teachers. Northern philanthropists and Southern educators have not taken the education of the Negro seriously. Men who couldn't even pass the entrance examinations for Yale or Harvard were placed as presidents of and professors in State and denominational colleges. Colleges and universities were established in the South which were not as high in grades as a New England high school or academy. Normal schools were established which were no higher than New England grammar schools. And graduates of these schools, possessing a mere smattering, would strut around with the sophomoric pride and peacock air that graduates of Yale and Harvard would never dream of assuming.

I believe that graduates of these schools have done valuable pioneer work. They have laid well the foundation upon which their successors may build.

But they have not the talents nor the training to enable them to successfully champion the cause of the higher aspiration of the Negro, or to successfully cope with and answer the arguments and assaults of Vardaman, Tillman, Tom Dixon, Tom Watson, the late Henry Grady, John Temple Graves, Hardwick and Hoke Smith. They have done their work well. But they should not stand in the way of those graduates of Yale and Harvard who, by virtue of their grasp of psychological, sociological and economic problems, by virtue of the slashing vigor and poetic beauty of their style, by virtue of their oratorical and literary gifts, are able to command the attention and to challenge the admiration of the world, because of their brilliant leadership of the Negro and their splendid handling of the critics of the race. It is better for those whose days of real usefulness are practically over to be put on the retired list if their jealousy of younger and more gifted leaders causes them to hinder the advancement of and place obstacles in the way of men more talented than themselves, and more capable of leading the Negro at this crisis in his history.

When the American comes to the Negro problem, he settles that offhand, without any thorough investigation. He merely passes it by, with a contemptuous wave of the hand, or toss of the head. Why, any petty clerk, or office boy or newsboy or bootblack, knows what ought to be done with the Negro, knows what kind of education the Negro needs! The prevailing sentiments seems to be that anyone, no matter how ignorant, is fitted to grapple with the various Negro problems.

A traveler who goes to Europe or Asia or Africa wouldn't presume to pass final judgment upon any countries of the far East from a bird's-eye view or passing glance. But all the Northern tourist has to do is to recline comfortably on the cushioned seats of a Pullman palace car, gaze tranquilly out of the window as he is being borne along by the iron horse through the Sunny South, and he is ready to write an elaborate treatise upon the Southern Negro, when in reality he has only surveyed a few loungers around railroad depots from a distance.

If we seek to get the Irishman's opinion regarding Ireland, we don't go to the ignorant immigrant fresh from Ireland; but we generally go to the Irishmen of the finest minds, who have had the best training. It is the same way with regard to the Philippines, Cuba, India, China or Japan. We don't solicit the opinion of the Chinese laundryman or the illiterate Filipino, and Cuban, or the untutored Hindoo, but that of the educated Japanese, the educated Chinaman, to get the best thought of natives regarding themselves and their country. And we ought to do the same with regard to the Negro. We ought to regard the men who represent the brains and scholarship, the moral stamina and manliness of the Negro race, as the real leaders.

The current belief is that the teachings of history and sociology can be ignored when we approach the Negro problem, that it doesn't require careful and serious study to understand the race question in its deeper issues.

Of all the subjects that command the attention of the country, none are more flippantly and carelessly discussed than the race question. When men discuss the tariff question, the currency question, socialism, imperialism, the trusts and the momentous problems growing out of the relation of labor and capital, they focus upon these grave issues all the concentrated light that history, philosophy, sociology and political economy can give. To understand the tariff question they must not only go back to the beginning of feudalism and trace the history of protection and free trade from the middle ages, when the manor system prevailed, but they must go back to the time when the Phoenicians were the traders of the world. To properly understand the currency question, one must not only be familiar with the history of American and European currency, but he must go back to the ages when money was not the medium of exchange—when barter was the method of exchanging goods. So, to understand the claims of the imperialists, one must not only go back to the period when Spain began her infamous policy of oppressing the Mexicans and Peruvians, but he must go back to the days when Athens and other Greek cities began to plant colonies. So we might take up other political, social or educational problems and find the genetic method of explaining the present by the past—the only satisfactory way of dealing with any problem. The reason is obvious. The present is the outgrowth of the past, and has its roots deeply grounded in the past. Hence, the present can only be understood in the light of the past. And we cannot understand things as they are save as we understand how they came to be.

The Negro problem is a complicated one. Unless a man is a profound student of psychology, sociology, political economy and history, he cannot begin to comprehend and understand, or grapple with its phases and aspects. Hence, the Moses who will lead the Negro race out of the wilderness and into the promised land must come from the centers of learning in New England. The race is doomed if the jealousy of those who haven't the courage to fight for the race impedes the progress of those who have.

My advice to the light-weights, feather-weights and bantam-weights of the race would be, "Clear the track and give the right of the way to the heavy-weights, the intellectual giants and the strong men of the race. They will sweep down the line and will toss aside the arguments of the critics of the race. They will go to the front and fight your battles for you." It may seem pedantic for me to say that we must look to the colored graduates of Yale and Harvard for the champions of the civil and political rights of the Negro. But three of the four men thus far in the twentieth century who have been the boldest, most fearless and most uncompromising in asserting the claims and demands of the Negro, three of the four men who have been the keenest, most penetrating and most searching in their analysis of and criticism of the arguments of the Tuskeegee sage and his followers, are graduates of Yale and Harvard universities. These four are Clement G. Morgan, Harvard's colored class orator; William Monroe Trotter, a Master of Arts of Harvard; W. E. Burghardt DuBois, a Ph.D. of Harvard, and George W. Forbes, the first editor of the *Boston Guardian*.

So, we see, that not from Tuskeegee, Hampton, or any of the Southern schools and colleges, but from Yale and Harvard have come the big four who will go down in history as the four saviors and deliverers of the Negro, as the four men who saved the day for the Negro, as the four intrepid leaders in the struggle for Negro liberty. Think what a calamity and a misfortune for the Negro race it would have been if these four men had never been born! Why, the intellectual and moral progress of the race would have been impeded a century.

And then there is a brilliant and distinguished graduate of Howard University, private secretary to the late Senator William M. Evarts, who, while not so conspicuous in the charging of the center against the intrenched position of Booker T. Washington, nevertheless did some magnificent fighting upon the right wing in successfully challenging the constitutionality of the Maryland Jim Crow law, so far as concerns the interstate colored passengers. I refer to Professor William H. H. Hart, of the Howard University Law School.

Dr. F. J. Grimke of Washington was not in the thick of the anti–Booker T. Washington fight. But what a brave stand he made upon the left wing when he sent a letter of sympathy to William Monroe Trotter, in his supreme hour of trial, and cheered the men engaged in a life and death struggle for Negro manhood. If DuBois was the Wellington, Lawyer E. H. Morris of Chicago was the Blücher in the battle for Negro rights. Just as the Boston coterie and DuBois were winning the day for the Negro, a new champion swept across the field, and in an address upon "Shams," mercilessly exposed the fallacies in Mr. Washington's doctrine of the inherent inferiority of the Negro, and made the rout of the Washington forces complete.

It may be that Douglass, Crummell, Downing, Grimke, Hart, Morris, Morgan, Byron, Greuner, DuBois and men of that stamp will be remembered by the colored people when the walls of the Tuskeegee of the proscribed curriculum are crumbling into ruins and a mass of dust and clay indicates the site where Tuskeegee once stood. The tale of how, when the Negro was being stripped of his rights and dehumanized, four young colored graduates of Yale and Harvard buckled on their armor, entered the lists, and, single-handed and alone, amidst the curses of the white people and jealousy of petty Negro leaders, unhorsed, overthrew people and hurled back the Goliaths of race prejudice, and brought dismay to the ranks of the black man's enemies; the story of how, when Sumner, Garrison, Phillips, Douglass, Crummell, and Downing were dead, four young colored scholars routed and put to flight, like Elijah of old, the black prophets of Baal, breathed their own dauntless spirit into the discouraged and disheartened sons of Ham, and taught them to look up and be men, will be told by grandsires on many a winter's evening by the fireside. Generations yet unborn will look back in grateful remembrance to the four colored men who made it possible for dark complexioned persons to be men and women in America. Their names will be forever enshrined in the hearts of the colored people of the world. Poets will sing their praises and orators will repeat and reiterate their eloquent words.

If ever a Negro writer hoped to color and flavor his writings with his own personality and individuality and write with the slashing vigor of a Carlyle, it is the writer of this volume which is only the first installment of a series of Negro histories that is projected. What Homer did for the heroes of the Trojan War, what Carlyle did for Cromwell and his other heroes, I am going to try to do for the great men of the Negro race. I am going to try to rescue from the dust and dusk of obscurity and oblivion, and surround with the halo of immortality the names of those heroic men and women who braved unpopularity and misrepresentation for asserting their manhood and womanhood. If life and health be spared me, I will endeavor to write the Negro histories that will inspire the colored youth of the land. I hope that the future historians of the race will build upon me and see through my spectacles. I trust that they will accept my point of view and take their cue from me.

If every other Negro in the land had bowed the knee in servile submission to the Baal of American caste prejudice, if every other Negro in the land had crouched and cowered and cringed like a cowardly cur, and confessed his inferiority, if every other Negro in the land had degenerated into a fawning, bootlicking sycophant, there would have been one colored man who, by the grace of God, would not have lost his faith in humanity. I would have continued to believe that somewhere in this wide, wide world, somewhere on God's green earth, it would have been possible for a Negro to live in peace and comfort, and be a man.

Other Negroes may do as they please, but I hope to develop into a full-fledged, well-rounded man. I intend to fulfill the law of my being. I don't believe that it will be necessary for a colored man to go to England, France, Australia, to the wilds of Africa, the jungles of Asia or the isles of the sea. I don't believe that it will be necessary for a colored man to endure the winter's frost and cold of the frigid zone or the torrid heat of the equatorial region in order to be a man, and draw a free breath. But I believe that the time will soon come in America when a colored man can live at ease and be frank, manly, straightforward and honest at the same time.

Sad is the fate of the world's great men. Columbus, the discoverer of America, died in poverty and disgrace in prison. Savonarola, Huss, Latimer, and Ridley were burnt alive at the stake. Athanasius was hunted and pursued like a criminal. Themistocles and Aristides were banished, Phidias and Anaxagoras died in prison. Miltiades, the hero of Marathon, was thrown into prison. Socrates, the peerless philosopher, was forced to drink the cup of hemlock. Luther was under the ban, Dante was exiled. Milton was hated. Webster, Clay, Calhoun, Horace Greeley, Sherman and James G. Blaine died brokenhearted, because they could not become presidents of the United States. Roscoe Conkling and Thomas Brackett Reed, thwarted in their political ambitions, retired from politics in sullen rage. The seekers of life's prizes emerge from the race baffled and empty-handed. He who pursues fame, grasps at mist and vapor. Many of the world's great men have died poor and unpopular. But we can all do something to broaden and elevate men's conception of life, and lighten the sin and evil, the misery and unhappiness in the world. I trust that this volume will be a bugle call. I hope that it will ring out the clarion note and arouse the dormant manhood and womanhood of the race.

NOTE.—We must not ignore the work of Hon. Archibald H. Grimke, President of the American Negro Academy, author of "The Lives of William Lloyd Garrison and Charles Sumner," and the work of Dr. William E. Sinclair, organizer of the Constitution League and author of "Aftermath of Slavery." Like the Grecian gods in classical mythology they have frequently come to the aid and rescue of the black Ajaxes and Diomedes who were performing superhuman deeds of valor while battling against superior numbers.

# Further Reading


Burkett, Randall K. *Black Redemption: Churchmen Speak for the Garvey Movement.* Philadelphia: Temple University Press, 1978.

Ferris, William H. "Individuality Is Race's Greatest Need." *Pittsburgh Courier*, November 27, 1926, Section 1, 8.

———. "Douglass as Orator." In *Blacks at Harvard: A Documentary History of African American Experience at Harvard and Radcliffe*, edited by Werner Sollors, Titcomb Cadwell, and Thomas A. Underwood, 113–22. New York: New York University Press, 1993.

Gaines, Kevin K. "The Crisis of Negro Intellectuals: William H. Ferris and Black Nationalist Thought." In *Uplifting the Race: Black Leadership, Politics, and Culture in the Twentieth Century*, by Kevin K. Gaines, 100–127. Chapel Hill: University of North Carolina, 1996.

Moses, Wilson J. "Afrocentrism, Cosmopolitanism, and Cultural Literacy in the American Negro Academy." In *Afrotopia: The Roots of African American Popular History*, by Wilson J. Moses, 169–92. Cambridge: Cambridge University Press, 1998.

———. "Eurocentrism, Afrocentrism, and William H. Ferris' *The African Abroad*, 1911." *Journal of Education* 173 (1991): 76–90.

"Obituary of William H. Ferris." *Journal of Negro History* 26 (1941): 549–50.

Shepperson, George. "Introduction to the Negro." In *The Negro*, by W. E. B. Du Bois, vii–xxv. New York: Oxford Univesity Press, 1972.

Sollors, Werner, Cadwell Titcomb, and Thomas A. Underwood. *Blacks at Harvard: A Documentary History of African American Experience at Harvard and Radcliffe.* New York: New York University Press, 1993.

# Index